Car Wars

The Age of Giant Corporations
AMEX: A History of the American Stock Exchange
NYSE: A History of the New York Stock Exchange
The Entrepreneurs
Inside Wall Street
The Fallen Colossus: The Great Crash of the Penn Central
The Worldly Economists
IBM: Colossus in Transition
ITT: The Management of Opportunity

Car Wars

The Untold Story

ROBERT SOBEL

T·T

A Truman Talley Book

E. P. DUTTON • NEW YORK

Published in the United States by
Truman Talley Books · E. P. Dutton, Inc.
2 Park Avenue, New York, N.Y. 10016

Library of Congress Cataloging in Publication Data

Sobel, Robert,
Car wars.
"A Truman Talley book."
Bibliography: p.
1. Automobile industry and trade—United States.
2. Automobile industry and trade. 3. Automobile industry
and trade—United States—History. 4. Automobile
industry and trade—History. I. Title.
HD9710.U52S62   1984   338.4'76292'0973   84-10133

ISBN: 0-525-24289-9

Published simultaneously in Canada by
Fitzhenry & Whiteside Limited, Toronto
COBE

DESIGNED BY MARK O'CONNOR

10 9 8 7 6 5 4 3 2

First Edition

FOR EDMUND, ALICE, ANN, AND DAVID BERRIDGE

Contents

CONTENTS

PART III

Reinventing the Automobile

Preface

*Imagine a modern-day Rip Van Winkle falling asleep in 1942
and awakening today. Considering what he would see in the way
of consumer electronics—and especially with automobiles—might
he not be forgiven for having concluded that Japan had won
World War II?*

—HERMAN KAHN,
1980

Research on *Car Wars* was begun when the American industry
was in shambles; these words are being written during a period
of revival. Profits are at record levels, prompting the boards of
directors of the Big Three automakers to bestow huge bonuses
on their top management—all of whom sit on those very
boards—which came to $181 million at General Motors alone.

In 1985 the four American firms will have completed an
$80 billion revamping and restructuring program begun in

1979, and all are now characterized as being "mean and lean." So they are—compared with what they had been in the late 1970s. But nagging questions remain. How will the industry do during the falloff in sales many industry analysts anticipate will transpire by late 1985 or the following year? Will General Motors and Ford be able to realize their ambitious global strategies? Can Chrysler come up with a successor to the K-car? And can American Motors, now effectively a subsidiary of Renault, generate profits to go along with boosts in revenues?

Finally, what of the Japanese? Can anyone seriously believe they won't mount a major sales offensive when and if restraints are lifted? Conversations with executives in Toyota City, Yokohama, and Tokyo leave no doubt on this score.

Such would seem to be the message behind the current expansion of the industry. At a time when interest is coming to be centered on the Japanese challenge in computers, it would be good to consider that Toyota spends more on research and development than does any other Japanese firm, and that four of the top fourteen investors in this area are auto manufacturers. This segment of the economy accounts for one quarter of all the industrial robots in Japan, which has approximately 70 percent of the world total. Toyota's Tahara No. 2 plant near Toyota City is perhaps the most modern and automated in the world, but may yield this designation to the soon-to-be-completed facility at Hofu being erected by Toyo Kogyo (renamed Mazda Motor Corporation in May 1984).

Moreover, of the top six Japanese exporters, four (Toyota, Nissan, Honda, and Mazda) are car companies (the other two being Nippon Steel and Matsushita Electric). That Japan's powerful Ministry of International Trade and Industry (MITI) will continue to exert pressure on their behalf is beyond doubt.

Suggestions about where the industry is heading will be found in Chapter 17: The Shape of Things to Come. But before one can appreciate the problems of the present and the possibilities of the future, it is necessary to know how it all began. The origins were in the period immediately following World

War II, when Detroit's outlook was bright, the horizon pleasing, and no one thought there was anything but success ahead for this uniquely American industry.

Notes on my sources can be found at the end of the book.

ROBERT SOBEL

July 15, 1984

It is meaningless to develop a motor vehicle industry in Japan. Now is the time of international division of labor. As we can get inexpensive motor cars of excellent quality from the United States, why don't we rely upon them?

—HISATO ICHIMADA,
Governor of the Bank of Japan,
in a speech given in 1950

The American
Imperium

1

The Age of
Detroit Baroque

Last year a Yale University physicist calculated that since Chevy offered 46 models, 32 engines, 20 transmissions, 21 colors (plus nine two-tones combinations) and more than 400 accessories and options, the number of different cars that a Chevrolet customer conceivably could order was greater than the number of atoms in the universe. This seemingly would put General Motors one notch higher than God in the chain of command.

HAL HIGDON,
"The Big Auto Sweepstakes,"
The New York Times Magazine,
May 1, 1966

"The most important thing that's happening in the automobile business, all Detroit is telling the world, is the return of the 'good old competitive prewar buyer's market.'"

So wrote an anonymous *Fortune* essayist in late 1953, as he

3

surveyed what remained of that year's model run and analyzed prospects for the next slew of offerings. "Well, competition is back," he reflected, "and the industry does need a lot of better salesmen."

To him, and many other industry observers both then and later on, 1953 did seem a turning point of sorts. And so it was. Postwar experiments with small cars had ended, as such firms as Hudson, Studebaker, Willys, and Kaiser-Frazer bowed before the verdict of the marketplace, and only George Mason of Nash was willing to continue in that direction. As though to symbolize their collective defeats, these independents entered into mergers. Willys was purchased by Kaiser-Frazer, and in 1953, negotiations began between Nash and Hudson, which merged to form American Motors, to be headed by Mason. Meanwhile J. J. Nance of Packard held a series of meetings with Studebaker's Paul Hoffman, and out of their talks came a new corporation, Studebaker-Packard. But neither man thought the firm would reenter the small car market.

Rather, they would emulate Harlow Curtice, who became General Motors' Chief Executive Officer in 1953, and who would come to symbolize the new era. Starting out slowly at first, Curtice would lengthen, broaden, and superpower the General Motors lines. And it was what the public seemed to want. "A few years back the man who drove a 100-hp car was considered a dashing fellow," observed *Time* a few days after Curtice took over. "But this week, when General Motors rolled out four of its new 1953 lines, the 100-hp auto was almost as dated as the linen duster."

That year, for the first time, a majority of American-made automobiles were powered by eight-cylinder engines, and this was the reality behind the symbolism.

That the public approved of this could be seen in the imitation of the GM line. But there were critics of the new dispensation. Ken Purdy, who made a good living testing cars and writing about them for a variety of magazines, was one. Purdy bemoaned Detroit's baroque designs and called for a return to basics. "Remember the cars of father's day?" he asked wistfully. "Cars that set a man up where he belonged, like a knight on a charger, and let him see where he was going?" "Cars that really turned when the wheel moved, instead of suggesting, sluggishly, that after a bit they might change direction?" Purdy went on to decry the industry's obsession with appearances, lashing out at designers who seemed more concerned with the placement of chrome on grille and bumper than with passenger comfort, accessibility of components for repair, and ease of handling. Purdy clearly believed the cars on the American roads were rolling insults to the intelligence of those who drove them and reflected poorly on the taste and perception of the industry that turned them out.

In content and tone, the article seems quite contemporary, for ours is a period in which Detroit has become the scapegoat for many of the country's real and imagined ailments. But Purdy wrote this piece—"I'll Shift for Myself"—for the February 1953 issue of the *Atlantic Monthly*, for a readership that at the time seemed quite content with its automobiles. Moreover, the cars of this period were approximately a foot and one-half shorter and several hundred pounds lighter than their counterparts would be a decade or so later. The specifications for the 1953 Chevrolet, to cite the most obvious example, weren't markedly different from those of some of the GM compacts of a later period. If Purdy and those who agreed with him believed that year's products to have been overblown, they were positively vitriolic when the time came to assess their successors. Raymond Loewy, whose Studebaker designs won dozens of awards, observed in 1955 that Detroit always claimed it was giving the public what it wanted. "And 'what it wants' is being translated into the flashy, the gadgety, the spectacular." In *The Insolent Chariots*, his best-selling assault on motordom released three years later, John Keats posed the Shakespearean question: "Whence, and what art thou, execrable shape?" and went on to catalogue Detroit's many sins as he saw them.

The fact remained that the public seemed to like those shapes. In the very year Loewy was criticizing the ballooning behemoths, Americans purchased a record 7.9 million cars, which was 1.3 million more than in 1950, the previous high, when almost anything that Detroit offered was snapped up. All of GM's 1955 cars were larger than they had been when Curtice assumed command two years earlier, and the industry leader also established a record by accounting for slightly less than 4 million of that total. Fewer than 200,000 of Loewy's Studebakers were sold that year, and in 1963, the company closed its South Bend, Indiana, facility for good.

Anyone who examined the 1963 cars would have concluded that the public, indeed, wanted "the flashy, the gadgety, the spectacular."

General Motors was the clear leader in this phase of automobile history, accounting for styling changes that Ford and Chrysler first reluctantly, and then enthusiastically, embraced. To appreciate this, one must understand what Curtice inherited and the alterations he ordered, and this could best be seen at Chevrolet, the corporation's volume leader.

The 1953 Chevy was a gussied-up version of a car that had been introduced four years earlier, when the industry was still uncertain about consumer tastes and turned out conservatively designed models. In fact, it utilized some components developed and used prior to World War II, including its six-cylinder engine (of the lower-priced cars, only Ford was available with an "eight" in this period). All in all, it was a solid, dependable, but unexciting vehicle, prompting one critic to complain that the Chevy looked "as though it had been designed by Herbert Hoover's haberdasher."

The Chevy weighed in at slightly less than 3,300 pounds, with a wheelbase of 115 inches and an overall length of 198 inches, and GM claimed it could get 25 mpg out of its 92-hp engine. The four-door version sold for $1,659, which was a few dollars less than a comparable Ford.

Curtice considered the revamping of the Chevy his first priority, and what he did to that car changed the direction of the industry for the next decade and a half. It began with a look over the fence at Ford, which had introduced a new model in

1952. Although its overall dimensions approximated those of the Chevy, the Mainline's six-cylinder engine was more powerful than any in its class. More to the point, however, the Ford was a sleek car and *looked* more expensive than it actually was. In fact, one of the company's problems that year was Ford's cannibalization of sales from Mercury. All of which was known at GM, when Curtice set about reversing not only this situation but also the image of the Chevy in America.

With Curtice's blessing, division manager Thomas Keating restructured his design team and added several new members, the most important of whom was Edward Cole. An engineer by training, Cole had already been singled out for special attention as a possible executive. Prior to arriving at Chevrolet, he had been the lead designer at Cadillac, where he was largely responsible for fashioning that division's new models—tail fins and all. Cole and the others could do little about the 1954 Chevys, since the plans for them were already off the drawing boards. But the design team was given a great deal of leeway with the following year's models, so long as they possessed the kind of flair that would dampen any inclinations Chevy owners might have to switch to the new Fords.

Few automobiles had been released with as much publicity as were the 1955 Chevys, and for good reason. A sharp departure for a division not known for experimentation, whose products were safe, economical, and conventional, in the past they appealed to individuals with those same characteristics. Not that the sedan's exterior dimensions were that much different from those of the 1954s. Although a future generation might remember the 1955 Chevys as being larger, heavier, and flashier than their predecessors, the basic sedan, in fact, was almost two inches shorter. It weighed 185 pounds more only because of its new 162-hp engine. But the 1955 Chevy still *looked* larger, plusher, and more expensive than it actually was—$2,100 with automatic transmission, which came to some $300 more than the six it replaced.

This car, arguably the most important GM was to offer in the 1950s, was designed to serve two purposes, and it succeeded. First, the Chevy eight was to retain the loyalties of GM customers who otherwise might have been won over by its Ford counterpart because of Ford's power and performance. The Chevy eight offered both, covering a quarter-mile test track from a standing start in 19 seconds, compared to 22 for the previous year's model. And it did so at what, for the time, seemed only a minor cost in overall gasoline mileage; in an independent test, the car managed a fraction better than 23 mpg at a steady 30 mph.

With its 1955 line, Chevrolet bowed to the all but inevitable triumph of the eight-cylinder engine. That same year Plymouth, Nash, and Hudson offered eight-cylinder–powered cars for the first time, realizing that without them they would lose sales to autos possessing such engines. One might have purchased a Chevy six, with the same body as the Chevy eight, for $170 less, obtaining better fuel economy at the price of power. How much power? That year's six advertised 123 hp, or 39 fewer than the eight. Slightly more than $4 per horsepower. It seemed a bargain. Customers rushed to buy the eight, and toward the end of the model year, industry experts were predicting the smaller engine's share of the market would decline steadily, and although never completely disappearing, would account for a relatively minor number of sales. At mid-decade, then, Detroit was committed to a sales war based more on power and performance than economy of operation and initial pricing. The Chevy eight legitimized the change as no other car could.

Styling was at least if not more important than power. The old Chevys had the look and feel of low-priced vehicles, and as indicated, stamped their owners as individuals who, although they may have been on the way up, were still pretty low in the socioeconomic pecking order. They would rise, according to that key tenet set down by Chairman Alfred Sloan a generation earlier: from Chevy to Pontiac to Buick to Olds and then—if they had what it took—to the pinnacle of Cadillac. To be sure, there were some overlaps—a fully equipped Chevy could cost as much as a stripped Pontiac, but this didn't alter the status arrangement a whit.

8

The new Chevy changed the situation somewhat. Cole had designed a car that seemed every bit as luxurious and powerful as most Pontiacs and even a few Buicks, but that cost several hundred dollars less; and in the process, he had turned back the Ford challenge. The following year's contest was even more sharply defined. Cole boosted horsepower and added a few cosmetic touches to make the car seem more glamorous, while the admen boasted, "the hot one's even hotter."

Ford's response was somewhat unusual, to the point of being daring, if misbegotten. This was a period when some parts of the press were becoming concerned about the hazards of driving, and Ford Division President Robert McNamara decided on a strategy of outflanking GM on this issue. The company announced that henceforth its cars would feature "lifeguard" design through improved doorlocks. There was to be a deep-dish steering wheel to protect drivers against impalement, in case of a head-on crash, and optional padded dashes. For the first time, American drivers might order factory-installed seat belts—another option. All these innovations failed miserably. Within Detroit automotive circles it was said that "McNamara is selling safety and Chevy's selling cars." General Motors had close to half the market that recession year and outsold Ford 3 million to 1.6 million.

The new Chevy and its impact during the 1955/56 season shook up the industry, now well-entranced in the high noon of the Curtice era. Even at GM, it had become evident that Sloanism was fading and that the image of each of the corporation's products was bound to change in the wake of Chevy's upgrading.

The Pontiac, which was the car Chevy owners were supposed to fantasize about, suffered immediately, as owners did their upgrading from the relatively spartan 150 and 210 series to the impressive Bel Airs, with more than a half million sold in 1956. Meanwhile, Pontiac Chieftain sales shrank. The entire division turned out 332,000 cars that year, compared with 591,-000 in 1955, and it had trouble moving these. Further declines were in the making, and in 1958, production slipped to 220,000, the lowest in the postwar period. Outside the industry there were rumors that GM would soon merge Pontiac into Buick and permit it to go the way of the Oakland and the LaSalle, two other models the corporation no longer produced because consumer interest had declined.

Industry executives knew that this was not so, that Pontiac was to receive the same kind of face-lift as Chevrolet. What Keating and Cole had accomplished at Chevy, a new team, Semon "Bunkie" Knudsen and John DeLorean, were charged with doing at Pontiac. Knudsen, the son of one of GM's most distinguished leaders, was to head Pontiac, while DeLorean took charge of the design team. When they arrived, Pontiac had the reputation of turning out what the flamboyant DeLorean called "an old lady's car," which was his way of saying it handled sluggishly and looked stodgy. DeLorean claimed credit for having changed this. The frame was lowered, the tread widened, more chrome was added, far more powerful engines (which mandated power steering and power brakes) and harder suspensions were provided, and the body was elongated, in the case of the Star Chief convertible, by tacking on an exterior-mounted spare wheel with a special bumper treatment. Now the Pontiac had tail fins of its own and came in splashy paint jobs. DeLorean added 400 pounds to the car and made it a foot longer. But those powerful eight-cylinder engines, although wasteful of fuel, also made Pontiac a "hot" car. Acceleration was much improved, and Knudsen and DeLorean entered Pontiacs in stock-car races in which they performed quite well. Ads featuring families in four-door sedans gave way to others in which young, handsome teenagers in convertibles smiled out at readers, as though inviting them to come to Pontiac as they might to a fountain of youth. DeLorean thus transformed the car into a symbol of excitement, adventure, and power—and in the process made it bulkier and gaudier than ever. What Cole had achieved with the Chevy, he had done—in spades—for Pontiacs.

It worked. Pontiac sales for 1959 came to 380,000. They were 450,000 the following year, and in 1962, they passed the half-million mark.

If Pontiac went from being an old lady's car to a car for youth, then Chevy advanced from an automobile with aspiring family men at the wheel to a wide range of models, at the top of which were hardtop convertible Impalas, considered equal in luxury and status not only to Pontiacs, but also to Buicks and Oldsmobiles. And there was more to come. In 1959, the car sprouted a pair of gullwing tail fins, more lavish and bizarre than anything yet seen. The Bel Air of that year had a wheelbase of 119 inches and an overall length of 211 inches. It weighed 3,880 pounds, featured a 185-hp engine, and cost $2,757 at the factory. Compare these statistics with those for the aforementioned 1953 Chevy. That car's wheelbase was 115 inches and its overall length 198 inches. It weighed 3,385 pounds, had a 92-hp engine, and cost $1,659 at the factory.

All of this in six years.

The transformations at Chevrolet and Pontiac affected all of GM's automobile divisions, except Cadillac, which as usual, remained the most impervious to such influences of all the corporation's units. Upsizing, developing more powerful engines, and adding power steering and braking and even power-driven seats and windows, became the rule. Functionalism was deemed boring, and numerous design flaws were plastered over by layers of chrome and paint.

Although the divisions continued to share bodies and components, a new period of competition began, which redounded to the benefit of Chevrolet. By 1959, a top-of-the-line, fully equipped Chevy cost appreciably more than a stripped Olds or Buick—and looked it. The Chevy was still the "everyman's car" talked about two decades earlier, only now it seemed that everyman wanted to appear lavish and ostentatious rather than proletarian or even middle class. Young drivers no longer had to think of graduating to other GM cars. Instead, they simply purchased larger and more powerful Chevys, to the point where that division threatened not only to crush Ford and Chrysler but also to crowd out its stablemates at GM. By 1959, when total American sales came to 5.9 million, Chevy's were 1.4 million, which is to say that slightly less than one out of every four cars purchased that year was a Chevrolet. Who could blame others within the industry for following its lead?

That Chrysler and Ford attempted to do so was transparently evident, but the results of their embraces of Detroit Baroque were hardly as auspicious.

Chrysler's longtime CEO, K. T. Keller, insisted the company turn out boxy, economical, mechanically advanced, and comfortable cars, designed "to sit in, not to piss over." In 1949, these were advertised as being "bigger on the inside, smaller on the outside," as though that was a virtue. Plymouth, for years, had been known as "the schoolteacher's car," which in the context of the time inferred that it was eminently practical, and Keller insisted that the roof be high enough so a male driver could wear his hat inside.

Lester "Tex" Colbert, who succeeded Keller in 1954, thought such ideas quaintly antique and out of touch with the realities of the marketplace. Arriving in the executive suites by virtue of his successful management of a facial tissue company, Colbert's background was law and marketing, and he had only a spotty knowledge of engineering, long considered Chrysler's strong suit.

Shortly after assuming command, Colbert told the press of his intentions to capture one American car sale out of five and indicated that this would be achieved by "out-Curticeing" GM. If long, low, heavy, and powerful sold cars, he would present the longest, lowest, bulkiest, and most powerful vehicles in their classes. If two-tone paint jobs were good, three must be better, and some Chrysler models were available that way. Designer Virgil Exner experimented with placing the automatic shift handle on the dashboard, and then push buttons replaced the shift entirely. How these improved performance or provided a better way to get the car into motion wasn't clearly explained. Change was exciting, thought Colbert and Exner, and excitement sold cars, so under their guidance Chrysler meant to provide both.

As with Chevrolet, Chrysler began in 1955 with what its advertising agency called "The Forward Look." This turned out to be cars that were longer and lower than anything that had previously emerged from the corporation. The public liked what it saw. Sales rose in all categories, with those for Plymouth hitting an all-time high. Chrysler's market share expanded from less than 13 percent in 1954 to slightly below 17 percent in 1955.

This success, along with that at Chevy, sealed the industry's fate. "The stodgy car died in 1955," wrote John Jerome in his 1960 study, *The Death of the Automobile.* "All our clinging Calvinistic sensibilities of practicality, economy, simplicity, and the cramped guidelines of American Gothic were junked." Few had a greater share in this than Colbert and Exner.

Later, it would be recognized that Chrysler reached a major turning point in 1957. In his attempts to outdo GM, Colbert designed that year's models with more powerful engines and the longest, highest, and, to critics, most bizarre tail fins yet seen. Chrysler spokesmen somewhat lamely tried to explain that these would provide the cars with greater roadability, but no one took this seriously. Once the most conservative of the Big Three, Chrysler was now the most flamboyant. And flamboyance sold cars.

There was a price for all of this, however. Colbert drove his design and production teams mercilessly in his campaign to provide novelty, woo customers, and expand market share. The 1957 models were rushed into production to take advantage of the mania for power and fins. The engines were balky, the bodies leaked and rusted, and an unusually large number of vehicles literally fell apart. Sales declined soon after. Under Walter Chrysler and K. T. Keller, Chrysler had earned a reputation for advanced engineering and sound construction, both of which were frittered away during the Colbert years.

By 1960, when Lynn Townsend took over the corporation, Chrysler held only 10 percent of the market and was slipping lower. A financial man who knew how to read both the numbers and the market, Townsend recognized dry rot when he saw it, and he would devote his time to pruning, consolidating, economizing, and regrouping, his ambitions seeming to center on survival rather than expansion. Early ads of the Townsend years read, "We intend to fix what's wrong, keep what's right, and move ahead." But how might this be done in the face of the GM challenge and Chrysler's now-ingrained need to rely on gimmicks to sell cars? The outlook was bleak, and for a brief period Townsend considered a merger with Studebaker, which, of course, had troubles of its own, but rejected the notion. "I'm not sure that Chrysler will be around in 1980," Townsend told Studebaker chairman Sherwood Egbert. "Ford might not even be around."

There was a nice symmetry about the Big Three insofar as size was concerned. General Motors was approximately twice as large as Ford, which, in turn, was twice as large as Chrysler. Executives at the last two companies often spoke airily of moving up in the pecking order, whereas GM's leaders solemnly analyzed the difficulties of remaining at the top in a highly competitive industry. Competitive it was—in design, advertising, and showroom. But at the end of the 1950s, as during the decade's earlier years, no one seriously thought the ranking would change. And Townsend's dark thoughts to the contrary, no one thought that any of the Big Three was in danger of failing or disappearing by any other means. General Motors was impregnable, Chrysler capable of withstanding even the calamities of 1957, and, as will be seen, Ford had managed to struggle through the greatest product blunder in automotive history.

During the early post–World War II period, Henry Ford II labored to place his stamp upon a flabby corporation on the verge of disintegration. This he did, with the aid of a group of returning Air Force managerial experts known as the "Whiz Kids," but more important, Ernest Breech, a GM veteran whose most recent post had been CEO at Bendix. Part of the rejuvenation was the creation of a strategy to enable the company to wrest second place from Chrysler, and perhaps even challenge GM in some areas. This didn't present much of a problem: like other automobile industry leaders, Ford would seek to imitate Alfred Sloan's GM, both in organization and product diversification.

His prospects were mixed, as was his legacy. The strongest element was the Ford line itself, which had managed to slug it out with Chevy on an almost equal basis during the 1950s, and on occasion, even surpass it in sales. Like GM and Chrysler, Ford had embraced the essential elements of Detroit Baroque, entering into the horsepower and chrome contests, its cars becoming longer, lower, and wider with the passing years. Ford's designers diverged from the mainstream somewhat in not wholly accepting tail fins, which at best were halfhearted efforts on the mid-decade models. And as was the case with Chevy, Ford upgraded its once-modest cars so that more affluent drivers might purchase them instead of moving up in the corporation's stable.

For GM this was a matter of deliberate choice. Less so at Ford, because once customers got beyond Ford there wasn't much else to choose.

Ford Motors had introduced the Mercury in 1938 and the car was continued after the war, designed to go against GM's Pontiacs and Buicks and Chrysler's Dodges and DeSotos; the hope also was that it would be the next step up from Ford. Although sales were respectable, the Mercury was rarely more than an elaborate Ford, without a strong personality of its own —doing better than the Chrysler models, but lagging far behind Pontiac and Buick.

There was even more trouble at the top of the line; Lincoln and Continental sales combined never reached 50,000 in the 1950s, and in most years were a third those of Cadillac or Chrysler. Not that the corporation did not try. The Continentals were the longest and heaviest passenger cars on the road —227 inches and more than two and a half tons toward the end of the 1950s. Ford did not seem able to make up its mind whether the Lincolns and Continentals were to be sold to "old money," which might consider Cadillacs a symbol of crass materialism, or try to overtake the GM car by making them a trifle sportier.

The corporation had much more success with the Thunderbird, which was designed as a sports or personal car. Disdained by purists, it was enthusiastically embraced by the general public. The Thunderbird also represented Ford's only important victory over GM in this period, and was perhaps one of the three or four best examples of Detroit Baroque.

Around 1950, Detroit became interested in the market for small and expensive sports models, such as Britain's MG. At GM, Harley Earl created the Corvette, which, in 1953, came only as a convertible, in only one color (white), and was powered by a Chevrolet six-cylinder engine. It was an experiment, with its fiber-glass body and novel suspension, the kind that only an enormously wealthy company could afford, and, at first, hardly a successful one. Only 315 Corvettes were produced in 1953, and 3,640 the following year. Over the years, it became larger and much more powerful, and by the late 1950s, it was deemed the only true American sports car. Although a critical and competitive success, the Corvette was never more than that because its price and design characteristics eliminated it as a contender for a wider audience. In no year of the 1950s did sales exceed 10,000, and GM made little effort to do better than this.

Compare GM's experience with the Corvette with Ford's during the early period of the Thunderbird. General Motors designed and built the Corvette from the ground up; it did not resemble, nor was it related to, any of the corporation's earlier models. In contrast, Ford opted to enter the field as inexpensively as possible, which meant utilizing existing components and designs. The result was a small, sporty-looking, powerful car (driven by the Ford V-8 engine), which had the unmistakable Ford look, the road feel of a sedan, and was thoroughly conventional in most other respects. Lewis Crusoe, who had once attempted to win approval for a small car to undercut Chevrolet and who had helped bring the Thunderbird into being, said it wasn't really a sports car, but rather "more truly a personal or boulevard car for the customer who insists on comfort and yet would like to own a prestige vehicle that incorporates the flair and performance characteristics of a sports car." An automobile writer of the period took a quite different view. "It's like driving up to a motel with your wife and registering under phony names and addresses. You may think you're fooling people, and maybe you are, but don't fool yourself."

Enough people apparently did, however, to make the Thunderbird a hit. Ford turned out 3,546 of them in 1954, topping Corvette by a few hundred, and sales took off the following year when more than 15,000 were purchased. Knowing they had a winner and trying to expand its appeal, Ford took the path that by then was becoming familiar—the car was lengthened, widened, made heavier, and loaded with options. The 1958 version, which came with a hardtop as well as a "rag roof," sold almost 38,000 units, and looked more like a jazzed-up, two-door sedan than a sports car. Sales topped 70,000 in 1961, by which time the Thunderbird had been transformed into a conventional car, which resembled a cross between the Ford and the Lincoln.

The Thunderbird experience was to have a profound impact upon Ford in the 1960s and beyond, and one with mixed benefits at best. On the one hand, it gave the corporation a background in small-car manufacturing, distribution, and advertising, which served it well, and the glamour associated with the Thunderbird would rub off on future models. But the Thunderbird also convinced a cadre of executives, designers, and marketing men that *small* connoted *sports* and that this market differed considerably from that for sedans. The only way to get from one to the other—to travel from the specialized to the general—would be through size. In their minds, the original Thunderbird was a nice second car for the wealthy and a first car for youth. By 1958, however, Thunderbirds were being purchased by families who wanted to upgrade from Victoria Club and Skyliner sedans.

This thought remained even when Ford pioneered small sedans, and achieved great success by doing so. When they should have been considering the possibilities of "another Model T," the Ford leadership wanted to repeat the Thunderbird. And, it should be added, avoid the Edsel, arguably the greatest new model flop in American automobile history, and one from which the corporation also learned the wrong lessons.

The Edsel was the result of the same forces that led to the new Chevy, namely, the upgrading of expectations on the part of car buyers. Individuals who, prior to World War II and during the reconversion period of the second half of the 1940s, had been quite content with their Chevys, Fords, and Plymouths were now in the market for automobiles that conferred greater status upon their drivers, had larger engines under their hoods, and more chrome on their bodies. As indicated, Chevy owners moved up to Pontiac, Buick, and Oldsmobile, whereas people who once drove Plymouths now considered Dodges and DeSotos, and even Chryslers. But those who once had been satisfied with Fords and now wanted a car with more status had to leave the Ford family. As Crusoe put it, "we have been growing customers for General Motors."

Discussions regarding possible new models began in 1948, but nothing came of them until four years later, when a special committee was established to report on market conditions. Initially two new models were considered, both additions to the existing Mercury line, with one priced below and the other above cars then on the road. The successes of the 1953 Ford and the 1954 Chevy led the committee to drop the former and concentrate on a car that might be larger, more powerful, and higher priced than the Mercury. For a while thought was given to a plan to mount a Lincoln body on a Mercury chassis, but this was quickly abandoned in favor of a far more ambitious program to start from scratch. For identification purposes, this new car was designated "E"—which some Ford people say stood for "Experimental," but others say was short for "Edsel," who had been Henry I's son and Henry II's father.

Ford wanted a car that would be conventional enough to attract sedan customers, but sufficiently different to create excitement within the industry and at the showroom. In other words, it was to contain elements of the old and new—in effect, a compromise. This was what Ford got; the Edsel was a compromise in virtually every area.

Overall planning was entrusted to Richard Krafve, a youthful assistant general manager at the Lincoln-Mercury division who had been with the corporation since 1947 as a management consultant, with no technical training and little in the way of experience. The design leader was Roy Brown, a thirty-eight-year-old Canadian whose experience had been in such products as radios and colored glass goods, and who had never created a car, but who had some background in components. Krafve said he wanted a "distinctive" car, immediately recognizable on the road and internally "the epitome of the push-button era without wild-blue-yonder Buck Rogers concepts." Brown was told to design models that would appeal to Ford owners, but not take sales from Mercury. He was to figure out why Americans preferred Pontiacs and Buicks and then create a car that incorporated some of their qualities, but also offered something different. Along the way, Krafve and Brown consulted advertising agencies, psychologists, sociologists, and even a poet. There was a national contest to select names for the models, with millions of dollars expended in promotion. When Manhattan dealer Charles Kreisler switched from Olds to Edsel, the news was greeted with as much publicity as when a baseball free agent today signs a multimillion-dollar, long-term contract. Literally everything was done to interest Americans in the car—except in the areas of design and manufacture.

Nearly 3 million Americans crowded into showrooms on September 8, 1957, to see and sit behind the wheels of the four Edsel models—Corsair, Citation, Pacer, and Ranger. They saw a car that bore the unmistakable stamp of Ford design, whose most distinctive exterior differences were an oval grille and unusual paint and chrome treatments. Reviews from critics were mixed, but not from the public. If many came to look, few remained to buy. The Edsel had all the signs of a flop, although Ford executives continued to exude confidence that it would be accepted.

Later, the Edsel would be remembered as the quintessential creation of High Detroit Baroque, a near-perfect example of conspicuous consumption and corporate foolishness. But while the car was surely garish and certainly a failure, it really was not the utter fiasco insofar as design went that critics made it out to be. The Ranger, for example, which was matched against the Pontiac Catalina and Dodge Custom Royal, was shorter, lighter, and less powerful than these two, cost less, and was more fuel economical. Neither were its paint job and chrome treatment that much more bizarre than those found on GM and Chrysler models. The Edsel's major problems were not so much in the matters of design and production as they were in areas beyond Ford's control; these included timing, in particular.

Automobile sales had slumped badly in 1958, the result of a general business slump and overselling in the 1957 model year. Only 4.2 million passenger cars were sold, the lowest since 1948, as dealerships throughout the country closed down and Detroit experienced its worst recession since the end of World War II. Moreover, customers switched from middle-range cars to lower-priced ones. Chevrolet, Ford, and Plymouth sales were off, but not nearly as much as were sales for Pontiac, Olds, Buick, Dodge, and DeSoto. As for Edsel, only 63,000 of its cars sold in the 1958 model year, far less than the projected 200,000. More in panic and despair than as the result of careful judgment, Ford incorporated Edsel into the Lincoln-Mercury division and transformed it into a more luxurious Ford. Nothing seemed to help, however, and in 1960, the model was discontinued.

At the time, Edsel's demise was taken to indicate that the Age of Detroit Baroque was over, but this proved not to be the case. If anything, the 1960 models were more in that tradition than were those of the 1950s. Had the Edsel been introduced in 1955 rather than 1957, it might not only have survived, but also flourished. Indeed, the car might have become popular if the release date could have been moved up by a couple of years.

That the American automobile industry learned no lasting lesson from the Edsel experience wasn't because of ignorance, stupidity, or insensitivity. Rather, the Detroit Establishment had only fragmentary evidence that a significant number of their mainstream customers had permanently changed their attitudes toward cars. But the sharp decline in sales for medium-price models during the 1958 recession was duly noted, as were the two success stories of that year. There were still waiting lists for Volkswagens, as potential buyers offered bribes to salesmen who might get them Beetles within weeks of the order rather than months, and this at a time when Detroit's models were being heavily discounted, with few takers. And one American car did spectacularly well in 1958: Rambler sales that year were 186,000, more than twice the 91,000 of 1957. In 1959, they would rise to 363,000, only a few thousand below sales for Plymouth. Taken together, the VW and Rambler experiences couldn't be ignored. The only problem that remained to be solved was whether the response was a temporary aberration from mainstream thinking or a permanent change in the basic thinking of the American car buyer. It wouldn't be going too far to suggest that this was the most important issue facing Detroit since the end of World War II.

2

Miracle at Wolfsburg

I am happy that due to the abilities of the superb designer Porsche and his staff, we have succeeded in completing preliminary designs for a German people's car, so that the first models will finally be tested by the middle of the year. It must be possible to make the German people a gift of a motor vehicle which will not cost them more than they have heretofore been accustomed to paying for a medium-priced motorcycle and whose gas consumption will be low.

ADOLF HITLER,
1935

The vehicle does not meet the fundamental technical requirements of a motorcar. As regard performance and design it is quite unattractive to the average motorcar buyer. It is too ugly and too noisy. . . . To build the car commercially would be a completely uneconomic enterprise.

The [British] Rootes Commission
assessing the Volkswagen,
1946

To the average American of the early 1950s, the adjective *small* connoted inexpensive and inferior. The Chevy, for example, was a small car and the Cadillac a large one, and the latter was thought of as more desirable. Price was directly correlated to size, and size was related to status. One should not be ashamed of driving a small car, but a small car certainly wasn't thought of with pride—by most Americans, that is. The idea was to move from small to large as rapidly as possible, large being a symbol of success. Such a concept, together with the belief that next year's model would be better than this one's—and more desirable—was at the very bedrock of Sloanism.

The Americanization of the Western world proceeded apace during the postwar era, and to large numbers of Europeans and Orientals, the large, flashy, powerful Detroit product came to symbolize the strength and self-assurance of the United States. Those who had met Americans learned of their belief that bigger was better in most things. They understood this, but didn't necessarily accept it—in the matter of cars, that is.

For a different kind of automobile culture had taken root in Europe, one in which size was a consideration when it came to gauging status, but not the only one. During the interwar period, the British, to cite the most obvious example, knew that drivers of the small Morrises and Austins were inferior socially and financially to those who owned the likes of Jaguars, Humbers, Rovers, and that quintessential luxury vehicle, the Rolls-Royce, and all of these were larger than that period's version of the minicar. Nonetheless, the most expensive European models, for the most part, were smaller than intermediate-size American cars. The typical American drivers of the 1930s may not have been aware of this, having never seen a Rolls. When Americans arrived in London as tourists in the early 1950s, however, they were often surprised on first viewing them at close hand. The Rolls was so obviously solid in appearance, so boxy, so well-appointed, so elegant—and so short. Further amazement would come when the Americans learned that the Rolls was powered by a six-cylinder engine. This puzzled them. Why should a car that cost three or four times as much as a new Cadillac or Packard be so small and underpowered?

The answer was simple and became obvious upon reflection. For one thing, gasoline had always been more expensive in Britain and the rest of Europe, and the per capita disposable income in most countries was lower than in the United States. Thus, small cars were more affordable. Accustomed to driving long distances on occasion, the Americans preferred those "land battleships," which weren't necessary or, for that matter, even desirable in most parts of Europe, where, in any case, there were fewer highways for a population still wedded to the railroad. Relative affluence, geography, and custom made the difference between the two automobile architectures and cultures, and this continued into the 1950s, when American cars became larger and more powerful, while the reborn European industry turned out models not that much different in size than those of the prewar period.

The Detroit Establishment didn't believe any European car could make a dent in the American market. Ownership of a foreign car in the early 1950s marked one as an eccentric, a snob, or a spendthrift, and probably all three. Because of economies of scale, foreign cars tended to cost more than similarly equipped domestic vehicles. In 1953, for example, General Motors alone turned out more cars than all of Europe's automakers combined. In the United States, the Big Three (GM, Ford, and Chrysler), and what might be called the "Little Six" (Studebaker, Packard, Nash, Hudson, Willys, and Kaiser-Frazer), which soon would be down to two marginal survivors, American Motors and Studebaker-Packard, turned out cars, whereas in Europe there were no companies even the size of Chrysler.

The United Kingdom, however, had the largest, best-developed automobile industry outside of the United States, which, in 1950, produced 522,000 vehicles, more than twice the output of France, which was in third place. Furthermore, the United Kingdom was the most important exporter of motor vehicles (again, France was a distant second). Although the vast majority of American drivers of this period had no intention of purchasing a foreign car, one might have thought that if any country had a chance in the domestic market, it would be Britain. Large segments of the population, especially the educated and affluent on both coasts, had long been Anglophiles, a sentiment reinforced by the wartime alliance. The Rolls continued to be the symbol of quality motoring, and many Americans simply assumed that the British possessed the knack of turning out cars like so many fine jeweled watch movements, in comparison to the highly mechanized, but impersonal domestic models. Small British sports cars were in vogue during the interwar period. Firms such as Morris and Austin had pioneered in several technical areas and were generally thought to be well-managed operations whose products were sturdy, even if their design was a trifle unimaginative. In the immediate postwar years, several parliamentary experts thought these companies and others might do well to manufacture larger cars as well, not only to safeguard against an anticipated American push into overseas markets once domestic demand was sated but also for shipment to the United States, where they might expect a decent reception. Nothing much came of this, but nonetheless, when it came to small cars, it would appear the United Kingdom had a decided edge against all would-be competitors of the time.

Yet even so, the British automobile industry could hardly be considered efficient or modern. Scattered over the English countryside were a score of small companies turning out handfuls of specialty luxury vehicles of the likes of Allard, Alvis, Aston-Marton, and Armstrong-Siddely. In addition, several middle-size operations—Rolls, Rover, Jowett, Singer, and Jaguar—slugged it out for a luxury clientele that was steadily shrinking in number. More than nine out of every ten British cars were manufactured by six companies—Austin, Morris, Rootes, Standard, and two American-owned concerns, Ford and Vauxhall (GM). The American industry, with well over twelve times the output of Britain, could support only three major concerns, while in Britain there was twice that number.

Mergers did take place—Austin and Morris would form British Motors, which, in 1954, would have approximately 38 percent of the domestic market and was thought to have the best chance of any foreign company to crack the American market (between them, they accounted for more than 90 percent of Britain's 106,000 automobile exports in 1953), but it was the wrong merger in terms of efficiency and economies of scale. Others would follow, which would eventually lead to the creation of British Leyland in 1967, a major concern that brought together Austin, Morris, Jaguar, Standard, and Rover. Had such an entity been created in the late 1940s, and had management rationalized the product line, with labor cooperating, the British might have been a formidable entry for the American market. None of this happened, of course. By then, the British automobile industry was not only smaller than that of France, but was behind Japan, West Germany, and Italy. British Leyland even lagged in the domestic market, where Ford had taken the lead, with imports from Japan and the Continent increasing their market share at the expense of British companies.

None of this could have been imagined in 1953, a year in which the "hot" import was the Jaguar. The plant operated on double shifts to fill American orders, and would-be owners of that luxury car were willing to wait four to six months for delivery. The small, peppy, but mechanically temperamental MG sports car was the top import that year, partly because there really was nothing quite like it, but also because of the cachet it bestowed on its owners. More interesting, insofar as the total market was concerned, was the second most popular import, the Hillman Minx, produced by Rootes Motors. For of all the cars available to Americans that year, it alone might have established itself as a permanent part of the automotive landscape.

Despite its name, the Minx was an ordinary, unimaginative, stodgy vehicle, nearer in appearance to that year's Plymouth than to the sleek Studebaker. But it was also small (160 inches long versus 181 for the Hudson Jet, the shortest American car that year), light (2,290 pounds versus 2,511 for the

Willys Lark and 3,215 for the Chevy), and stingy on gasoline (30 mpg on the road, which was close to one-half again as economical as a Ford six). Americans who test drove it found the Minx quite conventional in terms of handling and structure. In other words, at first blush, it seemed that the British had delivered a nice small car for those who thought the American models were too large, too overpowered, and too conventional and who wanted a bit of exotica in their lives.

But there were drawbacks, some of which were evident at time of purchase, and even more so after the car was delivered. For one thing, there was the matter of price. The Hillman cost $1,699 POE New York, which made it slightly more expensive than a stripped-down Chevy six. Thus, there was no price advantage at a time when small cars were supposed to cost less than larger ones. Or to put it another way, the Chevy, Ford, and Plymouth carried a lower per pound and per horsepower price tag than did the Minx. Then there was the matter of service. Although some American car franchisees took the Hillman under their wing, most of them were sold by independents, who often were undercapitalized and who seldom could perform more than routine servicing and minor repairs.

That the car was underpowered by American standards was understood, and a driver accustomed to taking long trips may not have been comfortable in the smaller and lighter vehicle. More important, however, the Minx proved not to be a rugged car, and breakdowns were painful affairs. Parts could take months to arrive from Britain, and when they did, the undertrained mechanics often did not know how to install them. If a Minx went out of commission on the road, the driver would be hard put to locate a nearby dealer or even a mechanic who had metric-size tools with which to work on the car. Tire dealers didn't carry the Hillman size, and auto supply stores didn't stock so simple a thing as replacement windshield wipers. Drivers who had grown up thinking their cars could be serviced anywhere in the country, at almost any gasoline station, became frustrated with their Hillmans, which seemed to spend more time at the dealers than on the road.

The same might be said of other small British "economy" cars of the period. The Morris Minor, which sold for only $1,445 POE New York, seemed tinny, and its interior was spartan by American standards. The Ford Consul made a better showing. Longer, heavier, and with a more modern appearance than either the Minor or the Minx, it could also be serviced at some Ford dealers in the United States, and parts might be obtained from Detroit, rather than from Ford's Dagenham plant in Britain. The Consul cost only a few dollars more than the Minx, and was as economical to run. Had it been offered by Austin or Morris, it might well have caught on and developed a following. But Ford didn't promote the car, believing that every Consul sold represented a sale stolen from Ford U.S.A., rather than incremental earnings. Finally, there was the Austin A-40, heavier and longer than the Minor, but also more expensive at $1,795. The fuel economy advantage over the Chevy, given the cost of gasoline at the time, came to $50 per 10,000 miles, hardly a substantial amount and one that could be wiped out with a single repair.

None of the British small autos did well on the used-car market, an indication of the disgust of their owners and the wariness of potential buyers. The "British Invasion" proved little more than a foray into the United States, timid, half-hearted, and badly conceived and executed. The American public came to realize that these cars were old-fashioned, often badly assembled, and unsupported by a service network. The British cars, which once had an undeserved reputation for quality based on the Rolls, now became the brunt of jokes within the industry. Dealerships folded, and owners of these cars found them to be "orphans" no one seemed capable of servicing. Thus, sales of British cars in the United States declined steadily after 1953. By 1960, the Triumph had replaced the MG as the volume leader with its popular TR-3 sports car, but only 11,683 of them were purchased by Americans, and the company's vehicles were in sixth place on the import list. Altogether British imports accounted for less than 14 percent of the total, one-third of the record compiled by the leader, which was Germany's Volkswagen, a phenomenon that puzzled but still didn't overly trouble the tycoons of Detroit.

More so than even Toyota and Nissan, Volkswagen demonstrated to the world that it was possible for a foreign automobile manufacturer to challenge Detroit successfully, not only in its domestic market, but also in the United States itself. Furthermore, without the VW example to serve as a guide, the Japanese companies might not have dared to mount their assaults.

Although VW had turned out automobiles and other vehicles during the 1930s—Hitler himself laid the cornerstone for the original Wolfsburg factory, and there is a picture of him smiling behind the wheel of a VW convertible with its inventor, Ferdinand Porsche, looking on approvingly—the company's true beginnings go back to the immediate postwar period, when Detroit ruled supreme and when it appeared that American-owned subsidiaries would dominate the markets in which they operated. Such had been the situation prior to the war in most countries. Why should things change now, when America was stronger and more respected than ever?

Germany had pioneered in the development of the automobile. The first true gasoline-powered car is thought to have been invented by an Austrian, Siegfried Marcus, who used an engine designed by a German, Nikolaus Otto. Automotive historians are familiar with the contributions of such men as Karl Benz, Gottlieb Daimler, and Rudolf Diesel. Germans, along with Frenchmen and Britons, but not Americans, led the way in the late nineteenth century, although this was to change later. In 1936, Ferdinand Porsche came to Detroit to worship at the shrine of Henry Ford, who he considered the father of the industry; at the turn of the century, Americans had traveled to Europe—especially Germany—to learn about automotive developments.

During the two decades between the wars, however, American companies, and GM, in particular, crowded out the Germans in their domestic market. As was the case in Britain, there were dozens of manufacturers in the 1930s, but four dominated the field—Adam Opel (owned by GM), Auto-Union, Ford Motor Company AG, and Daimler-Benz. Of these, Opel was by far the largest, and on the eve of World War II, the American companies, between them, had well over one-half the market for cars, this at a time when Porsche was still busying himself with prototypes.

Representatives of American corporations were in Germany even before the war had ended, following the advancing armies a few days after an area had been secured, investigating the conditions at plants seized by the Nazis, and putting together plans to reopen them as soon as possible. General Motors was well represented, and Ford sent its people, too, although little in the way of expansion was expected from that company, which had enormous organizational and financial problems in Detroit to occupy itself.

Three years later, Ford's leaders, headed by Henry Ford II and Chairman Ernest Breech, arrived in Germany on an inspection tour, but also to listen to a proposition from the British occupying authorities and Heinz Nordhoff, an Opel executive before the war, who had arrived at Wolfsburg two months earlier to take command at VW. The factory complex, which was in the British Zone, was still in ruins, but one assembly line had been put into operation, and from it, some 20,000 copies of an unusual small car, beetlelike in appearance, had rolled. The company was an orphan, and the British were seeking a suitable parent. "Perhaps it would be best," reflected Nordhoff. "Perhaps the only hope for this company is to be taken under the wing of a powerful American manufacturer." General Motors, which had reconstructed Opel and seemed destined once again to dominate the market, would not have been interested. But Ford, a distant second, might be in the market for a company that could complement its other operations. This was not the case, however. "Mr. Ford," said Breech, "I don't think what we are being offered here is worth a damn!" Henry Ford II, grandson of the man Porsche had idolized, agreed. So it was that Ford Motors rejected the opportunity to assume ownership of Volkswagenwerk AG.

As it happened, Breech and Ford were turning their backs on VW at a time when the fortunes both of the company and of Germany itself were taking a pronounced turn for the better, although it didn't seem so at the time. While Breech might not have thought much of the VW automobile, he must also have been worried that Germany might still become part of the Soviet empire, and although there was a waiting list for VWs, this was because the other German auto companies had yet to enter the field. Thus, the outlook was not particularly promising.

Then, in quick succession, came currency reform, the Berlin Blockade, Marshall Plan assistance, and a growing awareness of the Soviet threat and a dedication on the part of the West to defend Germany against the Soviets, all of which resulted in the creation of the Federal Republic in September 1948. Soon the world would be talking of the "German economic miracle," as that country not only rebuilt itself at an amazing pace and created democratic political forms, but also showed signs of regaining many of its pre-Hitler markets.

Volkswagen was in the vanguard of this effort. In 1948, it manufactured close to 65 percent of all German cars, a figure that would drop as Opel, Ford, Auto-Union, and others increased their production. Not only did the company retain the loyalty of most of its customers, with demand expanding faster than supply, but it also emerged as the largest industrial concern in the nation, which at the end of the 1950s posted revenues of $1.4 billion.

There were two reasons for this: Nordhoff's strategy and its implementation and the product itself, either of which would have come to little without the other.

As has already been indicated, VW had the jump on the other German automakers, but it also had a product that suited the circumstances of the nation during the immediate postwar period. The price was low: 990 (old) Reichmarks, and although the translation into dollars would mean little, given the unsettled nature of the German economy in 1946 and 1947, it was well within the reach of individuals fortunate enough to have what went for middle-management positions—and of American soldiers who were paid in dollars. By bartering successfully, a sergeant might get a VW for the equivalent of a month's pay, and demand from this source was one reason why the company had a waiting list from the first. It was not at all unusual for a person to purchase a VW, drive it around for a year or so, and then sell it at a higher than new price to someone who didn't care to wait on line at Wolfsburg. American soldiers, completing their tours of duty, also shipped their cars home. Perhaps spare parts wouldn't be available, and they must have thought that the cars would become inoperable with the first breakdown. They were more souvenirs than viable automobiles, something to show relatives and friends while the owner tooled around in a Chevy or a Ford.

Those 1947/48 versions didn't differ much in appearance from the prewar prototypes, and for that matter, would not change significantly over the next three decades. Describing its shape probably is not necessary, for few in the Western world can be said not to have seen many of them over the years (a 1970 poll indicated that the VW Beetle was second only to the Coca-Cola bottle in instant recognizability). And it did resemble a bug more than any car then on the road; this was heightened by the fact that in the early years so many of them were painted black.

It might be more useful to compare the VW to the Hillman Minx, the car that once seemed to have had the best chance of capturing the interests of those Americans who wanted to own a small, foreign-built sedan. To begin with, the Hillman looked conventional; from its oval grille to its humped trunk, it was the kind of car that would attract little attention, either on the road or parked along city streets. The Hillman had a water-cooled four-cylinder, 37-hp engine and a gearshift lever mounted on the wheel, the kind most Americans were accustomed to. Those drivers familiar with Chevys and Fords would have little trouble adjusting to its drive, and although mechanics might not be able to work on the engine because parts or proper tools were not available, at least they would recognize the various components and perhaps be able to improvise tools and adapt American parts.

In contrast, the VW had a rear-mounted air-cooled, four-cylinder, 25-hp engine. Its design was unusual too; the cylinders were horizontally opposed, a layout most American mechanics had never seen, and they must have been at a loss even to locate them on first sight. There was a small trunk area under the front hood, with additional space behind the rear seat—about the same as in the Hillman and other small cars, although this was not apparent. The gearshift was on the floor, where it had been in American cars in the early 1930s, and younger drivers had to learn how to use it. Moreover, the four speeds were not synchronized, and Americans who had become accustomed to automatic transmissions were certain to have trouble with this.

The VW was a *small*, small car. At 160 inches, it was as long as the Minx, but its interior dimensions were less generous. The Minx had four doors, and although its rear-seated passengers would not be as comfortable as they might have been in an American sedan, at least they would have little trouble getting in and out. Adults had to go through contortions to enter the back seat of the two-door VW, and they underwent what to those accustomed to domestic cars must have seemed agonies during a long trip. The Minx, at 2,290 pounds, was more substantial than the VW at 1,610, but paid for this with fewer miles per gallon (30 versus 34). And the VW carried a lower price tag—at $1,395, it was the cheapest "conventional" transportation available for those who did not patronize used-car lots. But American observers did not believe price and gas mileage would overcome VW's drawbacks. Even eccentrics would think twice about driving so unusual appearing a vehicle, especially one imported from Germany.

Those who examined the car, rather than the dimensions, prices, and other figures, came away with a different view, and test drives convinced others of the VW's superiority over the Minx and any other foreign model in its class. First and foremost, its finish was far superior, from an excellent paint job (years later VW would boast that whereas other manufacturers painted their cars, they painted their paint as well) to extraordinarily precise fittings. Volkswagen owners were amazed to find they had difficulty in shutting their doors unless the window was open, so airtight was the vehicle. After becoming accustomed to the gearshift and the noisy engine, drivers came to enjoy the easy handling and steering, not to mention the exceptional front vision over the sloping hood. Compared with American sedans, the VW Beetle seemed a nimble, precise, jewel of a car. Some may have purchased it as an economy vehicle, the alternative to a used Chevy, but they quickly came to realize that economy, lower price, and size didn't have to imply cheapness or loss of status. In these, and in many other ways, the VW blazed a path for other foreign manufacturers to follow.

Quality, recognizability, and novelty by themselves would have meant little were it not for the strategy Nordhoff used in bringing the car to America. And had it not been for the way he implemented that strategy, VW might have enjoyed a brief spurt of popularity and then faded—which is to say it could have gone the way of the Minx.

There was little in Nordhoff's career before he arrived at Wolfsburg to suggest that he would become perhaps the most important German industrialist of the immediate postwar years. His life had been similar to those of scores of other managers of his generation. His father was an insurance executive, having taken a post with a Berlin-based company, after the small bank at which he had worked failed. Heinz, born in 1899 the second of three sons, had a technical education, entered the army toward the end of World War I, was wounded and mustered out, and then returned to school. On graduation from college with a technical degree in 1927, he was employed as an engineer at the Bayerische Motoren-Werke (the Bavarian Motor Works, better known to Americans as BMW), which at that time was designing aircraft as well as producing automobiles. Nordhoff found cars more interesting than airplanes, and thinking he could progress further at a larger company, looked to the United States for employment. He wrote to Nash in this regard, and might have come to America to take a post at that company had not the 1929 crash caused cutbacks at that firm. Then he applied to Opel, thus making the transition from German to GM control. He started out writing service manuals, but soon rose to middle management in the engineering department. In 1936, Nordhoff took a seat on the board, with shared responsibilities for turning out a *Kleinauto*, Opel's response to the VW Hitler so admired. During World War II, he managed a large plant in Brandenburg, fleeing to the Harz Mountains with his family in late 1944 to avoid being captured by the Red Army. After the war, Nordhoff had hoped to return to Opel, but he soon discovered that the once-largest German automobile manufacturer had all but ceased operations. At the time the British contacted him to learn whether he was interested in heading VW, Nordhoff was running a small repair shop. Naturally he leaped at the chance, and arrived at Wolfsburg in late 1947.

As has been indicated, VW had little trouble selling its Beetle in Germany, since initially, at least, there was no competition. This in itself might have encouraged Nordhoff to turn out the cars as rapidly as possible, with little heed for quality control, and in addition, to forgo the regular if not annual model changes. He did neither. Instead, Nordhoff actually tightened up on quality and sacrificed sales for reputation, knowing this would be needed once other companies entered the field. Thus, the low-priced VW surprised its purchasers— even those American soldiers then stationed in Germany—by the value it offered.

Early on, Nordhoff determined that there would be evolutionary rather than radical alterations in both the appearance and the mechanical aspects of his car. Not that he had much choice in these early years. Volkswagen simply couldn't finance model changes, for one thing, and for another, it would have been virtually impossible, given the kind of car with which it had started.

In most cars, annual changes had been more cosmetic than anything else. Those shiny, flashy new models that came out of Detroit every autumn may have looked different from their predecessors to potential purchasers, but more often than not, most of the components under the thin metallic skins and chrome overlays were the same. It wasn't unusual for an American company to retain an engine for well over a decade, virtually unchanged, while the body design and dimensions went through several alterations; this was also true for transmissions, suspensions, and the like. Thus, an eight-cylinder engine originally designed to power a 3,000-pound car might wind up in a car coming in at 4,000 pounds. It may have started out being a trifle too powerful, but wound up providing sluggish acceleration for the vehicle in which it was used.

It would be useful to think of Porsche's design as being "holistic," as opposed to "atomistic," which is to say that to alter one major component or to add weight would have required changes in most of the others, whereas the atomistic American cars could be easily changed, component by component. The Americans knew what they were doing, and so did Porsche. His mandate from Hitler had been to create a low-priced car for the masses, who would forgo cosmetic changes in return for a reliable, inexpensive performer. In fact, this was to be the German version of the Model T, the most famous of the holistic cars. Ford's basic design hadn't changed in appearance in the two decades of its run. Rather, Ford improved it continually, not waiting for the end of a model year to do so. Technology, not fashion, dictated the history of the Model T.

Ford and the Model T, not Sloan and the postwar Chevy, were to be Nordhoff's ideal. He had a car in which every part was matched to every other. Did customers dislike the sloping hood? Could VW transform it into one that looked more conventional? Of course it could, but this would create more drag, and so require a higher horsepower engine, which, in turn, could mean changing the transmission as well. So the idea was rejected, in favor of evolutionary changes that didn't affect the basic body design. Nordhoff presented his rationale in an interview several years later:

> I brushed away all temptation to change model and design. In any sound design there are almost unlimited possibilities—and this certainly was a sound one. I see no sense in starting anew every few years with the same teething troubles, making obsolete almost all the past. . . . Offering people an honest value, a product of the highest quality, with low original cost and incomparable resale value, appealed more to me than being driven around by a bunch of hysterical stylists trying to sell people something they really did not want to have. . . .

While Sloanism triumphed in the United States, Fordism was reborn in Germany.

Yet there were small changes in the design and trim. The carburetor and dashboard were redesigned in 1949, and hydraulic brakes replaced the balky mechanical ones the following year. Cosmetic alterations came in 1951: chrome molding for the windshield and the Wolfsburg crest on the front hood. During the next two years, vent windows were added, the window crank was redesigned, and an oval, one-piece rear window replaced the split one. Most important, all the gears were synchronized, making the car far easier to drive for anyone who hadn't put in time on trucks. Still in 1953, a year in which VW turned out more than 180,000 Beetles, fewer than 1,000 of them were sold in the United States. The Minx still ruled—although its domain was minuscule. The British Invasion was sputtering out. The German Onslaught against Detroit had begun, although almost no one outside of Wolfsburg knew it.

3

The German Onslaught

For decades, no one believed that European cars could ever be a success in the United States. Then, after the war, the British showed that it could be done. I knew that we could do the same.

HEINZ NORDHOFF,
1959

An American friend of mine helped me stage a press conference aboard the freighter. We got a lot of publicity—all of it bad. I even tried calling the VW the "Victory Wagon" to take the curse off it, but the press referred to it only as "Hitler's Car."

BEN POL,
1948

Never in the sales history of the automobile has so much been accomplished by what, at first glance, seems to be so little. The Volkswagen sells because it is, more than anything else, an honest

car. It doesn't pretend to be something it is not. Being an honest piece of machinery, it is one the owner can be proud of. One just can't imagine, for instance, a Volkswagen with a fake air scoop or tail fins to make it look like an airplane in flight.
> Car Fact Book,
> 1957

> *Half Car, Will Travel*
>> Sticker on the back of a VW Beetle,
>> 1957

Ben Pol, a middle-aged, paunchy, convivial Amsterdamer, was Nordhoff's most trusted and talented advance agent. He had been able to talk several Dutch automobile dealers into taking Volkswagens on consignment at a time when anti-German sentiment still ran high and the cars were selling, to the point that, in late 1948, they dominated the market in Holland. For this reason, and because Nordhoff felt Pol's hearty backslapping demeanor would be appreciated by the Americans, Pol was entrusted with the initial foray into the United States.

Pol arrived with one car and a list of possible dealers in January 1949. Both he and the Beetle received publicity, none favorable. Americans may have been hungry for cars, but they drew the line when it came to considering this unusual model turned out by their recent enemy, especially when it was being presented by a man who looked and sounded German. None of the dealers with whom Pol spoke was interested in carrying the car, and most were downright hostile. Dispirited and out of money, Pol sold his demonstration model and spare parts to a New York imported-car dealer for $800, used the money to pay his bills, and returned to Wolfsburg to report to Nordhoff. Undeterred, VW's chief executive traveled to the United States late that year to scout the territory himself. He met with the same kind of reception; in his own words, the expedition was "an utter failure."

Still, Nordhoff wasn't prepared to abandon his hope of selling VWs to Americans, and in fact, he was able to glean several important lessons from what he saw and heard in the United States. For one thing, he quickly perceived the twin problems of sales and service, which would have to be overcome if foreign manufacturers, other than those of luxury cars, were to have an impact in the United States.

In those years, such foreign cars as the British Hillmans and Austins, the French Renaults and Citroens, and the Italian Fiats were distributed in one of two ways. The companies would grant dealers for non–Big Three companies exclusive franchises within fairly large territories, hoping to encourage them to push their models. Thus a Packard, Studebaker, Nash, or Hudson showroom might have a corner set aside for Hillmans or Fiats, placed there on consignment. The dealers thus had another product for practically no outlay of cash or time. Other showrooms—most of them in large seacoast cities—sold only imported models. Such "foreign car dealerships" would stock a large array of disparate cars, from Jaguar to Renault and Fiat, and several others in between. Thus, anyone interested in owning a foreign car (and they were grouped regardless of price and country of origin) could find something to his liking at these veritable supermarkets.

Cars, yes, but not knowledge or service. That Packard dealer or the salesmen at the foreign car distributorships more often than not knew little more about these vehicles than what they might glean from manuals and brochures. They rationalized that this was all that was needed. Customers sufficiently motivated to think about purchasing a foreign car probably had done some research on their own, and had come through the door presold on a particular model. More than one dealer confessed to learning more about their cars from their customers than from any material supplied by the manufacturer.

Service was virtually nonexistent. It was one thing for an American car dealer to provide floor space for a European model or two, and quite another to maintain a full stock of parts and provide training in maintenance and repair for his mechanics. None was prepared to make this kind of investment, and just as these dealers had casually entered into agreements with Renault, Rootes, Fiat, and the others, so they abandoned them in the same way.

The situation at the foreign car supermarkets was only slightly better. At least their managers had some experience with handling these cars and some commitment to them. But here, too, prospective buyers faced a shortage of parts and mechanics who often could not handle their particular models. Owners of British, French, and Italian cars were well advised to expect long delays for almost all repairs. "We'll have to send to the factory for parts" became a familiar refrain—and a vexing one, for that particular warehouse might be somewhere in Europe, the part to arrive by sea rather than air. The car might be off the road for weeks, even months, before the part arrived, and imagine the owner's frustration on learning the Europeans had forwarded the wrong part and that the process would have to be repeated. Indifferent service and repairs drove many owners of foreign sedans back into the arms of Detroit's Big Three. Little wonder, then, that loyalty was so weak or that the resale prices of Hillmans, Austins, Fiats, and Renaults were so low.

All of which Nordhoff came to realize in 1949. Used Beetles were fetching premium prices on the Continent; but if the company imitated the sales and service examples established by other manufacturers of foreign cars, Beetles would surely fail in the United States—assuming the Americans decided to purchase them, in the first place. Nordhoff knew what was needed, but he also realized that VW lacked the capital to establish the kind of support facilities provided by Studebaker or Nash, not to mention General Motors or Ford.

Nordhoff also knew that older, better-known, larger, and more affluent British, French, and Italian companies, with executives experienced in the American market, had made their ways to the United States, and although none had much success as of 1950, in time one or more of them might find the formula for marketing small cars there. When and if that happened, the others might have to withdraw, perhaps never again to have this chance to sell their products to affluent Americans.

All the signs were that Detroit had no intention of moving into this segment of the field. Thus, the market for small cars (assuming one existed) was wide open, and the scramble was on.

Unable to mount the kind of effort he felt necessary, Nordhoff improvised, believing that even a flawed start was better than none at all. He would have preferred establishing his own network of dealers, trained by VW to offer superior service to what he was certain would be an ever-growing number of satisfied customers, but at the time, this was neither called for nor possible. Instead, Nordhoff took the path blazed by others, seeking American agents accustomed to importing European models and then distributing them to the foreign car supermarkets. He offered them the usual concessions to enter the field, only to be rejected by many established dealers betting on the likes of Hillman and Renault, who didn't care for VW's appearance or ancestry.

Nordhoff finally found several dealers willing to take a handful of Beetles on consignment. Max Hoffman was the most important of the lot, but his experience was typical of others at the time. The owner and proprietor of a foreign car supermarket in Manhattan, Hoffman had a clientele of affluent, sophisticated urbanites whose interest in cars ran from sports models to status symbols—from the MG and Triumph to the Humber and Jaguar. Hoffman was intrigued by a new sports car designed by Ferdinand Porsche, then being handcrafted in small quantities. Powered by a rear-mounted, air-cooled engine, reasonably priced and more trouble-free than anything else in its class, the car was already being sold in Europe where demand was strong and notices excellent. Hoffman wanted to carry the Porsche, and Nordhoff was agreeable to the idea—provided he take the Beetle as well. Hoffman accepted the terms, and in 1950 became the exclusive VW importer for the eastern United States.

This meant that Hoffman would get some Porsches for his established customers and others who read or heard about the automobile's rave notices, place some Beetles on the floor, and try to sell more to other dealers east of the Mississippi. In practice, Hoffman would take orders and attempt to ensure prompt delivery. In 1950, some 150 Beetles were placed this way, with 200 more taken the following year. Fewer than 400 arrived in New York in 1953, by which time the total registration was just under 1,000.

As with the Minxes and the Renaults, dealers might carry the VW, but they offered little by way of service or support. Yet even then, they noticed that this car was different. For one thing, it was being sold by word of mouth. People who were bold enough to purchase this car were also the kind of people who enjoyed tinkering with them, and they liked what they found. Moreover, the car proved quite sturdy, needing little in the way of servicing. Without really attempting to spread the news, Hoffman also acquired a following on the West Coast. Nordhoff was delighted to give him this territory, and by early 1954, the Beetle was well on its way to becoming the "fad car" in Southern California, the first of many trends that would start out there and then spread to the rest of the country.

Did Hoffman truly realize what was happening? Did he ever appreciate the potential of the VW? Apparently not, if one is to judge by his actions. Hoffman did next to nothing to promote the car, remaining content to be an order-taker from his enclave in New York. Had he put some of his personal and financial resources to work backing the Beetle, his might have been one of the great success stories of American business, and in addition, he would have amassed a tremendous fortune. As it was, Nordhoff soon grew impatient with Hoffman's lack of dedication and interest. In late 1953, he named John von Neumann, a California dealer, exclusive agent for the western United States and didn't renew Hoffman's contract for the rest of the country.

Although Hoffman had hardly been a dynamo when it came to promoting the VW, he was the symbol of the company to those dealers who were carrying the car. Something had to be done to assure them that the supply would not only be continued, but also that service would improve under a new regime. Moreover, Nordhoff felt that the time was ripe for a stronger and more definite commitment to the American market. Articles on the Beetle were appearing in automobile magazines and even the general press, and most were favorable. The VW cult was in its infancy, and Nordhoff meant to nourish it as best he could. Two factory representatives were dispatched to America, one to head an organization in San Francisco, the other to remain in New York, and they were charged with franchising new dealerships and working with the old ones to upgrade service. As it turned out, the New York office was to become the more important, not only because this was the major urban market and the city was closer to Germany, but also because the man sent to head operations there, Will van de Kamp, was just about perfect for the tasks ahead.

Despite his name and courtly appearance and manner, van de Kamp was not of aristocratic lineage, but rather came from a solid middle-class family. He had flown in the Luftwaffe during World War II and had worked for several German companies afterward before coming to VW in 1951, where he rose rapidly in the sales area, with wide responsibilities for overseas development. Within the VW organization, van de Kamp had a reputation as a perfectionist and as something of a martinet. One American who worked with him during the mid-1950s thought van de Kamp modeled his behavior after that of the pre–World War I Junkers—or at least what he thought it had been. Whether this came to him naturally or was a pose didn't really matter. More important was van de Kamp's unique abilities at translating Nordhoff's concepts into strategies and tactics suitable for the American markets, and creating an organization to carry them out. More than anyone else, van de Kamp infused the VW organization with an élan that served it well during the next two decades.

Shortly after arriving in New York in January 1954 and establishing a makeshift headquarters, van de Kamp set out on a nationwide tour of VW dealers. He found them a mixed crew, ranging from several efficient foreign car supermarkets that carried a full line of parts and were overseen by competent mechanics to motorcycle shops run by amateurs who knew next to nothing about cars and didn't want to learn. Van de Kamp withdrew franchises, demanded upgrading, berated those who ran slovenly operations, and rewarded efficient dealers with larger territories. New dealers were required to demonstrate financial capabilities and a dedication to VW. Specifically, they had to maintain complete inventories and pass muster as repair and service shops. Van de Kamp was supported in this by Nordhoff, who dispatched scores of instructors, salesmen, and inspectors to the United States in 1954 and 1955, while continuing to improve the Beetle to enhance its attractiveness to Americans further.

The effort paid off. More than 20,000 Beetles were sold in the United States in 1955, a year that marked the beginning of the car's takeoff in this market. It was truly a phenomenon, one Detroit noted, but about which it would yet do nothing. Volkswagen clubs appeared, there were magazines devoted to service tips, anecdotes, and even the history of the car. Drivers would beep their horns when they saw another VW. It all was somewhat puzzling to drivers of domestic cars. There was the "VW bore," a species encountered usually on the East and West coasts at cocktail parties, who insisted on imparting to others tales of his car's stamina and economy. By 1959 (when there were more than 120,000 Beetles on the American roads), the car was well on its way to symbolizing the youthful revolt against what many considered a crass materialism that was corrupting the American dream, a consumption ethic run amok. Whereas middle-Americans celebrated earthly successes by purchasing and polishing ornate and large Detroit products, intellectuals at prestigious colleges and universities (and those who aped them) flaunted contempt for such values by driving about in their VWs—unwashed and a trifle dented at that. All of this occurred years before the media discovered "the generation gap." Ironically, what once had been "Hitler's car" became a touchstone of sorts for the political left in the United States and would remain so through the hectic 1960s.

There surely was more to it than that, however. The Beetle wasn't merely a symbol of a rejection of Sloanism in all its cultural manifestations, or a return to the essentials of Fordism. The simple fact of the matter was that the car was almost as good as its most dedicated defenders believed it to be. In design and machining—if not in power and comfort—the Beetle was better than comparably priced American cars. The refusal to change models annually actually benefited its reputation and enhanced its desirability. This was taken to mean that the essential shape was close to perfect—*classic* was the term most often used to describe it by 1969, by which time the VW was no longer called "ugly." Moreover, the continuation of the basic body design translated into higher resale prices for used models. It wasn't unusual for a three- or four-year-old Beetle, which cost less than a Chevy or Ford, to fetch a higher price than a Buick or Mercury of the same vintage.

Finally, the VW had succeeded where the Minx had failed —in the matter of reputation. The British sedan started out by appealing to Americans who thought it a quality product from the same people who had given the Rolls-Royce to the world. Of course, the Minx and other small British cars failed to live up to expectations, and by the late 1950s, they were deemed inferior to their American counterparts. In contrast, the Beetle was initially looked upon as an economy model, but unlike the Minx, its image was enhanced by time and familiarity, and it came to be considered a quality automobile, the equal, in its own category, to the prized Mercedes. By the early 1960s, the Beetle had become the preferred car for many individuals who might have been able to afford more expensive automobiles. This experience, as so many others of the VW, would serve as a guide to the Japanese when the time arrived for them to enter the American market.

The Japanese might also have profited from studying VW's sales and distribution structure. Almost from the start, van de Kamp had realized that the company's American efforts lacked a firm centralized structure, and he meant to provide one. The time to act arrived in the mid-1950s, when Wolfsburg no longer had to seek out and convince American dealers to carry the VW, but rather had the luxury of weeding out the less promising candidates and awarding franchises to proven, well-financed individuals. Even so, each dealer worked out his own arrangements with the factory or the American representative, and van de Kamp believed this ad hoc approach was damaging. In June 1955, with Nordhoff's blessings, he organized Volkswagen United States, which was to be the sole importer of cars into the country. Soon after, it was restructured and a new name, Volkswagen of America, was selected, which, in addition to importation rights, had a mandate to set standards for dealers.

For starters, van de Kamp insisted on new standards of cleanliness and service. Mechanics working on VWs would have to undergo formal training on a regular basis. Promises to customers in regard to deliveries and repairs had to be honored; frequent complaints might mean the termination of the franchise. Van de Kamp then informed several foreign car supermarket owners that they would have to make a choice between the VW and their other cars, or at the very least, erect separate buildings in which the VW would be exhibited and from which it would be sold and serviced. These structures would be designed by VW of America and carry its logo. In this, as in all things, van de Kamp strove to create for VW an image of efficiency and pride, an image he may have felt was increasingly rare in GM, Ford, and Chrysler dealerships.

It seemed to work. By establishing and maintaining higher standards, VW of America transformed grease monkeys, who had previously worked on a wide variety of cars and hadn't mastered any of them, into highly skilled, proud mechanics, who became experts on that single VW engine and other VW components. Some service shops were fitted with large plate glass windows so that customers could watch while uniformed young men treated their cars with painstaking care in an almost antiseptic setting, making certain every spot of grease was removed before sending the Beetle on its way. They couldn't help but contrast this with traditional American practice. There was no more haggling over price, for one thing, and for another, factory-caused defects were not only corrected but also apologies arrived from Wolfsburg as well as from the dealer. And there were seldom many of these. The owner of a Detroit-made "lemon," unable to obtain satisfaction from the company or dealer, might learn from friends of the VW treatment and become a prime candidate for a Beetle. It was truly an American success story, but it must have been galling for other dealers to realize it had been orchestrated from Germany.

Even so, Detroit felt it had no real cause for alarm. All indications pointed to the fact that the vast majority of Americans had no interest in foreign cars—especially small foreign sedans. During the mid-1950s, almost all American automobile executives were willing to concede VW and whatever imitators came along a small market on both coasts, along with eccentrics in between. Detroit's response to the foreign sedan continued to be the used American car, which competed with it in terms of price while offering traditional power and comfort. That this was so isn't surprising, given the temper of the times, the situation within the industry, the market, but most of all, the temperaments of the executives charged with deciding the future of the American automobile. One might wonder, however, why American manufacturers didn't bring to market the small cars turned out by their foreign subsidiaries, so as to capture at least a segment of this market at very little cost. Of the Big Three, only Ford made the effort, a feeble one at that, selling a handful of imports from British Ford, but not encouraging its dealers to offer the models.

Yet this apparent blindness can be explained, if not forgiven. Detroit chose to view the VW as an aberration, a unique product whose success couldn't be imitated by others, and the numbers bore them out. For example, in 1961, not a particularly good year for Detroit, VW sold 177,000 cars in America, most of them Beetles, which represented almost half of all foreign sales. Renault was in second place, with 44,000 cars, the bulk of which were the poorly received Dauphines. Then came

Mercedes, with 13,000 of its high-quality, status-conferring models. Was Detroit concerned? Not when more than 142,000 chrome-laden, powerful Cadillacs were purchased. In fact, the motor industry was even more intrigued with the Volvo, a medium-size Swedish import in tenth place in 1960, which leaped to fourth the following year, posting slightly less than 13,000 sales. The Volvo had a reputation for ruggedness and value. It was larger, more powerful, and more expensive than the Beetle, and part of its appeal was to VW owners anxious to move up the ladder. Since Wolfsburg had nothing else to offer in the way of sedans, some buyers were switching to Volvo. Not that VW had anything to worry about insofar as American placements were concerned, but the American manufacturers thought that rather than challenging them, Nordhoff might be hard put to protect his flanks against Volvo and other such cars that might come along in the 1960s.

To place the matter in perspective, one should consider that, in 1961, none of the European manufacturers was able to sell even a quarter as many cars as did VW, but that highly successful company with its well-publicized and received Beetle, had only 3 percent of the American market. Volkswagen dominated its segment, with Renault, Fiat, and Volvo knowing they couldn't hope to challenge the leader, whereas the British had all but left the arena. What were 177,000 sales, however, compared with Chevrolet's 1.6 million or Ford's 1.3 million? Or for that matter, the 371,000 Ramblers sold by that apostle of the small car, George Romney, of American Motors?

Even so, VW had demonstrated its power, and this evoked a response from Detroit. It was halfhearted and ill-considered, but the fact that the Big Three had deigned to recognize VW as a serious challenger was considered a compliment. Heinz Nordhoff had stirred GM, Ford, and Chrysler into action, something Kaiser-Frazer, Willys, and the British had never been able to do. Each of the large corporations intended to teach the Germans a lesson in production and marketing, drive them back to the Continent, and reclaim what was rightfully theirs, namely the beachhead staked out by the Europeans. Or at least, this was what they seemed to have had in mind.

As it turned out, the Americans were hardly in a frame of mind to teach anyone anything, and in fact, they had learned little from the VW invasion. This could be seen in the misbegotten efforts to enter the small car market during the late 1950s and early 1960s.

·4·

The Coming of
the Compact

*It is utterly ridiculous to use a four thousand pound car for the
wife to go down to the grocery store and get a loaf of bread.*
GEORGE ROMNEY,
1958

*What he did for American Motors he might well do for Michigan,
and it is quite likely that Michigan is in no greater trouble today
than his company was some years ago.*
*Wyoming (Michigan) Advocate,
June 21, 1962*

*It is readily apparent that foreign compact-car owners are of a
social class higher than that of domestic compact-car owners.*
WILLIAM CUNNINGHAM,
*Segmentation in the United States
Compact-Car Market, 1972*

Henry Ford, Walter Chrysler, and Alfred Sloan were well known, celebrated men in the 1930s. The first two had their names on the factories, whereas Sloan headed the nation's foremost automobile corporation. Among industry leaders and students, however, George Mason was considered their equal, if not their superior when it came to turning out cars and running a company.

Mason was less well known more because of the smaller stage on which he operated than anything else. Although most Americans looked to the Big Three for automobile leadership, Detroit monitored developments at Nash's Kenosha, Wisconsin, facility, where Mason was engaged in transforming that once-moribund and almost bankrupt company and creating a new kind of car.

Mason has been largely forgotten today, and others have been credited with his vision and achievements. Vindication for both wouldn't arrive until after he died. It wouldn't be too much to say that in the 1930s the American automobile industry passed from the Age of Ford to the Age of Sloan, and that today we have gone far into the Age of Mason. The reason is simple: Mason was the father of the compact car.

Although he hadn't exactly worked his way up from the factory floor, Mason was of the generation that did and he shared many of its experiences. He started out as a part-time salesman for his father, a Briggs-Detroiter dealer, and, on graduating with an engineering degree from the University of Michigan, took a job at Studebaker. This was followed by stints with other automobile companies, and by 1926, Mason was heading production at Chrysler. At the age of thirty-five, he seemed well on the way to a top management post, if not at Chrysler, then somewhere else.

This he achieved, of course, but not before his career took a significant detour. Mason left the industry that year to assume leadership of the ailing Copeland Products, which manufactured Kelvinator refrigerators, which he soon returned to profitability. His performance at Copeland brought offers from other troubled companies, and Nash Motors was one of them.

Founder Charles Nash was seventy-two years old and seeking a successor. His company, which had sold over 115,000 cars in 1928, had come within a hair of bankruptcy in 1932, when only 20,000 were purchased. The company was solvent with 43,000 sales in 1936, but was still struggling to maintain itself in the face of intense competition. Mason seemed close to ideal for its leadership, but he refused to come unless Kelvinator was part of the deal. Nash agreed reluctantly, and Nash-Kelvinator was formed in 1937.

As it turned out, the refrigerator-maker saved Nash, its steady earnings compensating for the occasional red ink of the auto division. This wasn't because the Nashes of the late 1930s were poorly designed or shabbily manufactured, but rather because the kinds of economies of scale possible at General Motors and Ford couldn't be achieved in Kenosha. Like the companies it most resembled, Studebaker and Hudson, Nash was obliged to keep its prices close to those established by the Big Three's comparable models, and so usually had far lower profits per unit. And in common with them, Nash relied upon a small base of loyal customers who for decades had driven cars turned out by the company, and would have nothing else, and others attracted by prices or innovations not available elsewhere.

Mason didn't believe this could last. Concluding that the next generation of drivers would switch to the Big Three models unless the independents came up with improved cars and better production economies than they had during the early 1930s, he set about changing the line he inherited from Charles Nash. Of course, this had to be done on the cheap by Detroit standards, for Mason always was short on financial resources. Engineers from Budd Manufacturing, a leading factor in the railroad car business, worked with their Nash counterparts— and Mason himself—to develop a sedan body in which the frame and chassis were united, welded in a single unit rather than bolted together as was standard. This eliminated many of the rattles drivers had complained about, permitted important production savings and shortcuts, lessened the amount of steel used in cars, and also simplified fabrication, an important matter at a plant generally conceded to have the most inefficient work force, save for Studebaker's at South Bend.

Mason employed this principle first in the "600," a pioneering vehicle introduced in 1940. Although its exterior dimensions were approximately those of the standard Chevy, Ford, and Plymouth, the 600 weighed little more than 2,600 pounds, which was far lighter than the Big Three cars. In part this accounted for its fuel economy, which Nash claimed was 30 mpg at highway speeds. Since the 600 came with a 20-gallon gasoline tank, it could travel almost 600 miles between refills. Rumor had it that future 600s would have additional novel features, such as a front seat that might be converted into a bed, and even air conditioning, known to be a priority item at Kelvinator.

By Nash standards, the 600 was a huge success. The company reported sales of almost 76,000 units in 1941, its best showing since the onset of the Great Depression. Although this didn't mean that Mason might now contemplate challenging the Big Three (the smallest of which, Chrysler, posted sales of 143,000 cars that year), Nash was now second among the independents, behind Studebaker and ahead of Hudson and Packard, in terms of market share.

Mason had to forgo plans for innovations and new models when World War II broke out. During the war, the Nash and Kelvinator facilities concentrated on manufacturing aircraft engines and related parts. In those years, however, he had time to think about where the corporation might head once automobile production was again possible. Along with most of the industry's executives, he had come to believe that none of the independents would long be viable against the Big Three and that they would have to unite to survive. Studebaker showed little interest in such an arrangement, since, of all the independents, it had the most complete line, but a plan to bring together Nash, Hudson, and Packard was discussed. Each company would concentrate on a different segment of the market —Packard the upper end (against Cadillac, Lincoln, and Chrysler), Hudson the middle (against Buick, Olds, Mercury, Dodge, and DeSoto), and Nash the lower part of the spectrum (Chevy, Ford, and Plymouth). Economies realized through integration of plants, product lines, and distributorships would allow this new entity to compete successfully in an aggressive market.

Nothing came of this particular plan, but it is important to note that Nash was positioned in the "economy" area, which was where Mason wanted to be. He had already concluded that whether as part of a larger firm or on its own, Nash would concentrate on lower-priced, lighter, and even smaller cars. The company would continue turning out vehicles for its established customer base, and when it returned, the 600 was every bit as long and wide as the Big Three entries. But it was also lighter, with significantly higher fuel economies.

Mason wasn't the only person thinking along these lines, or Nash the sole firm willing to enter the field with a smaller car. The man and the company did lead the way, however, at a time when the Big Three were going in the opposite direction, and the VW challenge was yet to come. Mason even selected the name for the car that was to embody his ideas, Rambler (after a Nash model of the pre–World War I period). And it was he who decided not to call it a small car, perhaps because he knew American buyers frowned on the word in most things, and cars, in particular. Rather, the Rambler would be advertised as a "compact."

Mason organized a team to design and then to create this car, the key member of which was Meade Moore, who was Nash's vice-president in charge of engineering and research and who also took a hand in production. But the individual who was to become more closely identified with the Rambler in the public consciousness wasn't Moore or even George Mason. Rather, when Americans of the 1950s and beyond think of the car they recall George Romney, a public relations man and lobbyist who joined the company in the spring of 1948.

Romney was one of those individuals who it is sometimes said merited a more favorable assessment than the one usually afforded in the history books. After leaving the automobile industry when his reputation was at its peak, he became an effective and highly popular governor of Michigan, and in 1964, was talked about as a possible Republican presidential nominee. Romney was the front runner for the designation in early 1968, despite growing concern over his intellectual and political abilities. Then he claimed to have been "brain-washed" regarding the Vietnam War, and the press lacerated him for this remark. Romney was made to appear a well-meaning bumbler and soon after dropped from the campaign, in the end backing Richard Nixon for the nomination. He then served as Nixon's Secretary of Housing and Urban Affairs, retiring into relative obscurity in 1972.

Most Americans who have any recollection of the man probably picture him as an energetic, smilingly attractive lightweight, who might have lacked many of the qualities needed for the White House. Perhaps so, but these were attributes that served Romney well when he mounted the last domestic challenge to the Big Three's hegemony based on the heritage left him by George Mason. For a few years in the 1950s, Romney seemed a giant killer, who not only might turn back the VW assault but might also force GM, Ford, and Chrysler to accept his vision of the American automobile. Not until the emergence of Lee Iacocca as Chrysler's savior, more than a generation later, would the automobile industry have a folk hero of his magnitude.

Romney was born in Mexico in 1907, the son of American Mormons who had gone there in search of greater economic opportunity and religious freedom. The family returned to the United States soon after because of growing anti-American sentiment in Mexico. Several other moves followed, with the Romneys winding up in Salt Lake City, where George attended school and worked as a plasterer during vacations. Always a religious person, he spent a year in the United Kingdom as a missionary. In 1929, Romney went to Washington to take a post as assistant to Senator David Walsh, a Massachusetts Democrat, and this was the beginning of his political career.

Pictures of Romney at the time show a strikingly handsome, clean-cut young man who wouldn't have been out of place in newspaper advertisements for toothpaste or shirts. He was also personable, gregarious, transparently sincere, and eminently likable. Washingtonians with such qualities didn't remain aides for long; either they sought office themselves or entered the private sector. Romney chose the latter path, becoming a trainee at the Aluminum Company of America in 1930, rising not only to be its Washington representative and lobbyist but also to serve in a similar capacity for one of the industry's trade groups, the Aluminum Wares Association. By the late 1930s, Romney had become fairly familiar at congressional inquiries and along the social circuit, respected in association circles as an effective and articulate lobbyist with ambitions for better things.

Romney made the switch from aluminum to automobiles in 1939, but the work itself wasn't that different. He accepted the post of manager for the Detroit office of the Automobile Manufacturers Association. This turned out to be a position of no little power and visibility, for the industry was about to convert to military production and Romney was selected to be its spokesman in Washington. For the next eleven years, he met regularly with top auto executives, served on numerous boards, and learned how the industry was managed from the executive suite. Along the way Romney received bids to join several car companies, usually in a public relations role. All were rejected, for by then he had more exalted ambitions. These appeared to have been realized in early 1948, when he was offered the executive vice-presidency at Packard, with a pledge of the presidency itself after a two-year apprenticeship. Romney intended to accept, but at the last minute, rejected Packard in favor of a post with less status and pay at Nash-Kelvinator, where he was to be Mason's assistant.

While Mason directed the corporation and Moore led the team that was to develop the Rambler, Romney roamed the factory floor, learning how cars were assembled. This was a new experience for a man whose previous work had been far from such activities. This isn't to suggest Romney hadn't had anything to do with formulating and implementing corporate strategy—Mason included him in all the important discussions. But Romney was hardly equipped by training and knowledge to do much more than listen, learn, and comment in those first years. Not until 1950 did Mason elevate him to a vice-presidency and indicate that Romney was the heir apparent. By then the work on the compact had been completed, and the first models were in the showroom. Yet popular legend holds that he, not Mason or Moore, was the "father of the compact."

Not even his biographers and hagiographers would go so far. Rather, they stress his role as promoter and popularizer, which is to say he functioned well in his more familiar roles of public relations man and image-maker. As it turned out, this was precisely what was needed at that time and in the American market, as it was then structured.

Unlike the Volkswagen, the Rambler was a fairly conventional car and would never develop the kind of cult following and loyalty commanded by the Beetle. This wasn't Mason's intention, however. He didn't attempt to imitate the German car, but rather created a market for his own vision of the automobile's future.

The first Rambler, introduced in April 1950, was a convertible with a 100-inch wheelbase; it was some 20 inches shorter in overall length than its Ford and Chevy counterparts. The car was priced at $1,808, only $40 below the Chevy and $140 below the Ford, but the Rambler came equipped with a radio, heater, and other accessories usually demanded by purchasers, and as this package was worth approximately $150, it represented considerable savings. So the Rambler was cost-competitive, which at the time was the major selling point for smaller cars. Other models followed—a station wagon in June and a two-door hardtop a year later, and like the convertible, these were smaller than and meant to compete with Fords, Chevys, and Plymouths.

For all of this, the Rambler wasn't unusual by Nash standards. It shared many components with the 600, and its engine had been reworked from an existing unit. Like all other Nashes, it featured unibody construction. There was a new suspension and dashboard, but the driving public had no trouble identifying the Rambler as a Nash product. As was the case with the 600, it was economical to drive; tests indicated that the Rambler averaged better than 32 mpg at a steady 30 mph, which was more than 20 percent better than what was being claimed for Chevys and Fords.

The new Rambler was released with as much ballyhoo as Mason could afford, and was greeted with curiosity—and then profound indifference. Later on, this would be seen to reflect the economic and social climate of the period; but also, the Rambler didn't appeal to any particular market, being too small for one class of potential customers and perhaps too large for another.

The vast majority of Americans who wanted to own and drive domestic cars—and this was the group Mason was trying to reach with the Ramblers—still equated size with status. Thus, the smaller Rambler, no matter how well it handled, how trouble-free it was mechanically, and how inexpensive it was to buy and own, told onlookers that its driver wasn't as affluent and successful as the driver behind the wheel of an inexpensive version of a Chevy or a Ford. Mason's decisions to start out with the convertible was particularly unfortunate, because convertible owners were particularly sensitive to car size and status. If driving a convertible Chevy spoke well of the owner's modernity or his or her youthfulness and outlook, and indicated he was a cut above the person who owned a four-door Styleline sedan, then a Caddy convertible was far more desirable than its Chevy counterpart. People who thought like this would hardly be drawn to the Rambler. Nor would those who were wedded to the MG and the Triumph, those small, fast-handling British convertibles, for whom smaller size was a virtue, look on the Rambler as a typical product out of the Detroit Establishment. The same held true for the station wagon and the two-door sedan, neither of which made much of a dent in the market. In 1954, when sales were less than 36,000 units, there was talk of abandoning the Rambler as a lost cause.

Yet Mason wasn't ready to quit. Rather, he expanded the line, introducing both a larger Rambler and a smaller new car, the Metropolitan, to the American market.

That an upsizing of the Rambler would occur was almost taken for granted. All American cars seemed to get bigger every year of the 1950s, and why should the Rambler be an exception? In late 1953, Mason approved production of a 108-inch wheelbase Rambler, with interior dimensions that compared favorably with those of the Big Three low-priced cars, but that was approximately a foot and a half shorter in length. This car didn't do well at first, barely keeping pace with the 100-inch model, which was still in production.

The Metropolitan was a much more interesting and potentially important car. Working in conjunction with Britain's Austin, the Nash designers and engineers produced a prototype in 1950 that was dubbed the NXI—for Nash Experimental International. Designed to sell at $1,000, or two-thirds the price of a stripped-down Chevy or Ford, it weighed 1,350 pounds (over 300 pounds less than the VW). The NXI was a two-passenger car, however, and although it was designed to get 50 mpg, it did not suit the American market. Romney was placed in charge of publicizing the car, and under his direction, a market survey to determine potential demand was conducted. Mason entertained great hopes for the NXI, believing that eventually as many as 150,000 of them a year could be sold to young, relatively low-income urbanites, or to suburban families for use as a second or "station" car. But the study indicated that the car would not be well received, and the idea was scrapped, only to be revived three years later as a car to compete with the VW and other European models.

Now named the Metropolitan, the car was somewhat larger and heavier than the prototype NXI, but it otherwise was pretty much the same. And despite its presentation as an American car, the Metropolitan was really an English model, with both drive train and body manufactured by Austin. It was a two-seater, like the NXI, but the front space was more generous than that of most small imports, the VW in particular. Moreover the 52-hp engine was far more powerful than the imports, and the suspension had a decidedly American "feel." Its major appeal would appear to have been to single people or to married couples without children, who were attracted by VW's size and price, but still wanted a domestic nameplate. In 1953, when sales of foreign sedans were still minuscule, this hardly seemed a large market. But if the Metropolitan could have taken a sizable part of it, VW's invasion might well have been blunted, and by a car out of a company that wasn't of the Big Three.

The Metropolitan's statistics were impressive. Although it offered the same rough ride of other small sedans, at 1,880 pounds it was the heaviest of the group. Even so, its reported fuel economy was good—37 mpg at a steady 30 mph versus VW's 43 mpg. Moreover its price, $1,445, was even a few dollars less than the VW. Introduced in 1954, the Metropolitan attracted a great deal of attention and drew buyers into the showrooms. In time it did attract a loyal following, but it couldn't penetrate the market on either coast to any significant degree; the VW remained the car of choice there for those interested in small economy models.

This probably resulted more from image and financial matters than engineering or design. Although the Metropolitan was a generally well-designed car, which proved to be relatively rugged, it was after all, a Nash, and driving a model with that nameplate had no cachet for most Americans of the time. Then, too, the brief love affair with English cars had come to an end, and potential buyers who investigated the Metropolitan came to realize that most of its major components came from Austin, whose record of turning out trouble-free autos was tarnished. Nash's old distributorships, accustomed to dealing with conservative, lower-middle-class families, weren't enthusiastic about a car that was so different from any they had previously attempted to sell. Finally, Nash simply lacked the financial and personnel resources to promote both the Rambler and the Metropolitan. Mason and Romney both agreed that prime consideration had to be given the former, on which the future of the corporation might rest.

Nash-Kelvinator was a troubled firm, although in the immediate postwar period it was buoyed by the unsatisfied demand for cars. Revenues, which had been below $100 million for all but one year of the Great Depression, came to $250 million in 1947; profits were more than $18 million. In 1950, when Romney was being groomed for the succession and Mason believed his dream of capturing a significant part of the small car market could be realized, sales exceeded $427 million and profits were $28.8 million. From then on, it was all downhill for Nash-Kelvinator. Revenues for 1953, the corporation's last full year before its merger with Hudson, came to a record $479 million, but profits shrank to a mere $14 million.

The reasons were familiar, and most of them were beyond Mason's power to change. The Big Three were simply too powerful for any independent to defy. Economies of scale, large dealership networks, well-financed advertising campaigns, and an end to the period when demand outran supply all contributed to problems not only at Nash, but at Hudson, Studebaker, and Packard as well. General Motors and Ford were locked in a struggle for market share, and Henry Ford II's new team was out to prove itself at the expense of the GM line. Ford's sales did rise, but so did GM's, as both expanded at the expense of the independents. Before World War II, the "little four" had less than 10 percent of the market. When the Big Three products were in short supply, these firms, along with newcomer Kaiser-Frazer, had almost twice that percent. Then the shortages ended and the Big Three flexed their muscles, market share declined once more, and by 1953, it was once again less than 10 percent and falling.

Not only couldn't the independents match the Big Three when it came to pricing and advertising, they also failed in the increasingly important area of image. During the Curtice era, when flash, dash, and size were paramount, their products— even the streamlined Studebaker and the last of the Kaisers— lacked the necessary patina of prosperity and marked their owners as unfashionable, outdated, and more than a trifle dull.

Even this might have been withstood were it not for declining quality control. This was an industry-wide problem, but it was most severe at Studebaker and Nash. Loyal customers were willing to stay with their products and pay a few hundred dollars more for them because, in the past, they had considered them reliable and well-constructed. This started to change in the late 1940s, and by 1953, the independents' products were looked on as second rate, and most industry observers knew drastic action was needed if some or all of them were to survive.

Casting about for a means of survival, and by then willing to try almost anything, the other independents decided to follow Nash's lead and come out with smaller and less expensive models, thus avoiding direct competition with the Big Three. The outlook was hardly promising, however, since the Rambler hadn't caught on and sales for the Henry J were disappointing. Still, Willys entered the field with its Aero in early 1952, and in late 1953, Hudson introduced its 104-inch wheelbase Jet. Both failed. Not only were they downsized at a time when this wasn't popular, but also the cars were mechanically uninteresting and offered no significant innovations in design. Moreover, both cars carried higher price tags than comparably equipped, full-size Chevys and Fords. The Aero and the Jet proved to be the death rattles for the companies that produced them. Then Willys became part of Kaiser-Frazer, which itself was soon to leave the industry, while Hudson entered into negotiations with Nash.

By then it seemed clear to most industry observers that significant economies—and perhaps survival itself—could be realized only through merger. This would enable the new company to eliminate some similar lines, close down inefficient plants and become more productive, streamline the sales effort, and in other ways, cut costs so as to both lower prices and increase earnings. Mason led the way, reviving his long hoped for three-way merger of Nash, Hudson, and Packard into an entity he wanted to call American Motors. The combination would be near-perfect, he thought. "American Motors could produce seven series of cars with only two body shells. Body A could be for a basic-volume car. Body B would be used for the Hudson Wasp and Hornet, Packard Patrician and Clipper and also for the Nash Ambassador and Statesman." Duplicate facilities for the manufacture of transmissions, engines, and other parts could be closed down or consolidated. Mason felt certain that the resulting company would be the equal of Chrysler, if not GM or Ford.

Packard's leaders weren't interested in this plan, however, opting instead to merge with Studebaker. As it turned out, this proved fortunate, for of the four independents, Packard was the weakest and had the least promising future. Moreover, the withdrawal of this manufacturer of larger and more expensive cars permitted the Nash and Hudson executives to concentrate on those segments of the market they knew best, namely the low- and medium-price areas.

American Motors came into being on May 1, 1954. Even before then, however, Mason had set into motion plans for integrating plants and eliminating several models, one of which would be the Jet. The difficulties involved were well on their way to being overcome when Mason died of a heart attack on October 3. Less than six months after its birth, Romney became president of AM.

As was to have been expected, Romney pledged to continue his predecessor's policies, and in some respects he did. Rationalization of the model line proceeded, and Romney was even more severe in cutting costs than Mason had been. Although sales increased, rising from $400 million in 1954 to $441 million the following year, this was more the result of an upturn in the economy and a good year for the industry than anything Romney had done. Moreover, AM was awash in red ink, losing $11 million in 1954, $7 million in 1955, and almost $20 million in 1956. The company seemed to have inherited most of the weaknesses and few of the strengths of its predecessor companies. Like them, AM had difficulties financing model changes and large-scale advertising campaigns. Its dealerships were undercapitalized and, for the most part, second rate. The hoped-for amalgamation of Nash with Hudson didn't take place. Both the Rambler models—the 100- and 108-inch wheelbase cars—were also offered by Hudson dealers.

In 1955, the corporation sold a total of 161,000 cars, fewer than Studebaker-Packard, and Romney toyed with the idea of dropping the Rambler entirely and concentrating on the larger Nashes and Hudsons, which although also poorly received, at least seemed in tune with the prevailing taste for ever-larger cars. He did eliminate the 100-inch-wheelbase model and broke ground for a new engine factory to turn out a V-8, and this, too, indicated Romney's inclination at the time. Yet he did hold on. The Rambler remained the lightest and most fuel-efficient car in its class—and in the opinion of most purchasers, the homeliest.

Romney knew the Hudson line was doomed. Throughout 1955, 1956, and 1957 he dismantled that operation, feeding parts to the creditors while integrating what little remained into the Nash division. Within three years, all that remained of Hudson was a handful of executives, a few yet unsold facilities, several dealerships that were in the process of being absorbed by Nash, and a sheaf of paid bills, the funds for which came from the sales. It could be claimed that Hudson had saved Nash from bankruptcy—although not in the way Mason had thought it would when the merger took place. But this trend couldn't continue indefinitely. American Motors wouldn't last the decade unless something altered its image among the car-buying public.

For all his vacillations, Romney hadn't abandoned the idea of a company centered on the compact car. He monitored the sales of small foreign sedans, VW, in particular, and although more Ramblers than Beetles were sold in 1955, he knew that the latter car was penetrating more of the domestic market, with no clear end in sight.

With this in mind, Romney decided to gamble AM's future on the compact, but in fact, he had no choice in the matter. The corporation might go down with the compact, but it would also have failed if changes were not made.

In September 1957, AM announced that both the Nash and the Hudson would be discontinued. In their place—and as a sign of dedication to the small car principle—the firm would produce only one line of full-size cars, the Rambler, and would revive the old 100-inch-wheelbase Rambler, now to be called the American—not only after the company but also to attract buyers away from the Beetle.

This was a dramatic move, but hardly daring. Eliminating the Nashes and Hudsons would allow Romney to sell off more assets and concentrate all production in Kenosha. The 108-inch-wheelbase cars would have been matched against Chevy, Ford, and Plymouth, whereas the reborn American would have the compact category to itself and presumably offer some competition to the imports. Under Romney, AM all but abandoned the middle and upper levels of the market, becoming solely interested in compact economy models.

The American wasn't much different from the old small Rambler. It was powered by the familiar and conventional 90-hp, six-cylinder engine, at a time when the Big Three were engaged in a horsepower race. The car was plain, with little chrome and no tail fins, whereas the Big Three cars had three-tone paint jobs and splashy interiors. The American could seat six—barely—the Chevy, Ford, and Plymouth were becoming ever more spacious. On the other hand, the American claimed to deliver more than 20 mpg on regular gasoline in stop-and-go traffic, whereas some medium-price Big Three cars went less than 15 mpg on high test. Romney promised to retain the basic style from year to year (to save money as much as to deride annual changes for the sake of change). Most important, he lowered the price; the delivered cost of a new American would start at $1,789, which was approximately $300 less than the cost of a delivered Chevy, Ford, or Plymouth. For the first time since the end of the war, an independent had managed to gain a significant price advantage over the Big Three.

Drawing on his public relations background, Romney played an important, if not central role in developing a new advertising campaign, the boldest since the end of the war, and in the process became a highly visible spokesman for his company. Standard-size cars were derided as "dinosaurs in the driveway," and American Motors asked, "Why should a 110-pound woman need a two-ton car to take her three blocks for a package of bobby pins?" and "Do you drive your car or does it drive you?" The company's television ads were humorous, lively, and barbed, drawing much favorable comment and winning awards. But they didn't sell cars. Traffic in the showrooms did increase, but sales remained low.

That things changed late in 1957 was more the result of Romney's good fortune than anything else. As noted, the Edsel was introduced in September, with far more ballyhoo than Romney had been able to muster for the American, and initially at least, sales were good for this large, high-powered car that was available with gaudy paint jobs and many accessories. Then, less than a month later, the USSR shocked the nation by successfully launching a space satellite. This was taken to mean the Soviets had surpassed the United States in several key technological areas, and editorial writers and television commentators wanted to know how this could have happened. There was talk of thefts of American secrets and the genius of captured German scientists, but even more talk about what was wrong with American society in the 1950s. The most popular answer seemed to be that the nation had become crassly materialistic and overly sensate. And just as Sputnik became a symbol of Soviet success and American failure, so giant cars came to stand for much of what was perceived as being wrong with the country. From his desk at the Defense Department,

Charles Wilson attempted to belittle the achievement, saying that the United States wasn't interested in "playing basketball in space," and in any case, would have a satellite of its own shortly. To this Senate Majority Leader Lyndon Johnson replied, "Yes, and it will have a two-toned paint job and window washers." Again, the large car became the scapegoat.

It would be going too far to suggest that Sputnik was responsible for declining car sales in 1958, since this was to have been expected after the record-breaking pace set in 1957 and the developing recession. But at 4.3 million units, this was the worst showing in a decade and caused no little consternation in Detroit. But not in Europe, for foreign car sales in the United States jumped from 206,000 (3.5 percent of the market) to 378,000 (8.1 percent), with VW going from 65,000 to 79,000.

The AM story was even more dramatic. Sales rose from 106,000 cars in 1957 (1.8 percent of the market) to 186,000 in 1958 (4 percent). American Motors was the only domestic automobile manufacturer to increase revenues in that recession year—to $470 million, and the profits of $26 million were not only the first ever but larger than those posted by Nash in any year but one. *Consumer Reports* selected Rambler as its "Car of the Year," AM's stock sparked on Wall Street, and George Romney's name and face became familiar throughout the nation. Nor was this simply a flash in the pan. More than 363,000 Ramblers were sold in 1959 and 422,000 the following year, when AM had more than 6 percent of the market. The change in preferences, the VW revolution, the recession, Sputnik, good fortune—and Romney—had saved the corporation.

And it shook up Detroit more than at any time since the Great Depression. The automobile establishment had always believed the VW phenomenon wouldn't last, or at the very least would soon peak and then decline. Detroit just couldn't believe foreigners could ever understand the broad American market and appeal to owners of Chevys, Fords, and Plymouths. The Rambler presented a different kind of threat, and one that called for a response. This car was American, down to its very name, and over time it might appeal to large numbers of domestic drivers. National self-esteem remained high, Sputnik notwithstanding, and although the automobile executives might dismiss Heinz Nordhoff as an upstart German, they respected Romney as one of their own, a man who had come up with a successful product worthy of imitation.

The lesson of the American wasn't lost on Studebaker-Packard. The other independent also paid Romney the compliment of imitation; in 1958, Studebaker-Packard unveiled the Lark.

Like the American, the Lark was mechanically conventional and short on chrome and fancy interiors. It was a trifle more stylish than the older car, and to some it seemed a squat version of the 1957 Champion. The Lark was less economical than the American, but it boasted a more powerful six-cylinder engine and could be purchased with an optional V-8, which enabled it to outperform most standard models.

Just as the American had saved AM in 1958, so the Lark pulled Studebaker-Packard out of the red in 1959. The firm had sold 48,000 cars (1 percent of the market) in the previous year, when it lost $2.2 million. During the first full year of Lark sales, Studebaker-Packard sold 113,000 cars (2.2 percent of the market) and reported a profit of $28.5 million. For a few months in 1959, it appeared the company had carried out "the little miracle of South Bend," as one newspaper called it. But the Lark had arrived too late, either to save the company or to make important inroads against the American in the compact automobile market. Production declined steadily thereafter, and in 1965, Studebaker-Packard produced its last car.

Meanwhile AM found itself in a new struggle, one born out of its successes rather than its failures; this was the Detroit response to the American. The automobile show held in New York in late 1959 starred three new models—the Corvair, the Falcon, and the Valiant, out of GM, Ford, and Chrysler, respectively. The Big Three were prepared to take charge of this rapidly expanding segment of the market, in the process not only returning American Motors to its marginal position but also ejecting the Europeans—VW included—from the domestic scene.

───── 5 ─────

The Big Three
Think Small

The proposed Chevrolet lighter car project has been indefinitely deferred due to a continuing material shortage, both for new plants and car production, and the desire of the General Motors Corporation to devote all the productive facilities and available materials of the Chevrolet Motor Division to meet the overwhelming demands of the motoring public for the established line of Chevrolet vehicles.

General Motors press release,
May 15, 1947

Thus far it has not been practical from the standpoint of the economics to offer the small car . . . because you take the value out so much more rapidly than you can take the cost out.

HARLOW CURTICE, chairman,
General Motors,
1958

There were some small cars out, like the Falcon and Monza, but Lee [Iacocca] was looking for a distinctive kind of car. From cars already on the market you could buy only either a big car or a smaller, plain kind, and there wasn't a really nice smaller car available. If you wanted a nice car, you had to buy a Lincoln or Cadillac, but that was it.

HAL SPERLICK, designer and product planner, Ford, *1982*

Late in 1955, General Motors and Ford design teams went to work on compact car projects. This isn't to suggest that executives there were firmly committed to manufacturing them. As has been seen, the Rambler wasn't particularly popular that year, and although VW sales were rising, and waiting lists extended to more than half a year in some parts of the country, Detroit still did not see the Beetle as a serious threat to Chevy, Ford, and Plymouth. Rather, this was a form of contingency planning that was and is quite common within the industry. Then as now, the major companies experimented with designs and mechanical innovations, few of which were or are realized in production models. So it was with the small car projects. None of the original designs of 1955/56 made it to the showrooms, but the projects had been set into motion, to be aborted or implemented as conditions dictated.

Meanwhile, Detroit monitored the foreign car invasion, the feeling being that more than anything else numbers would dictate the decision, and so they did. Total foreign car sales for 1955 came to 58,460 units, four out of five of which were small sedans. The following year, when domestic sales slumped by 17 percent, the imports sold 98,187 units. Troublesome, but hardly dangerous, for this was still less than 2 percent of the total market. If it had stopped at that point, Detroit might never have acted, but the small cars kept coming, with almost 200,000 of them sold in 1957, by which time the imports had almost 3 percent of the total market.

This led to a response, or to be more precise, two of them.

First, Detroit accelerated research and development for compact cars, with production now a distinct possibility. Second, both as a stopgap measure and a potentially less expensive method of meeting the overseas challenge, they revived importation of small cars manufactured by their European subsidiaries.

As noted, Ford authorized the importation of a number of cars from Ford Ltd. in 1949, and these cars continued to be imported during the next few years, although the company did little to promote them. Even so, at mid-decade, Ford held third place in the import market behind Volkswagen and Renault, with sales doing well even during the 1956 slump. Close to 20,000 of these cars were sold in 1957, at which time Ford authorized an advertising campaign and conducted a survey to determine just what there was about the cars that appealed to American drivers. The results of both were about as expected. The ad campaign didn't seem to affect sales, and the survey indicated that many of the purchases were made by individuals who didn't want to wait six months or so for a VW and decided to compromise with an imported Ford. This implied that sales would decline sharply once VW's production caught up with demand. Concluding it made little sense to stress importation, Ford devoted more time and effort to designing a domestically manufactured compact.

The GM experience was somewhat similar. The company had recently turned out new lines of cars at its British Vauxhall and German Opel subsidiaries, and now decided to bring them to the American market. Like the British Fords, these cars were somewhat larger, heavier, and more powerful than the VW. And at around $2,000 each, more expensive too. In fact, the Vauxhall and the Opel were only slightly lower in price than the more spartan versions of the Chevrolet. What Curtice clearly had in mind was to bring in cars to sell to people who were on line for VWs. When and if sales dropped, so would the two cars. But if they managed to develop a market of their own, GM would pour additional funds into advertising and promotion. It was, then, an inexpensive way of entering both the import and small car areas.

Alone of the Big Three, Chrysler lacked overseas subsidiaries, although it did maintain a few small fabricating plants in Europe and Australia. Casting about for such companies, and finding the pickings lean, Colbert settled on Simca, an ailing French company in which Ford had once had an interest. Although Simca was second only to Renault in its domestic market, the company was poorly managed and its plants were chronically troubled by poor quality control. Chrysler started by purchasing a one-quarter interest in the company in the summer of 1958, took seats on the board, and proceeded to export small Simca sedans. These cars were approximately the same size, and had the same price tags, as the Opels and Vauxhalls and Ford Anglias, which is to say they didn't compete directly with the VW Beetle. Especially when it came to dependability; the Americans soon learned what the French had known for years, that Simca was an unreliable car. Arriving at a time when Chrysler itself was turning out low-quality models, Simca proved a headache and a money loser. So although GM and Ford presented their foreign cars at low cost and risk, Chrysler entered into an important commitment that turned sour, further weakening the corporation.

Meanwhile, development proceeded apace at GM and Ford, with Chrysler establishing a research team soon after. Designers at all three companies relished the idea of producing a model to compete with the VW, wanting not only to prove that they too could create a small, economical car but also to demonstrate that Americans were the world leaders in all aspects of the auto industry. Their enthusiasm wasn't shared by the Big Three executives, however, who in fact positively disliked having to move toward compacts. Although sales figures may have dictated a decision to manufacture these models, other sets of numbers indicated they wouldn't be anywhere as profitable as were the large cars and, in fact, might lose money

—a great deal of it—should sales fail to go above 500,000 or so for each company.

Unlike the decision to import cars from captive European companies, the one to convert American factories to small-car production would be most costly. For one thing, new assembly lines would be needed and this, together with research and development costs; the price of tools, dies, and so on; promotion, and related expenses, translated into a total commitment for all lines of the Big Three of close to $10 billion. Then, too, the labor time to turn out a small car was the same as for a full-size model, and the savings on materials would be relatively insignificant. To give the most obvious example, GM would have to create a smaller version of the Chevy, whose stripped-down Bel Air 6 was selling for less than $2,700, that would be marketed for less than $2,000 if it were to compete with the VW Beetle, or $2,400 to $2,500 to rival the American, and this would require cost-shaving that Detroit had not known since the Great Depression.

Then there were the other questions, such as the degree to which the small cars would cannibalize sales from their larger "cousins," rather than from the imports or the American. It would be disastrous if the compact Chevy failed—but perhaps worse if Bel Air sales slumped because would-be owners were attracted to the smaller model, causing GM to lose a large profit realized on such sales.

Finally, what would be the reaction to a small Cadillac? Would a generation that had learned to equate status with size conclude it was somehow inferior? And if this were so, would this adversely affect the entire Cadillac line? It was commonly believed that Packard's decline dated from the moment the company decided to come out with a medium-price six-cylinder car after the war, so that potential buyers turned to Cadillac. Might this experience not be repeated when and if Cadillac became available in a smaller "six"? And was a potential reward worth that kind of risk?

Years later, Detroit would be faulted for having responded sluggishly to the challenges of the VW and, in a somewhat different way, of George Romney's American. Perhaps so, but given the circumstances, the reluctance to downsize was not only understandable but also realistic and sensible. Critics noted that the market share taken by small cars and compacts expanded significantly in the 1950s, but they failed to appreciate that American automobile buyers indicated in many ways their preference for larger, more powerful, gaudier cars. Tail fins and other gimmicks may seem foolish, in retrospect, but then, customers seemed to crave them, and so they were provided. The failure of the Edsel and the success of the American shouldn't lead one to ignore the popularity of the Chevys and Plymouths when those models embraced Detroit Baroque.

Downsizing still inferred downgrading late in the decade, and this view prevailed even during the 1958 recession. The lessons could be seen in the public opinion polls, but more important, in showroom traffic and purchases. Those who argue that Detroit manipulated the market give far too little credit to the customers and ascribe too much power to the industry's leaders. Moreover, such criticism usually comes from individuals who would have been quite content if Detroit had attempted to impose *their* views in cars upon the market —by producing only small, economical vehicles, for example. What should be realized is that the same forces that led Ford to turn out the Edsel obliged the Big Three to take the far greater risks of going to the compacts, namely, consumer tastes as shown by consumer purchases.

By 1959, when the Big Three's compacts were ready to be introduced, the imports had more than 10 percent of the market, which was triple the 1957 share. One automobile industry executive was quoted as saying, "There will always be 5 percent of the car market that will be made up of individualists and nonconformists who cannot permit themselves to choose a car built by one of the Big Three." Clearly he underestimated the number of such individuals. What remained to be seen in 1958/59 was whether that extra 5 percent or so who had been won over to the imports would return once GM, Ford, and Chrysler entered the field, and whether the other 90 percent of "conforming" Americans would accept or reject the new cars. Even as they proceeded with plans for compacts, none of the Big Three was certain just how it wanted the majority of customers to react.

This ambiguity was seen in the statements of industry leaders throughout 1958, a year when final plans were completed and assembly lines were converted. In January, Curtice told a Senate subcommittee that "Thus far it has not been practical from the standpoint of the economics to offer the small car, on the basis that because you take the value out so much more rapidly than you can take the cost out," to which Colbert added, "up to this point all I can say is we at Chrysler have not given up, but we have not found a way yet to engineer, style, and build one of these smaller cars for enough difference in price to justify what we believe the American market demand for it is." At the end of the year, GM President John Gordon said the company was still "weighing the pros and cons" of small-car manufacturing, and the following March, when automobile magazines were reporting the dimensions of the Chrysler compact, Colbert claimed his company would enter that field only if the others led the way.

The reason for this lack of candor was obvious. Given the miserable market for cars in 1958, these men didn't want to do or say anything that might dissuade Americans from buying cars. Reports of new models might do just this, they believed, and so deceptive statements were made throughout the period.

In March 1959, at a time when auto sales were on the upswing and it appeared that that year's models would sell, each of the Big Three announced its intention to offer a compact during the 1960 model year. Compact rather than small, that is, for the new cars would have dimensions closer to the American than the VW. But the companies wouldn't go further than that. Little by little, over the next few weeks, additional details were released, this form of corporate striptease being quite common to maintain consumer interest, and so it did, even more than had that for the Edsel. By early June, anyone at all concerned with Detroit's plans could have discovered that the first of the compacts would bear the Chevy, Ford, and Plymouth nameplates and that the Chevy would feature an air-cooled, rear-mounted engine. Even the wheelbase figures were known: the compact Ford was to come in at 109.5 inches, the new Plymouth was to be 106 inches, although a trifle longer overall. The price tags were supposed to be just under $2,000, to undercut the American and offer stiff competition to VW, especially if, as anticipated, dealers discounted them a trifle.

If these new cars proved successful, the companies planned to upgrade them by transforming the basic shell into compact Buicks, Oldses, Edsels, DeSotos, and Chryslers in 1960. And then in the autumn of 1961, they would take their biggest gamble by bringing out compact versions of the Cadillac, Lincoln, and Imperial. Finally—always assuming continued successes—GM and Ford hoped to offer Americans truly small cars designed to compete head-on in size, performance, and price with the Beetle; this was to happen in late 1962. But it all depended on the reception afforded the first wave and the continuing development of the American marketplace.

Even as these plans were being leaked, structures and implementations were changing. At Ford, it was decided to drop the Edsel; not only would there not be a compact version of the car for 1960, but also the full-size model itself would be cut off at the end of that model year, with Ford absorbing a loss in excess of $300 million on the project. Although this cost the corporation dearly in the matter of reputation, it also meant that some Edsel installations and personnel could be switched to the manufacture of the new compact, now known as the Falcon. Because of this, Ford was able to enter the market before the others, and so garner additional publicity.

The Falcon was a genuine compact version of standard-size American cars. It surprised no one who had driven a variety of domestically manufactured vehicles, except perhaps for the manual choke of the kind that had been dropped by most American manufacturers during the immediate postwar period. The Falcon was three feet shorter than the Edsel (to which it was often compared) and at 2,500 pounds, more than 1,400 pounds lighter. It featured a 90-hp, six-cylinder engine; the Edsel 8 was more than twice as powerful. Yet the price differential, although significant, was not that great. A Falcon with an automatic transmission might cost a few dollars less than $2,300; a similarly equipped Edsel was listed for under $3,000, but was being discounted by several hundred dollars. Ford had striven mightily to hold down the price, which accounted for that manual choke, but couldn't bring it below the magic $2,000 figure.

The Falcon was a great sales, but not a corporate, success. More than 100,000 of them were sold in the last few months of 1959, and over 500,000 the following year, more than the GM and Chrysler compacts combined. But there was a price for this: Ford sales declined from 1.4 million to 917,000 in the same period. Clearly, Falcon had cannibalized sales from its larger parent.

What kind of person purchased the early Falcon? The simple answer might be one who wanted a compact, conventional car, but there was more to it than that. Although significantly smaller than the standard Chevys, Fords, and Plymouths, and mechanically far simpler, the Falcon wasn't that much different in size and performance from the Fords of the late 1940s. Perhaps people who purchased Falcons were indicating that the pride of ownership that came from owning the larger and more powerful cars wasn't worth the price in initial cost and maintenance. It came closer to the old, familiar "basic transportation" than anything the Big Three would offer after 1973, and the Falcon's success indicated that plenty of Americans wanted just that. But this caused no great joy at Ford headquarters, because the profit margins and net profits on Falcons were significantly below those for the standard-size vehicles. Even before the great success of the 1960 model year, Ford's designers were told to transform the Falcon into a larger, more powerful—and more expensive—car.

General Motors developed a compact that was, at the same time, less and more successful. This car, the Corvair, featured design and engineering that were both daring and clever—quite different from what one had come to expect from the Chevrolet Division—and if fully realized, it might have provided GM with a near-perfect compact from both the technical and marketing points of view.

The Corvair's air-cooled flat, or "pancake" engine, with its rear-mounting, would put some potential customers in mind of the VW, and perhaps allow it to take sales from the German company. That GM was taking aim at the Beetle was evident from the start, and there even were some improvements to lure owners of that car. For example, whereas the VW was most impressive in a wide variety of areas, its air-cooled engine didn't pump out enough heat to warm driver and passenger during the cold northern winters. The Corvair's design team —a number of whom were Europeans from Taunus who knew the VW—got around this by developing a gasoline-fired heater even more powerful than that found in standard-size cars. And although the trunk space in both the front and the rear was quite small, even when compared with the compact Ford and Plymouth, it was far larger than the minuscule space in the Beetle.

Beyond that, the Corvair was a low-slung, sporty-looking car. The name itself, derived from the Corvette, was selected to suggest speed and high performance—or so it was later claimed. Thus, GM was putting out an automobile that owners of standard-size Chevys wouldn't find appealing, and of course, this was precisely the idea. Of all the first-wave Big Three compacts, the Corvair alone did not cannibalize sales from the full-size parent.

The biggest problem facing GM was holding down costs, and this meant converting the original, all-aluminum engine into one that was half aluminum and half cast iron. In addition, some of the interior finishes would be plastic rather than metal. More important, Chevrolet's management decided to scrap a stabilizing bar that would have kept the car on course if the driver oversteered, which was quite common with vehicles with rear-mounted engines. Finally, the Corvair had 13-inch rather than 15-inch wheels. The total savings for all of these changes came to approximately $30. A small amount, one might think, but Cole was hoping for sales of around 500,000 cars a year, and this meant an additional $10 million in earnings. Or more likely, a lower price tag for the Corvair, to lure VW buyers and to maintain an edge against Ford and Chrysler.

The Corvair performed almost as well as Chevrolet's executives and designers had hoped. Although VW sales weren't unduly affected, the car did attract young, sports-minded individuals and did not affect the sales of the division's conventional-size models.

With its Valiant, Chrysler attempted to appeal as much to the potential buyer's image of what a sports car should look like, as to his expectations for a small sedan. The Falcon, however, looked like and indeed was a conventional family car; the Corvair looked like an interesting model that might appeal to some young people who otherwise would not consider a Chevy; and the Valiant represented a middle ground between the two. One executive remarked that the model was what one might have expected had a sophisticated European designer set out to create a car middle-Americans, with fantasies regarding exciting driving, but no real desire to own a low-slung powerhouse, might want. It had already happened at Ford, where the Thunderbird had evolved from a snappy two-seater into a sedan. Might an upgraded Valiant compete on a price basis with the T-Bird? The question seemed to have entered the minds of executives at Chrysler. The company was in the mood for compromise, and this came through in the Valiant. The car was expected to find favor with those who liked those high-finned Plymouths, a Ford owner who found the Falcon dull, or a GM customer who wanted a small car but considered the Corvair a trifle too unusual for his tastes. Many journalists who specialized in analyzing automobiles found the Valiant a smooth-driving car, the most powerful of the small sedans, which was almost as economical as the other two, but one with the flaws as well as the virtues of recent Chrysler products, namely, it was shoddily constructed. Chrysler engineering continued to be strong, but quality control there was the worst of all the Big Three.

Like the other smaller cars, it did the job assigned it, namely, to hold back the challenges both from overseas and American Motors. Chrysler sold slightly fewer than a quarter of a million Valiants, while Plymouth sales declined by 140,000 units. Here too the car was a compromise, but the Valiant did not cost Plymouth as much as Falcon did Ford, nor did it have the insignificant impact Corvair had on Chevrolet.

It would appear that a large number of these sales were taken from the imports, especially Renault, Volvo, and Fiat. But not from VW, however, which in 1961 sold more than 177,000 Beetles and Karmann Ghia sports cars in the United States and, ironically, was selling a larger model sedan—the Variant—in Germany. Volkswagen had close to one-half the import market and was enlarging its grip all the while. Sales came to slightly less than 200,000 the following year, when four out of every five foreign cars sold in the United States was a VW product. Even so, this was less than half the number of Falcons sold. In 1959, the Europeans had more than 10 percent of the American market; three years later, the figure had fallen to 4.9 percent.

American Motors' period of glory came to an end, once the Big Three entered the field. Rambler American sales wound up at 422,000 units in 1960 and then declined to 370,000 the following year. There would be a mid-decade revival, but by then all hopes of challenging the Big Three had ended. By the early 1970s, when sales were around one-quarter of a million units, the talk at AM dealt more with what was needed for survival than anything else.

That the Big Three would become complacent is understandable. Their executives had for years claimed they could throw back the foreigners any time they chose to, and now all but VW had been crushed. As for VW, Detroit continued to believe the company catered to oddballs whose business wasn't worth the trouble going after.

This attitude, combined with the success of the compacts, led GM and Ford to abandon plans for VW-size cars of their own. The Ford model, which was to be called "Cardinal," and GM's "Fisher" were kept on the drawing boards but never produced in the United States, although Ford manufactured its small car as the Taunus 12 in Europe and the Fisher influenced designs at GM's European subsidiaries.

The Big Three were to introduce additional compact models in the 1960s, many of which enabled customers to upgrade from those that came out in 1959 and 1960. Customers who were unhappy with the Falcon might have appreciated the Comet, for example, which carried a Mercury nameplate. Oldsmobile would have the F-85 and Cutlass, while Pontiac produced the Tempest and Buick the Skylark. At Chrysler, the Dodge Dart was a fancier version of the Valiant. Most of these cars were well received.

It was paradoxical, however, that with all this success, margins dipped precariously. Detroit now felt that it could provide just about any car—short of one to take on the VW— the American public wanted, but the experience with the Corvair, Falcon, and Valiant had shown that prosperity could be profitless. As one GM executive observed, more money might be made from the sale of a single "loaded" Bel Air than from five stripped Corvairs, and the same was true for the others. The companies hadn't been particularly happy with having to come out with those cars, but their successes meant they couldn't be abandoned.

They might be altered and "augmented," however.

The solution to this dilemma was already quite familiar to industry veterans: when in doubt, upgrade. Customers were prodded into equipping their new compacts with a wide variety of options, from special paint jobs to air conditioning, so that in the end these cars, designed as economy vehicles, might cost as much or more than the full-size models.

In addition, several of the compacts started to grow in size, while Ford and GM came out with additional compacts that were really full-size cars. This trend became obvious in 1952, when Chevrolet introduced its Chevy II. This car was a standard-size sedan, spartan and less powerful than its bigger brother, with styling reminiscent of the 1950–1954 Plymouths. It seemed conservative and cost slightly less than the full-size Chevy; although some called it a compact, it was really the first of a new breed, which would soon be known as "intermediates." Apparently GM hoped that the Chevy II would take some of the play away from the Falcon, and so it did, leading Ford to retaliate with the Fairlane, which was almost indistinguishable from the full-size Ford. At Chrysler, the Dart became more like the Dodge and less like the Valiant. And this was not the end of the proliferation. In 1963, Chevrolet introduced the Chevelle, which matched the mother car in cost, but offered a different body style.

By mid-decade, the potential customer for a GM car starting out at the bottom of the range might look at a Corvair sedan. Then he would move up to the Chevy II, with a half-step to the Chevelle. Next came a wide variety of full-size Chevys, with the top of the line models costing as much as an Olds. The Pontiac line began with two versions of the compact Tempest, followed by three lines of full-size models. The Buick came in three choices, one of them a seemingly contradictory "full-size compact," which was really an intermediate. Oldsmobile could be had in the large F-85 compact, the conventional sedan, or the pricy Toronado, an ultra-high-performance Grand Turismo model. Cadillac remained at the top of the line—but with several different body styles. Not even Cadillac's austere reaches were immune in this period of proliferation.

The Ford line was more limited, ranging from Falcon to Fairlane to Ford, then to Comet and Mercury, and onward to Lincoln. At Chrysler, the progression was from Valiant to Plymouth (in three models) and then to Dodge, Chrysler, and Imperial.

Not since the 1920s had there been so many different models of cars on American roads.

New ones were continually appearing. Ford's highly successful T-Bird indicated that there was a ready market for vehicles that looked like sports cars, but ran like conventional American sedans. Many wanted a Thunderbird, but its price was out of reach for the average car buyer. Lee Iacocca, then a thirty-nine-year-old Ford vice-president, led a team that developed a car that partially satisfied this craving, a low-priced vehicle that still was a status symbol of sorts: the Mustang, which appeared in the 1965 model year, when almost 560,000 of them were sold; more than 600,000 were sold the following year. General Motors responded with the Camaro, and the race was on.

All the talk now was of sporty-looking sedans, which seemed a near-perfect compromise between the small cars and the full-size models, which were usually purchased with many options, and returned good profits per unit to the manufacturers.

In 1965, Detroit sold Americans a record 9.3 million cars, and the field was littered with the corpses of abandoned showrooms of European car companies, and a dwindling number of foreign-car owners vowed never again to buy a car that might some day become an orphan.

Volkswagen sold more than 383,000 of its cars in America in 1965, accounting for two out of every three foreign sales. Renault, which four years earlier had been in second place with 44,000 sales, was now in ninth, having sold only 11,000 of its Dauphines and other unpopular models, usually at large losses. Britain's MG and Triumph sports cars were in second and third place, selling 44,000 cars between them. Next was the Swedish Volvo, still known as the car VW owners upgraded to. Opel was in fifth place because it was sold from GM showrooms.

Then a newcomer appeared on the list of top ten imports: Japan's Datsun, which accounted for 13,000 sales in 1965, virtually all in California. But the Datsun didn't trouble Detroit. Neither did the Toyota, which sold 6,400 cars in the United States that year. These seemed dull, uninteresting vehicles, the kind that might appeal to people who thought the Fiat an admirably attractive car or people seeking to draw attention to themselves.

In 1965, American automakers looking overseas studied Germany, and, possibly, Britain and France. None of them had any idea what awaited them from Japan.

The Japanese Challenge

6

Sunrise in Nippon

When Russia and China and India and South Africa come into consuming power, what are you going to do? Surely you don't think that Britain and America will be able to supply them? Surely you don't visualize Britain and America as nothing but vast factories to supply the world! A moment's thought will make clear why the future must see nation after nation taking over its own work of supply. And we ought to be glad to help the work along.

HENRY FORD I,
1930

For a brief period in the late 1940s, when it appeared that Japanese politics and economic life would take a more leftist course than proved the case, Suehiro Nishio was a figure of importance and contention. Ultimately, he would be forced from the public spotlight owing to complicity in a financial scandal, but in early 1948, Nishio was Secretary-general of the cabinet of Socialist Tetsu Katayama, a key post and a fine springboard for any aspiring politician.

Nishio was fifty-seven years old at the time, with a long record as a labor organizer and union activist. Within the Socialist Party, he was deemed something of an expert on industrial matters and was viewed as such by most educated Japanese. Even businessmen who were not particularly pleased with having a Socialist government knew Nishio had a deep and broad knowledge of the economy and a clear vision of its possible future. So when Nishio delivered himself of an opinion in this field, he was listened to with respect. He did this in 1948 regarding the potential for a Japanese automobile industry. Simply, he didn't think there was one. "Japanese motor vehicle manufacturers cannot compete internationally because equipment is too obsolete and the production method lags behind those motor vehicle manufacturers in advanced countries," he stated.

> I recommend urgently, therefore, not to produce Japanese motor vehicles as far as passenger cars are concerned. There is a 20-year or even 30-year gap between Japanese cars and imported ones in terms of design, performance, and durability. Prices of foreign motor vehicles are also half of their Japanese counterparts. From overall aspects, it seems to be that it will be the right policy to import motor cars.

The Socialists lost power a few months later to a conservative coalition, one of whose members was the sixty-three-year-old Hisato Ichimada. Respected within the ruling group as a leading financial expert, Ichimada was to serve in a variety of banking posts both in government and the business world. By 1951, he was governor of the Bank of Japan, which not only provided him with an important power base and political platform, but also gave Ichimada a say in the formulation of plans for Japan's economic future. His sentiments regarding the place of the automobile were pretty much the same as those of Nishio:

> It is meaningless to develop the motor vehicle industry in Japan. Now is the time of international division of labor. As we can get inexpensive motor vehicles of excellent quality from the United States, why don't we rely upon them?

Of course there were others, some in important posts, who disagreed, but a large majority of those in government, the bureaucracy, and the private sector agreed with the conclusions drawn by such experts as Nishio and Ichimada, and they demonstrated, with geometric logic, why Japan was not destined by resources, desire, or abilities to manufacture and market passenger cars.

The Japanese had no more than the rudiments of an industry, and of course, no thought of selling cars abroad. In 1952, the country turned out a grand total of 4,837 automobiles, and imported three times as many, most of them from the United States and Britain. One could hardly imagine circumstances under which this would change.

Before the end of World War II, there was little awareness, either in industry or elsewhere, of a Japanese automobile industry. Newsreels of Tokyo filmed in the 1920s and 1930s showed scenes of streets packed with rickshaws and other man-powered vehicles, with only an occasional car. Americans—to whom Japan was a quaint country best known for silk, shoddy toys, and Madame Butterfly—did not think this unusual. Decades before anyone thought of coining the term *Third World*, they considered Japan a charter member. Between World War I and World War II, when the United States and Western Europe were turning to the automobile and building national road networks, Japan went its own way. In 1924, for example, when American companies turned out 3.1 million cars and registrations reached 17.6 million, Japanese passenger car registrations came to 17,939—in a country with 105,000 registered rickshaws, 3.7 million bicycles, and 374,200 ox- and horse-drawn wagons.

What need was there in Japan for automobiles? The answer seemed obvious: absolutely none. The country had few natural resources, and although statistics of the period are of little use due to uncertain collection methods, Japan certainly had no mass market for cars. Whatever arable land there was had to be used for agriculture; Japan lacked both capital and space for a road construction program. Some military officers spoke of the need for trucks to be used in case of war, and several businessmen saw how they might be adapted to segments of the civilian market. The former thought there was a need for national companies so the army would not have to rely on overseas suppliers, but civilians had no interest in financing what would be a very limited, probably highly unprofitable industry.

At that time, Japanese big business was dominated by the great financial aggregations known as the *zaibatsu*. Their foci were banks and other financial institutions, from which the *zaibatsu* controlled wide varieties of enterprises, from shipbuilding to factoring to merchant banking to mining and merchandising. American and European observers then had some difficulty comprehending their rationales, with many considering them vestiges of a peculiar national feudalism. During the 1960s, they were compared to the emerging American conglomerates that they superficially resembled. Of course there was more to them than that. The *zaibatsu* enjoyed an intimate relationship with the government and the bureaucracy. What later would be known as "Japan Inc." wasn't created in the post–World War II period. Rather, it existed, full blown, in the 1920s and 1930s.

Depending on how *zaibatsu* were defined, they numbered ten to twenty during this period, the most prominent being Mitsui, Mitsubishi, Sumitomo, and Yasuda; of these, only Mitsubishi showed more than passing interest in automobiles. Mitsubishi Shipbuilding made a brief foray into the industry in

1918, when with some reluctance it produced trucks for the military, but this project was abandoned in 1921. That year, the *zaibatsu* created a subsidiary to manufacture a small inexpensive car to be known as the "Automo-go," 250 of which were sold before the project was abandoned in 1927, after which Mitsubishi turned once again to trucks. Okura, one of the smaller *zaibatsu*, had earlier backed the Tokyo Automobile Works, a company that had had virtually no impact on the industry. The Mitsui Bank helped finance the Ishikawajima Motor Works in 1919, when that company, helped by Britain's Wolseley Ltd., attempted to develop truck models of its own. Such funding often precedes equity investment, as is the Japanese practice, but not in this case. The loan was recalled soon after, and Mitsui made no further move into trucks.

The *zaibatsu* didn't show any interest in motor vehicles until well after World War II, by which time it was too late for any of them—except Mitsubishi—to become even a marginal manufacturer. Just as America's entrenched businessmen failed to perceive the potential of the automobile in the early twentieth century, so did their Japanese counterparts of the 1920s and 1930s.

Instead, what little industry there was was dominated by feeble start-up operations, subsidiaries of larger, non-*zaibatsu* entities dependent upon the parent for financial and technical support, or overseas branches of foreign corporations.

The new, independent companies were the least promising. In 1904, Torao Yamaba turned out a two-cylinder, steam-powered car in a corner of his shop, known as the Yamaba Electric Repair Company. He knew nothing of automobiles, but learned enough from manuals and models on display at a foreign importer's showroom to produce what was intended to be a bus ordered by two entrepreneurs in seven months. Yamaba probably resembled his American counterparts of the period—a tinkerer fooling around with buggies which were regarded with curiosity, but little else.

The same might have been said of Shintaro Yoshida, a mechanic and businessman, who had been studying automo-

bile technology for several years. Together with an engineer
who understood motors, Komanosuke Uchiyama, he manufactured the first Japanese gasoline-powered auto, what amounted
to a carbon copy of an antique Ford, in 1907. Yoshida eventually produced seventeen of these vehicles, which he called the
"Takuri," which loosely translated from the Japanese meant
"little rattletrap."

Out of this came the first Japanese automobile company,
Kunimatsu Motor Works, which appeared in 1909, and after
several organizational changes emerged two years later as the
Tokyo Motor Works, Ltd. Capitalized at $250,000 (of which
only one-quarter was paid), it erected a factory with a floor area
of some 12,000 square feet and set out to produce a low-price,
small automobile. So it did, but few purchasers appeared for
what was called "The Tokyo Car," and the company soon
switched to trucks and buses. In all, Tokyo Motors turned out
fewer than thirty vehicles before it was dissolved around 1920.

Masujiro Hashimoto, a young machinist who spent nine
years in the United States studying internal combustion engines, returned home in 1911 to found Kwaishin Sha, a company that manufactured and marketed a 12-hp, gasoline-powered passenger car. This vehicle was called the DAT, an
acronym of the surnames of three associates, Den, Aoyama,
and Takeuchi. (A generation later, Hashimoto would turn out
a model known as the "Datson," or "son of DAT." But since
the sound "son" in Japanese was similar to that for "bankruptcy," he changed it to "Datsun.")

Kwaishin Sha had a difficult time of it, even though the
DAT was well received. After several reorganizations and
mergers, it appeared in 1926 as the DAT Automobile Manufacturing Co. that, although minuscule by American or European
standards, was one of the larger Japanese automobile firms of
the time.

Meanwhile, several established non-*zaibatsu* companies
entered the market, most by imitating Western models. Tokyo
Gas & Electric, a manufacturer of home appliances, turned out

some trucks during World War I. The Ishikawajima Shipbuilding Co. purchased an Italian Fiat sometime in this period and then tried to reproduce it for the Japanese market. Failing in this, Ishikawajima entered into an agreement with Wolseley to import that British car, and eventually manufactured Wolseley trucks in Japan. More important, it entered into a joint venture with Tokyo Gas & Electric to design and manufacture a passenger car. From this emerged the Diesel Automobile Co., which, in 1936, was Japan's third largest automaker. After further reorganizations and acquisitions, Diesel was reincarnated as Isuzu Automobile Co.

Of course there were others. Dozens of Japanese companies entered the field, which, although not as crowded as the American market, resembled it in having large numbers of extremely small entities, most of which were destined to disappear through mergers or failure.

There was an important difference, however. The failed American automobile companies lost ground because they had not perceived the needs of or met the demands presented by a rapidly expanding market. One of the major reasons for the Japanese failures was the lack of such a buying public. Almost from the first, the Americans gravitated toward a mass market —the road to the Model T was there at the turn of the century. Not so in Japan, when even during the 1920s the automobile was perceived more as a curiosity than a practical vehicle, and the only growing demand was for commercial trucks utilized by the military.

There were exceptions to this—companies founded by ongoing enterprises that almost from the first were able to find niches within a small and stagnant industry, in large part because of superior management, generous financing, and government bailouts. Westerners often perceive Toyota and Nissan as the Japanese versions of General Motors and Ford, implying that they resemble each other managerially and strategically. Such is not the case. Rather, from the first each pursued its own path.

Sakichi Toyoda—the grandfather if not the father of Toyota—made his mark on the Japanese business scene in the late nineteenth century. The son of a woodworker and cabinet-maker, Toyoda was born in 1867 and grew up during the early years of the Meiji Restoration when Japan was abandoning its feudal trappings and striving to become a modern industrial power. This was a period of relative social upheaval, during which bright, ambitious young men lacking the proper social and business cachets were able to create firms that, although not challenging the entrenched *zaibatsu*, became formidable in their own, somewhat limited spheres.

Then and throughout Toyoda's lifetime, silk was a cornerstone of the Japanese economy and one of its major exports. The silkworms were tended in thousands of small mulberry groves and their cocoons were processed on looms imported from Great Britain, then the world's leader in textile machinery. When still quite young, Toyoda perceived the need for simpler, less expensive machines smaller silk growers could afford. Encouraged by the passage of a patent law in 1885, he created a new handloom that was quickly accepted. Other models and patents followed; in 1897, Toyoda sold his first power loom, which over the years displaced its British counterpart, and within a decade he was exporting machinery to Europe—even to Britain.

As was the practice in Japan, Toyoda then allied himself with one of the old *zaibatsu*, while retaining his independence. In 1907, Mitsui provided some of the financing for the creation of Toyoda Loom, the understanding being that in return Toyoda would utilize the services of the Mitsui Bank. The arrangement worked well, and two decades later, the company was transformed into Toyoda Automatic Loom Works, the centerpiece of a new *zaibatsu* that embraced machine tools, industrial materials, real estate, and other diverse enterprises.

That Sakichi Toyoda would attempt to create a *zaibatsu* was natural enough, but the movement toward diversification doubtless was intensified by an industry-wide slump in textile machinery. Recession and growing protectionist sentiment throughout the world led Toyoda into new paths. In 1929, he made one of his most important moves, transferring several patents to Platt Brothers, a British machinery manufacturer, in return for royalties of approximately half a million dollars a year, which were destined to become the seed money for the company's automobile venture. Toyoda died the following year, but not before having prepared for the succession of his son, who was addressed in his will: "Your father served the country with spindles and looms; it is your duty, Kiichiro, to serve the country with automobiles."

Then as now, it is the Japanese practice to promote executives as much by age and "class" as by other criteria. Although there have been some exceptions, for the most part, major Japanese corporations are headed by what to outsiders appears a gerontocracy. Kiichiro Toyoda, then only thirty-six years old, would play an important role at Toyoda Automatic Loom, but the actual direction of the firm would be left to his elders. Rather, as Sakichi indicated, he would devote most of his energies to automobiles.

From the time of Henry Ford I to that of Lee Iacocca, Americans have been fascinated by leaders of automobile companies, more than those of almost any other industry. The Japanese tradition is quite different. Although they are not exactly unknown, automobile tycoons are a fairly anonymous lot, rarely featured on the covers of magazines or written about in full-scale biographies. This extends to Kiichiro Toyoda, the most successful automobile executive of his generation. He was a humble and self-effacing man who, early in his life, developed a passion for automobiles while displaying exceptional managerial abilities. Without large-scale funding from Toyoda Automatic Loom, Kiichiro's automobile company might not have survived, but had the enterprise been headed by a less talented individual it could not have succeeded as it did.

Its beginnings were hardly auspicious. A false start was made in 1931 with a small sedan that failed dismally. Toyoda and his staff then turned to a study of imported American vehicles, using them as a reference point for their next experiment. Attempts were made to fit a Chevrolet engine into a small, sturdy passenger car, but nothing came of this either. Members of the board protested that costs had gotten out of hand—Toyoda had spent more than $1.4 million in three years of effort—and pressed for a shutdown. Such protestations were brushed aside, and in 1934, Toyoda won approval for the erection of a separate factory in Kariya, from which he promised a new line of cars would soon emerge.

The first Toyoda product, a small sedan known as the G-1, appeared in 1935. Larger and heavier than other Japanese cars, the G-1 was clearly strongly influenced by contemporary American vehicles. Its major selling points were sturdiness and price, which was lower than that of imported models. Despite this, and the creation of a marketing arm and finance company, the G-1 passenger car didn't stir up much interest. The Japanese public simply wasn't prepared to purchase automobiles. Toyoda sold twenty of them in 1935, a year in which the company posted larger losses than ever before, and the outlook for the future was bleak.

The venture might have been liquidated soon after, were it not for a sharp alteration in the political climate. Japan had invaded Manchuria in 1931, and since then an expansionist group of young army officers had gained a following in the country. When successive cabinets led by Admirals Makato Saito and Keisuki Okada tried to curb its influence, the group retaliated with waves of terrorism, culminating on February 26, 1936, in a plot to assassinate members of the Okada cabinet and seize power. Former premier Saito and others were killed, but although the coup failed, Japan turned toward military adventurism. Koki Hirota became premier in March, and was replaced a year later by General Senjuro Hayashi. Both men were allied with the expansionists, and as part of their programs, authorized sizable increases in military spending.

This had an immediate impact on the automakers. For the past seven years, various governmental bodies had considered measures to encourage them, but little had been done. One of the first actions of the Hirota government was to enact the

Automobile Manufacturing Law, which placed the production of motorized vehicles under military control. Companies willing to manufacture trucks for the Army would be licensed and receive lucrative long-term contracts. Moreover, importation of foreign cars and trucks would be restricted to protect what little there was of a civilian market for domestic companies. This law, more than any other action, marked the true beginning of the Japanese automobile industry, which from the first had an intimate relationship with the government.

The large *zaibatsu* weren't interested in participating. Not only were their leaders still uncertain about whether Japan could support such an industry, but also most were wary of the militarists, fearing that they would lead the country into destructive and unnecessary wars. For a while, when discussions with Toyoda and others were fruitless, it seemed as if the government might have to establish its own company. But in September, Toyoda received a license under the Automobile Manufacturing Law, along with a contract to manufacture trucks at a facility then under construction near Nagoya.

As though to celebrate this event, Kiichiro Toyoda split off the automotive department from Toyoda Automatic Loom Works. He would continue to oversee operations, but his older brother, Risaburo, was made the first president of the Toyota Motor Co.

Why this change in spelling? The brush strokes for "Toyoda" came to a number some felt was unlucky, and it also looked somewhat stodgy. One of the executives who was with the company at the time has written that " 'Toyota' not only sounded clearer than 'Toyoda' but also seemed better in terms of advertising psychology."

The final split from Automatic Loom occurred in 1937. That year, Japanese truck production came to 7,643 units, of which Toyota manufactured 3,023.

Japan's other viable automobile and truck company of the period was Nissan, which, as indicated, had strikingly different origins. Nissan also benefited by receiving a license under the

Automobile Manufacturing Law, along with military contracts, and until the very end of the war, when some of its
factories were destroyed by bombings, it was the larger of the
two companies.

Yoshisuke Aikawa, the central figure in the emergence of
Nissan, was both quite different from and more conventional
than his younger rival, Kiichiro Toyoda. Whereas Toyoda had
become intrigued with automobiles while still a student and
would remain so for the rest of his life, Aikawa had hoped to
create and then lead a multi-industry entity, which is to say,
imitate the most prominent model available, the *zaibatsu*. He,
too, would be successful, for Nissan became involved in chemi-
cals, construction, insurance, lumber, foundry products, and a
variety of other enterprises in addition to automobiles. Aikawa
became a spokesman for and prominent leader of the automobile industry, but the automobile was only one of his many
interests. Toyoda, in contrast, was content to remain wedded
to that one industry. Thus, Toyota is readily comprehensible
to Americans who have analyzed General Motors, Ford, and
Chrysler. Nissan more strongly resembles the likes of International Telephone & Telegraph, Litton Industries—and to
those who know the Japanese business scene, Mitsui and Mitsubishi.

Shortly after graduation from Tokyo Imperial University
in 1904, Aikawa opted for the kind of postgraduate training
many ambitious and educated Japanese men of his generation
preferred, namely, an extended trip to the United States to
work and learn about manufacturing and management techniques. In his case, this involved studying recent developments
in the cast-iron and steel industry. During a second visit in
1909, Aikawa purchased sufficient machinery to open a facility
in Japan. In 1910, he had organized Tobata Casting Company,
which from the first was the largest in its field.

Tobata turned out castings for a large number of companies and provided Aikawa with an overview few businessmen
outside of the *zaibatsu* enjoyed. During the next ten years, he
purchased several small companies, took an interest in others,

and founded several, all of which were involved in some way with castings.

Tobata did some business with GM, Ford, Austin, and Morris, all of which were selling cars in Japan, and this sparked Aikawa's interest in the automobile industry. Like Toyoda, he thought the future for cars in his country could be bright; this would be yet another industry in which Tobata could play a role. Moreover, Aikawa perceived that the rise of the military would create a need for trucks, another growth area. But still, it was only one of several, and in the early 1930s, Aikawa was not yet convinced that motor vehicles should be his primary concern.

Meanwhile the industry was involved in a wave of mergers, with businessmen knowing they would have to grow in order to obtain army contracts. In March 1932, the leaders of DAT, Tokyo Gas & Electric, and Ishikawajima agreed to a loose working alliance, to be known as the National Automobile Union, which would manufacture trucks. This didn't go far enough to suit the military, which urged a complete merger. Discussions toward that end were initiated, but fell apart when Tokyo Gas & Electric withdrew.

By that time Aikawa had organized a corporate shell, which he called Motor Vehicle Industries, and had approached DAT with a takeover bid. DAT was still small and underfinanced, with a product that had not made an impact on the market (in 1931, DAT produced a total of ten vehicles). Tobata and another Aikawa-controlled company, Nippon Industries, purchased DAT in 1932, and then went on to merge it with the automobile interests of Ishikawajima. At the time, Aikawa hoped to produce trucks for the army while entering into some kind of arrangement with GM to manufacture passenger cars, but events moved swiftly and this plan was soon abandoned. Other changes and maneuvers followed, and in late 1933, Tobata and Nippon split off its motor vehicle units, which the following year took the name Nissan Motor Company. Now Aikawa controlled Nippon, which in turn controlled Nissan, whose primary company was DAT.

Unlike Toyoda, Aikawa thought Nissan lacked the where-withal and personnel to design and manufacture cars and trucks and that American know-how would be necessary. Even before the merger was complete, he contacted GM with a plan for a joint venture, in which the American company would provide capital and technology with the Japanese contributing marketing units and manufacturing facilities. At first GM refused, but after realizing that given import restrictions the alternative would be abandonment of the Japanese market, it came to terms. The joint venture would be organized with Nissan the senior partner. The plan had to be aborted, however, when the government vetoed the idea and asked Aikawa for an alternative plan. In the end, Nissan purchased the needed technology from Graham-Paige, recruited American engineers to work at the Nissan facilities, and turned out imitations of small American cars. Aikawa continued to hope for some kind of American connection—in 1939, he tried to work out an arrangement whereby Nissan would merge with Ford's Japanese subsidiary, but this, too, was thwarted by the military. World War II ended this phase of Nissan's history, which up to then, and after, lagged behind Toyota in technology, design, and innovation.

Its influence with the military did not wane, however. Aikawa's nephew (and one of Japan's postwar premiers), Nobusuke Kishi, was one of the dominant leaders in Manchukuo, which in the late 1930s became an industrial heartland for the Japanese war machine. Nissan was invited to establish factories there, and so it did. These factories produced a flood of trucks, ordnance, and related military gear. It is possible that had Japan won the war, Nissan would have emerged as one of the major *zaibatsu*, while Toyota would have been a prosperous, but secondary manufacturer of motor vehicles.

These two companies dominated the passenger car industry before and during the war, throwing back challenges from the *zaibatsu*—which too late decided it was a mistake to ignore the growing demand for cars, trucks, and related vehicles. Some attempted to obtain licenses and contracts, but to no avail—by then the military was quite satisfied with the way the industry had been organized. But Mitsubishi would be permitted to turn out a line of heavy trucks, while Mitsui continued its old relationship with Toyota as one of the company's more important bankers. Their failure to perceive the potential of the automobile in Japan was one of the more glaring errors of the *zaibatsu* in the interwar period. Under the circumstances, however, their unwillingness to commit large sums to such a chancy enterprise was understandable.

Between them, Toyota and Nissan accounted for approximately four out of every five motor vehicles manufactured in Japan from 1935 to the end of the war in 1945, with Nissan the larger producer. Most of the vehicles were trucks and buses; during World War II, the few government and military leaders who rated a passenger car made do with old Chevys, Fords, Austins, Wolseleys, Fiats, and the like. Even then, the Japanese truck and bus production was hardly impressive. In the peak year of 1941, the entire industry turned out 46,648 vehicles, of which 19,688 came from Nissan and 14,611 from Toyota. But this was only a fraction of the number of three-wheelers—really motorized tricycles—being turned out.

There was a Japanese automobile industry before World War II, and it was the only one of any consequence outside of North America and Europe. That it was feeble and fragile and might never have survived were it not for government intervention is both obvious and understandable. There no longer was any real doubt the automobile and the truck had roles to play in Japan, but even so, on the eve of World War II, there were more rickshaws than passenger cars in the country. At that time, it still appeared the Japanese would have to rely on others to produce their cars and trucks and that most of them would have to come from the United States.

The attitudes of Suehiro Nishio and Hisato Ichimada, sketched at the beginning of this chapter, were both reasonable and sensible, given the circumstances of the late 1940s. No one who understood the Japan of those years had serious doubts regarding the country's eventual recovery, although the dazzling successes came as a surprise, even to the Japanese themselves. Shipbuilding, construction, and the manufacture of machinery and a wide variety of other goods had already been revived. Knowledgeable individuals spoke of a time when Japan might export such goods to other parts of Asia. But not autos, and certainly not to the United States.

---·7·---

The United States
as Number One

If there is a law governing this un-cosmic world of the Japanese, both in his highest modes of being where he aims at the Absolute and in his everyday life where he is concerned with mere utilities, it can only be a law of inescapable change and universal imperma- nence. In no literature of a great nation is there less room than here for the pure radiance of the stars and for the geometrical order of their courses; neither the Pythagorean harmony of the spheres nor the Platonic idea of ideas speaks to the Japanese. Identity, Measure, Immutability do not correspond to the needs of his soul. For everything leads the Japanese back to himself; to him being is a circuit. His is the existence of a Monad leading a life that gravitates on an internal abyss of whirlpool-like forces.

KURT SINGER,
1945

An American economic colossus bestrode the world during the 1920s. Aggressive merchandisers from such firms as General

Electric, Westinghouse, Singer, Ford, and General Motors out-promised and outbid their European counterparts. The American petroleum companies started to elbow aside the likes of Royal Dutch, Shell Transport, and Anglo-Persian in the oil fields, and even in marketing on their home turfs. Radio Corporation of America, Western Union, and International Telephone & Telegraph bid fair to outdo the English and French in telecommunications, supported by Wall Street banks that overtook the once-supreme London establishment. Efficient managers from New York, Chicago, Detroit, and other American headquarters cities spoke glowingly of establishing beach-heads in the form of factories in which American-designed and -manufactured components would be assembled, offices and service networks that would offer a native variant of consumerism and industrialism for all, with ever-rising standards of living.

The Americans delivered on their promises. Their products were cheaper and more reliable than those from other countries. Americans seemed eager to please customers, granting concessions in order to open markets, guaranteeing products and services, and providing extensive backup facilities to ensure satisfaction. Buyers who purchased American goods because of their price remained customers because of their high quality. The British, French, and Dutch firms that were displaced by the Americans appeared stodgy and ineffectual. They were dismayed at the loss of overseas markets and angry that their own countrymen seemed to prefer the new American goods—often copies of European designs—to their own. They all but fell over themselves in a rush to study American manufacturing and marketing techniques, to learn the American secrets and then apply them at home.

This suggests that everything the Japanese appeared to be in the late 1970s, the Americans had been a half century earlier. There was even talk of what now seems like a 1920s version of Japan Inc., a triad of major corporations, international banks, and federal bureaucrats, all working together to seize and then expand overseas markets. What the awe-inspiring Japanese

Ministry of International Trade and Industry (MITI) was after World War II, namely, a highly successful organization for the coordination of Nippon's domestic industry and overseas ventures, so the U.S. Department of Commerce was for American business after World War I. MITI's more important leaders, such as Takayushi Yamamoto, Koshichi Ueno, and Shigenobu Yamamoto, had both a model and counterpart in Secretary of Commerce Herbert Hoover.

The United States and Japan had maintained cordial, but not always friendly relations with one another since 1853, when Commodore Matthew Perry opened the country to trade. After the Meiji Restoration in 1868, the Japanese looked more to Britain and Germany as models than to the Americans, whom they correctly perceived as their chief rival for hegemony in the Pacific basin. Japanese statesmen tended to believe that President Theodore Roosevelt had cheated them of some of the spoils of victory in the Russo-Japanese War of 1905 in the Treaty of Peace signed at Portsmouth, and there were clashes regarding America's racial exclusion laws, clearly aimed at limiting Japanese migration to California. The two countries were putative allies during World War I, and Japanese statesmen recognized in President Woodrow Wilson's refusal to include disclaimers of racism in the Treaty of Versailles a continued American belief in the inferiority of nonwhites. Yet on their part, the Japanese had always guarded against immigration to the home islands, and their own nationalism was based on a profound sense of racial superiority. Both the United States and Japan hoped to fill the void left by the expulsion of Germany from Asia, and realized that Britain would never again dominate that part of the world, seeing in this another opportunity for expansion.

Yet for all this rivalry, and the expectation of more to come, the two countries entered into a vigorous commercial relationship. Japan was a growing market for American manufactured goods, machinery, and foodstuffs. In 1925, the Japanese purchased $230 million worth of American goods, approximately half of the Asian trade, less perhaps than America's exports to

France, but far more than that to Cuba. For its part, the United States bought $384 million of Japan's products, or more than from any European country. Much of this was silk, a vital fiber in those prenylon years. But Japan also manufactured a wide variety of cheap, shoddy toys, hardware, and utensils, mostly for export to underdeveloped countries in Asia, but some of which found their way to the United States as well. "Made in Japan" on an item signified low price and poor workmanship to Americans of the 1920s and 1930s, and for good reason. So to some extent, each country perceived the other in terms of its exports. The Japanese admired and tried to imitate American technology, while the Americans concluded that although the Japanese might produce fine silk, they had no talent in most areas of manufacturing.

It is against this that one must view the Japanese-American trade in motor vehicles. In the early 1920s, when the Ford Model T was on its way to becoming "everyman's car" in the United States, the few that were imported to Japan were owned by aristocrats, considered not only objects of curiosity but also symbols of position and affluence. These arrived in an almost absentminded fashion, nearly all of them being sold by the export-import house of Sale & Frazar.

Henry Ford didn't devote much time to the Asian market, but his son Edsel thought it merited consideration. Ford-Japan was organized in 1925, initially as a unit to import, market, and service Model Ts. That year Ford sent 3,437 model Ts to Japan, which was almost ten times as many as the total Japanese production. In 1926, Japanese companies turned out 245 motor vehicles, while Ford-Japan imported 8,677 cars. The following year, Ford-Japan erected a plant in Yokohama, where Japanese workers uncrated car and truck parts manufactured in the United States and assembled them for the domestic market.

By then, GM had decided to establish a Japanese subsidiary. An assembly plant with a capacity of 10,000 vehicles was constructed in Osaka, and the first Chevys emerged from it the following year, when GM-Japan supplied 5,635 motor vehicles for the domestic market, when Ford-Japan's sales came to 7,033 units, and when the Japanese companies put together a total of 302 four-wheeled vehicles of all descriptions.

So it went. Between them, Ford and GM fabricated more than 26,000 vehicles in 1929; the Japanese companies turned out 437. By then each American firm had established dealer repair and dealer service to customers, an idea previously unknown in Japan, which Toyota and Nissan were later to imitate. Until the mid-1930s, the real contest for the emerging Japanese automobile and truck markets was between the Americans, with the native firms watching from the sidelines, hoping to gain market shares on the periphery. Nine out of every ten Japanese automobiles were either the Ford "Economy-Car" or the GM "Popular Car."

It is not known whether Toyoda or any other Japanese auto manufacturer tried to enlist government aid to suppress the Americans, but this would not have accomplished much. For one thing, the Ford and GM managers took great care to hire and promote Japanese engineers and laborers; for another, they purchased locally produced parts as soon as it was feasible. Then, too, the Americans were willing to work with established Japanese concerns. Indeed, in speaking at the dedication of his plant in 1926, a GM official remarked that the goal of his company was to promote the automobile in Japan, which would benefit all companies engaged in such manufacture. In this way, the Japanese companies too would prosper, perhaps to the point of outperforming the Americans. "When that day comes, we will transfer our business to them gladly." Hyperbole, perhaps, but in fact, both GM and Ford did negotiate with several Japanese automobile companies about joint ventures and, after the power of the military increased, mergers as well. The sensitivity of GM-Japan and Ford-Japan to cultural differences and their recognition of the need to be perceived as respectful of local traditions was unusual for the time, and most effective.

Little wonder, then, that the *zaibatsu* did not participate in the automobile industry, that Kiichiro Toyoda encountered opposition from board members at Automatic Loom when he attempted to produce his first automobiles, or that Yoshisuke Aikawa initially considered Nissan an appendage to operations at Tobata, among whose prized customers were GM-Japan and Ford-Japan. Were it not for the growing influence of the military in the mid-1930s and the decision on the part of the generals to encourage Japanese companies and curb the power of foreigners, what little there was of domestic automobile manufacturing might have disappeared. By 1934, for example, the Japanese companies between them accounted for less than one out of every twenty trucks and cars manufactured in or imported into the country.

All this changed with the passage of the Automobile Manufacturing Law of 1936. Not only were the American companies denied licenses, but the government also sharply increased tariffs on assembled vehicles and parts. Ford's application to construct a new facility at Yokohama was rejected; a company official believed that Aikawa was responsible. "He had convinced the government he could build a car," was the simple explanation.

This didn't mean the immediate and complete exclusion of the American companies, for Nissan and Toyota weren't prepared to assume the entire burden of supplying the military with vehicles. Indeed, Ford-Japan sold more than 18,000 cars and trucks in 1937, still more than all the Japanese companies, with GM-Japan a close second. Production declined sharply thereafter, and understanding what was happening, Ford and GM cast about for allies. As indicated, Nissan was interested in making a deal, as were Mitsubishi and other *zaibatsu* now hoping to enter the field, but nothing was accomplished. By late 1939, it had become evident that the government would not permit takeovers or mergers of any kind. Why do so when the American properties could be seized once the two countries were at war? Also, Toyota and Nissan had expanded sufficiently to lead the officers to believe they could handle their military requirements. Between them, the two companies manufactured almost 30,000 vehicles in 1939, and together with other Japanese firms, 46,000 the following year.

By then the American facilities in Yokohama and Osaka had been shuttered, to be taken over by the Japanese in early 1942 when the United States and Japan were at war. Thus ended not only the American domination of that market, but also all expectations that Detroit would maintain its beachhead in the Orient.

As it turned out, the generals had overestimated their need for motor vehicles. The army, much of which had not yet adjusted to the age of the internal combustion engine, still preferred horses and oxen for haulage in China and utilized only 20,000 trucks on the Chinese mainland. Neither was there much demand for vehicles on the South Pacific islands, where roads were poor or nonexistent. The Japanese forces had only 3,000 vehicles, in contrast to the more than 100,000 the Americans had. Trucks, however, were in demand for the war industries on the home islands. Even so, Toyota and Nissan were able to switch some facilities to tractor and earth-moving equipment manufacture by 1943. Then, when Japan came under heavy bombardment in 1945, the factories were dispersed, and production nearly halted. Toward the end of the war, production was less than 10 percent of what it had been before Pearl Harbor. The companies remained, and facilities still existed, although some were in sorry shape. The work forces were there, soon to be augmented by returning veterans. But to all intents and purposes, there was no Japanese automobile industry.

Or much of anything else. By some estimates, over one-quarter of the national wealth had been destroyed. One of every four buildings had been demolished, one of three machines was rubble. Over 1.2 million Japanese had died in the fighting since December 7, 1941, along with 670,000 civilians. This was what General Douglas MacArthur inherited when he arrived in Tokyo in September as Supreme Commander for the Allies and de facto viceroy of Japan. "Never in history had a nation and its people been more completely crushed," he was later to write.

MacArthur wasn't referring to physical damage, however,

for much worse had been visited upon several European nations. Rather, he alluded to the trauma associated with defeat. A homogeneous people, who believed themselves heaven-blessed, led by an emperor thought to have descended from gods, never defeated in war or occupied by a foreign power, had its collective ego shattered. Fortunately for both Japan and the United States, MacArthur proved a near-ideal viceroy, who not only understood the temperament of the conquered people, but also knew just how far he could go in rebuilding and reshaping the nation. As for the Japanese, they saw "Makassa-san" as a new shogun who, although a foreigner, knew their history and traditions and respected both. Under his direction, a new constitution was written, embodying American and British democratic practices; the agricultural sector of the economy underwent drastic reforms; and a beginning was made in smashing the *zaibatsu*. Liberal observers, such as I. F. Stone and Arthur Schlesinger, approved of his democratization efforts, and conservatives praised MacArthur for keeping the Soviets out. Within a few months it was clear that Japan would make a smooth transition to recovery, in spite of inflation and chronic shortages. Moreover, the nation had absorbed the MacArthur reforms while maintaining its essential social structures.

That MacArthur would dominate the Japanese landscape the way he did should have come as no surprise to Americans who knew of his earlier career. Those following the occupation through newspaper articles and magazine stories might have concluded he was running the nation single-handedly. Yet there weren't as many reports out of Japan as there were out of Europe, where the Soviet threat was stark and the Cold War more a reality. There was no equivalent of the Berlin Airlift in the Pacific—no Marshall Plan or Truman Doctrine, either. Americans hardly noticed that the *zaibatsu* really were restructured rather than dismantled, or that what one scholar called the "functioning command economy" and another the "plan rational system" was relatively unchanged from what had existed before the war. The industrial sector hadn't undergone the kind of redistributional revolution that had hit the agrarian part of the economy. For example, the powerful Ministry of Commerce and Industry, which had helped direct the war effort and which, through its offices, coordinated much of the Japanese economy was relieved of its top command, but the bureaucracy remained, to be transformed into MITI, one of the key governmental agencies and, in 1949, an important booster of a revived automobile industry.

That was the same year Joseph Dodge emerged to become one of the most important figures in modern Japanese history. Almost forgotten in his own country, he is credited by some Japanese historians with being the father of the amazing postwar economic expansion. A conservative, somewhat stodgy banker, Dodge was a man of limited intellectual abilities who, although a former president of the American Bankers Association, had spent most of his life in Detroit, where he helped finance several auto companies. Whether he ever truly understood the dynamics of the Japanese situation or even appreciated what he was doing is hard to say. Dodge saw a country with rampant inflation, an untidy budgetary process, and poor tax collections and set about providing what were essentially American solutions to these problems—and as it turned out, the solutions worked.

In April 1949, Dodge issued a nine-point program, aimed at balancing the budget, improving tax collections, cutting back on government subsidies to laggard companies, and most important, stabilizing the currency so as to obtain an exchange rate of 360 yen to the dollar, which made Japanese currency cheaper than open market rates might have permitted. It was bitter medicine, applied by an old-fashioned midwestern banker who believed that inflation was a sign of profligacy for which the only real remedy was a massive dose of belt-tightening, and for whom balanced budgets, favorable trade balances, and a high savings rate were signs of an advanced civilization. Known collectively as the "Dodge Line," the program plunged Japan into a recession. Unemployment increased, there was labor unrest, and Japanese politics took a decided turn to the left. By mid-1950, however, conditions had started to stabilize, and the economy was well positioned to benefit from the boom that accompanied the Korean War. In large part because of the undervalued yen, imports from the United States declined while Japanese exports expanded, which helped revive Japanese manufacturing. Unemployment then shrank, savings increased, along with investment, and Japan started to emerge as an economic power.

In retrospect, it can be seen that the Dodge Line, combined with other assistance from MacArthur, made possible a Japanese revival more spectacular than even the famous German "economic miracle" of the 1950s. This had a favorable effect on the renascent automobile industry—but not before its leader came perilously close to dissolution.

Up to then, all of this appeared irrelevant. In the late summer of 1945 the question had arisen as to whether the Japanese would be permitted to manufacture motor vehicles, since other needs were much more pressing and domestic requirements, such as they were, might be met by importing American cars and trucks. At the time it was thought that Japan's motor vehicle future rested with the small, underpowered, and inexpensive three-wheelers used before the war, what one American observer called "motorized rickshaws." But in September, apparently without giving the matter much thought, MacArthur decided to allow the companies to turn out several lines of trucks, with the understanding that volume would be limited to 1,500 units per month. This ceiling was established not to keep the Japanese companies in line, but rather to ensure that scarce resources not be used for so minor a requirement. With this decision, the companies came back to life.

A year later, Toyota and Nissan petitioned MacArthur for permission to manufacture passenger cars. It seemed a small thing at the time, since only a few Japanese had the wherewithal to purchase cars, and in the past, they had preferred American models. Detroit was in the midst of its postwar boom, however, with no models to spare for overseas. So MacArthur acceded to these requests, and in June 1947, Toyota and Nissan received the go-ahead.

In 1948, the Japanese companies turned out 28,700 four-wheeled vehicles, of which 381 were passenger cars. That same year, other concerns (some of which would later come to dominate the market for motorcycles) manufactured 16,852 three-wheelers.

All restrictions on automobile manufacture were removed in 1949, when Japan manufactured 1,070 passenger cars and 26,727 three-wheelers.

It wasn't much of an industry, and perhaps it should not even have been designated one. None of the companies believed it could survive without guidance and assistance—which meant imitation of American practices and, possibly, partnerships with one or another Detroit company. At Toyota, for example, the newly named president of the sales company embarked on a trip to the United States, to learn American ways. "While on that trip I became convinced that we not only had to push forward with our new installment purchase system," he recalled, "but that we also had to streamline our sales outlets, which meant firmly establishing a modern concept of sales for our marketing channels to the consumer." He did this by following GM's example. "I adopted the GM representative system, for example, using GM's manual on dealer management as my guide." When Toyota entered the field of lubricants, it did so through a joint venture with a Standard Oil of New Jersey subsidiary. During the occupation, there were talks regarding a possible union, first with GM, and then with Ford. Other auto companies—Nissan, Isuzu, and Mitsubishi in the vanguard—hoped for an American connection. Nothing came of this, more because executives at GM, Ford, and Chrysler were not interested in such matters than from any lack of willingness on the part of the Japanese.

Who could blame the Americans for ignoring Japan? The domestic market was strong in the late 1940s, and whatever overseas interests Detroit hoped to cultivate were in Britain,

France, and West Germany, not the Orient, which remained unfamiliar territory. General Motors and Ford didn't even attempt to revive their prewar assembly plants, in a period when they might have done so with ease and in this way shatter whatever there was of a Japanese domestic industry, possibly for good.

Outside of MITI and the companies themselves, there was no strong sentiment in favor of automobile manufacture. The Bank of Japan was adamant about helping the companies. Economic and business experts there and throughout the government continued to believe that Toyota, Nissan, and the rest could never produce a vehicle that was better in quality and lower in price than those already rolling through the streets of Japan's cities—the cars and trucks of the American occupiers. Moreover, the Americans were willing to sell surplus military vehicles to the Japanese, and some 22,000 of them were disposed of in this way during the first four years of American rule. Under the terms of the United States–Japan Administrative Agreement of 1949, military personnel could import their autos free of tariffs and excise taxes. So they did—and promptly sold them to Japanese nationals at inflated prices. Those who could afford cars were able to choose between a slightly used Chevy or Ford or a vehicle like the Toyota SA, a four-passenger model technologically inferior to the American cars and only slightly lower in price. It did not matter that the Detroit models had been created for larger people and that servicing was a problem. To the sensitive Japanese of this period, it appeared that these cars were manufactured by a people who had the necessary expertise to win the war, whereas the Toyotas and other Japanese autos were put together by losers. In a period when MacArthur was the most popular figure in Japan and all things American were admired, this was no small consideration. Little wonder, then, that the SA sold poorly—only 215 units were purchased from 1947 to 1952, when the line was discontinued, whereas secondhand American sedans became a symbol of affluence.

Add to this the hardships the companies had to endure in

the initial months of the Dodge Line and a crippling strike at Toyota in early 1950, and it would appear that whatever Japan's economic destiny was to be, automobile manufacturing would not be a part of it.

Toyota had gambled heavily on recovery, expanding rapidly, purchasing material on credit, and extending loans to suppliers. The tight money-induced recession caused a decline in sales, while Toyota's debtors were unable to meet their obligations. By mid-1949, the corporation had a large unsold inventory and a sheaf of due bills, but little cash, and its own creditors were clamoring for payment. For the six months ending in March 1950, Toyota showed a loss of $200,000 and was close to bankruptcy.

At that point, the two Toyota lead bankers, Mitsui and Tokai, agreed to restructure its debt and float a loan. The company was divided into two entities, Toyota Motors and Toyota Motor Sales, with the former producing cars and selling them to Motor Sales, which then offered the vehicles to the public. This arrangement allowed the bankers to assist each individually, the idea being that whereas one might fail, the other might survive, perhaps to be merged with Nissan or some smaller auto company, thus salvaging something from the wreckage.

As part of the agreement, Toyota Motors had to lay off 1,600 workers, which led to a short, but vicious strike. Production dropped off sharply, with only 304 vehicles turned out in May 1950. The following month, Toyota's management and union agreed to a settlement; by then, Motor Sales had been established as a separate entity.

The corporations survived. Management was shuffled, and Toyota hasn't had a strike since. As will be seen, the episode frightened labor and made management somewhat less venturesome. Of all the automobile companies, Toyota has the most conservative balance sheet and the closest relations with its bankers. Finally, the experience gave Nissan leadership of the industry, a position it was to hold for close to a decade as Toyota struggled to regain its old position.

Like most Japanese businessmen of the period, those at Toyota and Nissan and other automobile manufacturers took their marching orders from MacArthur. Except for Mitsubishi none of them was classified as a *zaibatsu*, and so they were spared substantial restructuring. Toyota and Nissan, however, were designated "restricted companies," and as such had to divest themselves of ownership of other concerns. Thus, Nissan's links with Tobata and other companies of the complex were broken, and the authorities took great care that Toyota Motors maintained its distance from Toyota Motor Sales.

The picture changed dramatically with the Korean War, in June 1950. Japan became the base from which the United Nations defense and counterattack would be launched, while there was pressure to draw up and ratify a peace treaty. The Korean War helped remove whatever animosities remained between the two people, and the tacit union of the countries against a common enemy brought them closer together. In five years, Japan had traveled the course from being a defeated and humiliated foe to a needed and even respected ally. The impact of all this on the Japanese psyche can only be imagined, but it surely accounted for the enhanced self-confidence encountered in Tokyo during the early 1950s.

American procurement policies tended to favor those Japanese companies capable of filling a wide variety of military orders. Toyota and Nissan produced trucks and other vehicles for the military, and although these were only a small fraction of what was used during the war, they turned things around at these and other companies. The Japanese manufactured 30,-817 trucks in 1951, of which more than half were purchased by the Americans for use in both Korea and Japan; more would have been taken had they been available. Nissan, Toyota, and other manufacturers ran their assembly lines on double shifts and still couldn't keep up with the demand. New facilities were rushed to completion, profits soared, and the companies started to pay dividends to their shareholders.

Nor was this all. The Japanese companies received contracts to rehabilitate damaged vehicles, many of them American, and so became more familiar with Detroit's technology. The demand for automobiles increased, and the Japanese responded by boosting production to 3,611 units in 1951, which was more than twice that of the previous year. Additional expansion was planned, and attitudes at the Bank of Japan and other formerly skeptical agencies began to change.

MacArthur had pressed for a peace treaty with Japan as early as 1947, but there was little progress toward that goal until the Korean War, when events moved swiftly to end the occupation. President Truman relieved MacArthur of his command on April 11, 1951, thus removing from the scene the most powerful figure in the nation, a man who had helped rebuild the country and was still overwhelmingly popular, but who nonetheless symbolized Japan's status as a defeated and occupied nation. A peace conference was convened in San Francisco that summer, and a final treaty was signed on September 8. This was followed by the drafting and ratification of a security pact with the United States. Both the treaty and the alliance went into effect on April 28, 1952, on which date the occupation officially ended.

That year, Japan's index of economic activity was still below what it had been before World War II, but growth was rapid. One could see it in the rise of steel mills, shipyards, machine tool shops, and factories where consumer goods were being turned out, some destined for the American market. For Japan's foreign trade was also recovering, with the United States a prime market. Still, Japan was hardly a major force in this field. Exports to the United States in 1952 came to $229 million—against $633 million in imports.

The automobile industry boomed. Capital investment that year was twice what it had been in 1951, and another doubling would take place in 1953, when the Japanese companies manufactured 49,778 four-wheeled vehicles, an all-time high. Japan now imported 27,406 vehicles, and exported only 1,098, with fewer than a dozen going to America.

None of this might have transpired had it not been for

MacArthur's occupation policies and American economic assistance and procurement policies during the Korean War. Japanese automakers would soon prove to be among the most intelligent, perceptive, and astute in the world. But they received technical guidance from Detroit and political and economic benefits from Washington during the occupation. A generation later, one industry observer would assert: "The United States created the Japanese motor vehicle industry." Exaggeration and sour grapes, perhaps. But not without a seed of truth.

8

The Japanese Difference

Japanese goods fall into a category widely referred to as "low wage goods," and the problems they present in our market, "low wage competition." Japanese wages certainly are much lower than American wages. This differential is unavoidable, given the wide difference between per capita production here in the United States and that in Japan. But low wages do not always mean low labor costs or low total labor costs. Japanese automobiles cannot match American cars. In fact, there are even large segments of the American market for cotton textiles where Japanese goods cannot compete effectively with American products. But when Japanese technical efficiency is closer to the American level than Japanese wages are, Japanese goods may be produced more cheaply than American. The trade record shows a long list of successful Japanese export products, a list that grows longer each year.

PROFESSOR WARREN HUNSBERGER,
Johns Hopkins University, *1961*

Periodically, Americans enter into combination debates and teach-ins on why some foreign economies and enterprises are so successful and their own so pitiful, and what can be done to turn the situation around.

This happened in the 1950s, when scores of businessmen and scholars traveled to West Germany to observe, to learn, and to digest masses of material. They then returned home to write articles and books and address gatherings on that country's economic successes. "What might Americans glean from the German experience to make our economy more productive?" they asked.

Then, with the USSR's orbiting of Sputnik in 1957 came wrenching questions about whether or not the Soviets had surpassed the United States in science, and the thought that the American Century had come to an end only a few years after the United States had been the only strong economy in the world, with its products universally admired. "What does Ivan know that Johnny doesn't?" was a commonly heard question in this period.

It occurred again in the late 1970s and the early 1980s, when the country still bore wounds caused by the Vietnam War and the Watergate scandals. In a period of great national self-doubt, scoured by inflation and then unemployment, in the midst of the worst recession since the end of World War II, Americans looked to Japan, a country with far fewer natural resources, and saw an economy with stable prices and a low unemployment rate, a people of seeming harmony little troubled by crime and drugs, which had come through the oil shock without major trauma. Indeed, they didn't have to study Japan to realize that that country was doing something right. All that was required was a glance at the American marketplace, where Japanese electronic products and automobiles dominated.

Once again a continued national decline was predicted. Americans went to Japan to observe factories there. Often the same individuals who had so admired the Germans a quarter of a century earlier returned to proclaim that Japan would be the world's dominant industrial economy within a few decades. Not only would the Japanese set the pace in such older technologies as radio, television, and automobiles, they would soon push aside the Americans in data-processing, telecommunications, genetic engineering, and other emerging industries. Politicians warned that unless steps were taken to change the situation, Americans would be reduced to growing foodstuffs and providing tourist services in order to pay for Japanese manufactured goods, and the best they could come up with by way of solutions was hard work, rededication—and that last remedy of the weak—quotas, domestic-content laws, and tariffs to protect jobs.

But there was another way. We might try to imitate Japanese management and labor, grafting onto our system those aspects that might improve productivity and quality. Articles on just such a possibility appeared regularly in national magazines and serious newspapers. Books dealing with the "Japanese Miracle" edged out diet and self-improvement books from the best-seller lists. Television programs attempted to dissect Japan in less than an hour. In the course of these, a variety of experts tried to explain and analyze the society and prescribe remedies for American ailments to an audience that may have sensed something was wrong in the United States and right in Japan, but couldn't quite come to terms with the situation. To those with long memories, it might have been a replay of earlier fears regarding West German economic and Soviet military superiority and eventual domination.

But there was a difference this time. Earlier, calmer experts with a sense of perspective were able to point out the paranoia inherent in most of the allegations being made. But not many such individuals were around to perform this function in the late 1970s. The evidence that the Japanese were indeed superior to their American counterparts when it came to producing a wide variety of consumer and capital goods was too great to suppose this was temporary. It was driven home almost daily, in many different ways. And the symbols of Japanese success were omnipresent, from Seiko watches and Canon cameras to Sony television sets, Panasonic video cassette recorders, and, of course, Japanese cars.

Especially Japanese cars. When in early 1983, GM and Toyota announced they would jointly manufacture Corollas in a shuttered California GM factory, a number of industry observers opined that both companies had much to gain from the deal. In this way, the Japanese might counter protectionist sentiment in the United States. As for General Motors, it would have a car to replace the outdated Chevette, but more important, because Toyota executives would operate the factory, GM would have an excellent opportunity to study and learn Japanese management techniques. No greater admission of American defeat and Japanese success could have been imagined. That GM, the world's largest industrial enterprise, once so widely admired for its managerial successes, should seek lessons from Toyota would have seemed absurd only two decades earlier.

It was no laughing matter in 1983, however, when Detroit had all but conceded that it had taken second place to Toyota, Nissan, and the other Japanese automakers in matters of quality and value. A German auto executive, Carl Hahn, chairman of Volkswagen, put it succinctly. "For 20 years the Japanese learned from us. Now we are learning from them."

The Japanese knack for combining high quality with low prices in almost all their products was not the result of secret methods or—as some appear to believe—genetic superiority. Rather, through good fortune and design, the Japanese were able to incorporate into their national culture many aspects of the industrial revolution, that prized experience of the West. What transpired in Japan from the last quarter of the nineteenth century onward, and most visibly after World War II, occurred in Europe and the United States in the early nineteenth century, namely, the transformation of an essentially agrarian-commercial society into one that increasingly depended on manufacturing and distribution. Although the

workings of what might be called "the technological imperative" had changed the ways workers lived and their expectations, it did so in the context of earlier values and expectations.

Economic historians have long been familiar with the notion that, in Europe, industrialization developed in a society in
which the social structure and attitudes were semifeudal,
whereas in the United States, the path taken by the industrial
revolution was partly determined by a population that had fled
from, and in other ways rejected, feudal and traditional ideas.
When one adds to this the geographic factor, the presence or
absence of raw materials, and the size and nature of markets,
one can begin to understand the differences between European
and American industrialization and the reasons why the
United States had forged ahead of Britain, France, and other
European nations in the late nineteenth century and became
dominant in the first half of the twentieth.

By and large, Americans had been more innovative and
pragmatic than Europeans in many industrial areas, more
suited by culture to mass production for a mass market. And,
of course, there was a huge market in the United States for a
wide variety of consumer goods. That an American style developed in manufacturing and sales was noted by Europeans and
others in the first half of the century when they came to the
United States to learn our methods and explore possibilities of
adapting them in their own industries.

Similarly, there is a Japanese style in industrial organization and operation, as different from the American as ours is
from the British and the French. But there are also important
similarities, and although most popular writers on the subject
stress the former, it would do well to consider the latter as well.

One of the more enduring clichés regarding the Japanese
is that no industrialized people are more skilled than they at
adapting technologies and techniques created by others to
their own needs. The German economist Kurt Singer, who
taught in Japan during the 1930s, put the matter succinctly and

with no little prescience in a work written shortly after World War II, but not published until much later:

> They invent few things, receive passionately, and excel in the art of adapting, adjusting, fitting. They are exceptionally shrewd in sifting and excluding. What they have chosen to undertake is often reduced in scale or scope but within these limits is carried to perfection.

During the 1950s, when Singer wrote these words, Japanese firms entered into almost 2,000 agreements with American and European corporations for technology transfers, and even now, Japan is a net importer of technology.

In fact, the concepts of *zero defects* and *Total Quality Control*, the much-paraded Japanese "secrets" of industrial efficiency, were developed in the United States in the early twentieth century and afterward, a fact the Japanese readily admit. As early as 1911, a translation of management philosopher Frederick Taylor's *The Secret of Saving Lost Motion* sold over 1.5 million copies in Japan. After World War II, the Japanese looked to such American management experts as W. Edwards Deming, Joseph Juran, and A. V. Feigenbaum for advice and leadership. Toyota, Nissan, Honda, and other automakers deserve credit for their accomplishments, but it should also be noted that a substantial part of the philosophical foundation upon which their methods were based was "Made in America."

Although it has often been said that Japan is the only major country in the world where "capitalism" isn't used in a pejorative sense, it hasn't been observed that the Japanese have perfected the trick of developing what Westerners recognize as the Protestant Ethic and Calvinism without embracing the religion that produced them, but as in all things, with a particularly Japanese form. In the West, Calvinism implies a belief that man must prove himself on earth, this being a sign of having been selected for election, or being in God's grace. The Protestant Ethic glorifies hard work and achievement and emphasizes competition and recognition, which had been interpreted in Europe and America as a rationale for individualism.

The Japanese are second to none when it comes to effort, the drive for success, and the desire for the good life on this planet rather than joy in heaven. But they eschew individualism and stress group membership. One observes this in social, as well as in business settings. Whereas Americans seem to strive to stand out from the crowd, their Japanese counterparts try to blend into their milieu. American executives often utilize the corporation as a vehicle for self-realization; the Japanese believe executives should serve the larger entity. To Americans, this seems very much like self-sacrifice. Not to the Japanese, for only through the improvement and advancement of the group can they be said to have succeeded.

This is not to suggest that Japanese society and industries are monolithic. To the contrary, in many ways there is more competition in Japan—and certainly in the automobile industry—than in the United States. Rather, the Japanese tend to think of loyalties as occurring in concentric circles, somewhat like an opinion.

The outer skin is the nation. The Japanese are a homogeneous people; unlike the people of every Western country, almost all Japanese belong to the same ethnic group, speak one language, and follow the same religion. Racial and religious strife, so common in the United States, and the varieties of separatist movements that plague Britain, France, and Spain, among others, are alien to the Japanese. And they intend to keep it that way: foreigners may visit, but they are discouraged from staying longer than absolutely necessary. They cannot hope to form close personal relationships with the Japanese, and rare indeed is the foreigner permitted to become a Japanese citizen. Finally, most Japanese have as great a horror of intermarriage as rabid Western racists. The nation, then, is the most unified of the world's major powers. And here, too, Singer says something to illuminate the situation.

The guiding principles of selection have been in most cases utilitarian and political. Throughout their history the Japanese have shown a preference for what promised greater power and prestige for the nation, and for what appealed to the curiosity and appetite for novelties of the individual; they have tended to eliminate everything, however great, if it was felt to threaten the continuity of Japanese life, to imperil the stability of their political structure, and to alienate the individual from his congenial group. There is a perfect logic of an organic nature in these processes of assimilation and exclusion.

The next layers are, in descending order, the workplace, the family, and friendships, all of which may be interrelated. Future Japanese executives plug away in school, with families making great sacrifices to ensure placement in the proper university. Once there, scholastic efforts are downplayed in favor of social life and political activism, often in radical and even anti-American causes. In any case, the undergraduate years are not meant for studying alone or for political activism, but rather as a shared experience with others during which invaluable contacts are made, a practice the Japanese call *gakkubatsu* —that country's version of the American "old school tie." But *gakkubatsu* is much stronger. Japanese students expect to maintain the friends they made at school for life; membership in the cohort is another layer of the onion.

Observers familiar with the best American and Japanese universities often have suggested that the pace is more intense and standards generally higher in the United States. This isn't to say that Japanese students are sluggards or anti-intellectual, but rather that academic achievement is demonstrated more by obtaining admission to the quality institutions than by performing outstandingly while there.

Middle-class marriages in Japan are entered into with great calculation and an awareness of the benefits and liabilities involved, although this has been changing in recent years in favor of a more romantic approach. Both partners understand this, and as a result extramarital activities on the part of husbands who are executives are tolerated more readily in

Japan than they might be in the United States, not only by wives, but also by business partners. As for the wife, from the first she "knows her place," which is in the home, although here too there have been changes. Still, American and European executives on business trips to Japan with their wives are briefed in advance not to expect their hosts to invite them to social gatherings. Once again, this is in the process of changing, as businessmen in one country learn more about the folkways and mores of the other.

The workplace is central to all this. The wife's role is to assist her husband, taking care of all domestic affairs so that he is free to pursue his career.

One is aware of this even in casual contacts with Japanese businessmen. Nowhere in the West is homogeneity and uniformity so prized. A group of middle-management personnel on an inspection tour will seem like a military platoon. All will be wearing similar dark suits and ties, white shirts, and black shoes. They will be approximately the same age. If permitted to explore further, the observer would discover that their educational and social backgrounds are similar, as are those of their wives. Most will also have the same aspirations. Originality has never been a prime attribute of Japanese management; imitation, especially of the United States, is a hallmark of Japanese practices.

The same conditions are found in Japanese factories. Unmarried assembly-line workers live in company barracks, eat most of their meals at company cafeterias, and wear company uniforms. At Toyota, all the workers have caps with stripes to indicate grade and status—one white stripe for a trainee, two yellow stripes for a regular worker, and a black stripe on a white cap for a foreman.

Much has been made of the Japanese policy of lifetime employment, combined with a paternalism unknown in the United States. This isn't a product of the post–World War II period, but rather has existed since the Meiji Restoration, although elements of it could have been found even earlier.

Moreover—as will be seen—elements of the practice were not unknown in the United States in the period between the two world wars.

The original reasons were both practical and sensible: Faced with labor shortages that couldn't be alleviated through encouragement of immigration, Japanese companies concerned with industrialization had to offer many benefits to the workers they cared to retain. So it is now, which is to say that not all executives or workers are covered by this guarantee. Nor does it mean that those who are feel assured that their jobs are safe. In stringent periods, an executive may find himself switched to the factory floor, and a foreman could return to the assembly line. That this practice can be effective in tying the workers to the firm is obvious. Lifetime employment usually leads to corporate loyalties beyond those found in most American corporations. Far less is heard, however, about the disadvantages of the system. Since during slack periods Japanese corporations may fire workers not covered by lifetime employment, but must retain those who are, fixed costs can be high, thus creating more hardships than would otherwise be the case. A manager or worker who isn't happy or efficiently utilized at his company will be reluctant to move elsewhere, not only because of tradition, but also because he knows that potential employers frown upon such practices and distrust those seeking change.

Not as well known as the lifetime employment practices is the Japanese system for promoting executives. Generally speaking, merit counts for less than in the United States and nepotism is rarer there than in most countries. Education and seniority are the prime requisites for advancement in large Japanese corporations. Thus, the emphasis on attending the "right" schools and meeting the proper people, once there. The typical Japanese chief executive officer may have graduated from Tokyo University or some other prestigious institution and gone on to what amounts to a training program at the corporation. Advancement might be steady, but not sudden;

bright ideas, successful innovations, a superb record combined
with the admiration of his superiors would lead to commenda-
tions and bonuses as well as prime assignments, but not to
promotion over his elders.

Such an individual would be given tasks to assist in his
development. Attendance at an American graduate school of
business would be paid for by the corporation, which is to say
this person would go to the head of his class—but not skip a
grade. He would arrive at the executive suite at a fairly advanced age, usually the late fifties or early sixties; rare indeed
is a chief executive officer under the age of fifty-five. And after
a stint at the top he—along with many others who entered the
corporation at around the same time—would retire to the government bureaucracy or consultant posts, as those behind
them moved up a notch.

Along with lifetime employment, the seniority system encourages loyalty and rewards service with steady advancement, while inculcating a sense of security. For these reasons,
some American managers have been tempted to consider
adapting some aspects of it to their own operations. But the
system also can reward mediocrity and frustrate those whose
ambitions cannot be encompassed by such practices. This, too,
is a particularly Japanese practice that would not survive a sea
change.

To return to the analogy of the onion, the American tends
to be "self-centered," and at the core of the American system.
Doing or dying for the company is an idea that receives lip
service, and some may even believe it, but most measure success not by the company's fortunes, but rather by their own
within the enterprise. Not so in Japan—or at least not to so
great an extent. The "Japanese onion" has no such center, but
rather has layer upon layer of relationships, and individualism
is frowned upon.

This is the key concept with which one must come to
terms in understanding the Japanese economic and political

forms and structure, which, in turn, is a necessary prelude to learning about the successes—and flaws—in that country's automobile industry during the postwar period.

Like American industrial corporations, those in Japan have boards of directors that oversee operations and are ultimately responsible for success or failure. But whereas American corporations in recent years have come to favor substantial representation of outside directors, the Japanese reject the notion, believing that only those who devote their complete attention to the firm (and perhaps some of the firm's bankers) can know what is transpiring, and that power and access should come with responsibility. Thus, in the automobile industry as elsewhere, approximately 90 percent of the directors are also officers in the corporation. They function through what is known as the *ringi* system, in which a suggestion put forth by an individual is circulated among the group, meetings are held for discussions, the draft is modified, and in the end the suggestion is set forth as board policy. Responsibility for the end product is collective, rather than individual. This assures the cooperation of all in its implementation, with success being shared by the group. And, of course, failure would be collective as well.

Supporters and defenders of *ringi* stress the desirability of unified support for agreed-upon policies, whereas critics observe that although failures in America often result in the firing or demoting of the responsible party, the Japanese might have to expel the entire board should calamity strike. Identifying weak links, a most important managerial problem, is not easily done in Japan. This could be seen in the misstep Toyo Kogyo—which changed its name in May 1984 to Mazda Motors—made with the rotary engine designed for use in the Mazda cars, which was followed by a company-wide reorganization. In contrast, the near collapse at Chrysler meant that the chairman and president, along with a relative handful of staff, were replaced, while those who presumably weren't directly involved in the debacle remained.

In the United States, boards are supposed to have a fiduciary responsibility, meaning that they are there to represent the shareholders, and this is interpreted as doing what they can to increase dividends and the price of the common stock. Executives often have stock options, which gives them a personal stake in quotations. They are constantly reminded that the New York Stock Exchange is a form of rating agency, telling them—and the shareholders—just what kind of job they are doing. This emphasizes short-term results, a problem that plagued many corporations during the great bull market of the 1950s and 1960s.

The Japanese outlook is different. Fundamental loyalty in Japan is to the enterprise itself, whereas boards consider their prime constituents to be those banks and other financial institutions with strong, permanent, almost symbiotic relationships with the corporation. The banks expect to help underwrite debts and provide other services for fees, and although they find it pleasant to see share prices rise, this isn't of primary importance. Taking a longer view of things themselves, Japanese financial institutions encourage companies to do the same. And so they did in the 1950s, especially in the automobile industry. More than a quarter of the shares of Nissan were owned by six such institutions, led by the Industrial and Fuji banks. Honda's initial backers in automobiles was the Mitsubishi Bank, which now owns 22 percent of its shares. As has been noted, Toyota once was wholly owned by Toyoda Automatic Loom; now that firm's equity is less than 5 percent, and four banks and one insurance company own 23 percent of the shares.

Such a structure tends to free corporations from fears of stockholder revolts, and provides them with a quite different perspective regarding their constituencies. As one Japanese visitor to the United States remarked:

I get the impression that American managers spend more time worrying about the well-being and loyalty of their stockholders, whom they don't know, than they do about their workers, whom they do know. This is very puzzling.

The Japanese manager is always asking himself how he can share the company's success with his workers.

Japanese automobile companies compete with one another, often fiercely, in the domestic and foreign markets, but they also cooperate when the occasion demands. They work with their bankers in harmony with the governmental bureaucracy, which is charged with coordinating efforts, as seen in MITI's concern with exports. Japan has antitrust legislation, which, however, isn't nearly so stringent (or arbitrary) as that in the United States. Under terms of their 1947 "Law Relating to the Prohibition of Private Monopoly and to Methods of Preserving Fair Trade," or more commonly, the Antimonopoly Law, the newly established Fair Trade Commission (FTC) could restrict stock holdings by financial institutions in industrial corporations. Outside employment of directors was also restricted, so as to guard against conflicts of interest and to make certain that corporations in the same industry did not fix prices. Holding companies were banned, as was dumping, and combinations in restraint of trade.

Much of this was changed or eased after the occupation, largely because the spirit that motivated American antitrust policy was alien to the Japanese environment. Moreover, the law conflicted directly with MITI's policies in the export area. During the period the Japanese automakers invaded the American market they were guarded against prosecution for collusion by the MITI bureaucracy. Although Nissan, Toyota, and the others didn't overtly unite in their export efforts, information was shared regarding marketing and related matters, this being very much in the Japanese tradition. Still, the FTC counteracts MITI. Although the ministry usually strives to create larger units that can compete effectively against foreigners, the FTC insists that such behemoths tend to be less competitive, more dangerous politically, and in any case, illegal. In its conflicts with MITI, the automobile industry often found a firm ally in the FTC.

Dedication to the corporation on the part of its executives

and their willingness to accept short-term financial losses in order to realize long-term gains would mean little unless the harmony and unity in the front office was matched by performance and a set of complementary institutions within the factory. So they were, and like the others, they flowed from the Japanese national character, along with borrowings from and adaptations of Western concepts. This, too, is typically Japanese.

This sentiment of unity manifests itself strikingly in the Japanese union movement. On the surface, unions in Japan strongly resemble those found in other advanced capitalist countries, which is to say, large numbers of industrial workers belong to them (in fact more than 30 percent of the work force is unionized, against 23 percent in the United States). There are national federations, regular meetings, collective bargaining, arbitration and mediation, strike calls, and pleas for solidarity. At one time, the unions were strongly socialistic and even communistic, but this situation had changed by the mid-1950s, and the general outlook of most Japanese union leaders isn't much different from their CIO-AFL counterparts.

There is one crucial difference. A union usually is organized within a single company, and its members tend to be as loyal to the firm as they are to each other—perhaps even more so, and in ways that would amaze their American counterparts. It isn't at all unusual for management to ask union leaders to accept speedups and wage freezes, with the reasons for the changes carefully explained. This happened after the Organization of Petroleum Exporting Countries (OPEC) oil price increases, at which time a number of companies argued that greater productivity was required so as to keep the prices of manufactured goods at current levels and to maintain overseas markets. The unions agreed, with relatively little in the way of complaints, yet another example of management-worker solidarity.

All attempts at creating a labor movement on the American model have failed. Shortly after World War II, a group of

Toyota employees who had earlier molded the Federation of All Toyota Auto Workers' Unions, helped develop the All Japan Auto Workers' Union. There followed a series of bitter strikes, most of which came about more through miscalculations than design.

In 1950, when Toyota was on the verge of considering entry into the American market, the Federation called for the aforementioned walkout to protest a wage cut. Mediation calmed the waters, however; but in the end Toyota was permitted to fire an additional 2,000 employees so as to operate its business more efficiently. This shocked the rank and file, for whom job security and identification with the company were paramount. "In 1950, when I was a young shop steward, the union ran a three-month strike," recalled Shiro Umemura, who now heads the Toyota workers. "It was then that I learned what a serious problem unemployment can be."

Other, similar conflicts erupted in the 1950s, but most of them were settled with a minimum of conflict. The All Japan Auto Workers' Union collapsed in 1954, after which the locals at Toyota, Isuzu, Hino, and Suzuki joined together to create a loose confederation known as the All Japan Federation of Automobile Workers' Unions. Datsun workers, ever aware of the rivalry with Toyota, didn't join. Rather, they tried to create an opposition organization, the Federation of Japan Automobile Workers' Unions, which never amounted to much.

Meanwhile, workers at Toyo Kogyo, Honda, and Fuji remained in their own unions, each of which worked closely with the companies. Then in 1972 a new organization claiming 500,000 members, to be known as the General Federation of Japan Automobile Workers, was created. Its leaders believed the new organization would perform for Japanese workers as the United Auto Workers had for the Americans; once again the Japanese looked to the United States for models. But it wasn't to be. Japanese workers proved more loyal to the companies than concerned with their own interests. Management-worker solidarity remained intact, at least for the time being.

Occasionally Americans read of militant, seemingly antibusiness labor leaders almost eager to lead their followers on strikes. Such individuals were often found in the textile and steel industries, and several prominent ones appeared in the automobile industry as well. Although a number of these were truly sincere in castigating management, most indulged in passionate rhetoric to impress negotiators with the strength of their convictions, but there was also another, more personal reason. Japanese corporations have a tradition of promoting troublesome union leaders into managerial posts, in the hope of obtaining a more tractable negotiator for the union the next time they meet. Approximately 20 percent of Japan's large corporations are today headed by former trade union leaders.

Clearly, the level of cooperation between managements and workers, as well as their mutual respect, is higher in Japan than in the United States, and far higher than in Europe.

The Japanese have also developed various techniques to maximize output and enhance the reputations of their products, and central to all is the institution of *quality control circles;* a form of these circles had existed prior to the war, but became institutionalized in the early 1960s. In its simplest form, the circles are groups of workers who come together in order to develop procedures by which quality and productivity can be increased. All are given the chance to contribute, the idea being that in the end a consensus will be reached, with everyone understanding just what has to be done and each enthusiastic to contribute. Not to do so—or to deviate from the plan—would bring shame upon that individual.

Essential to the concept of quality control circles is the simple matter of goodwill and trust. Management must believe that the workers sincerely have the best interests of the corporation at heart, whereas the workers must accept as axiomatic that they will be treated fairly. Each must accept that the other is wholly dedicated to the well-being of the enterprise. For example, at Toyota, some 200,000 improvement suggestions a year are pushed into those familiar boxes found in each factory, this set against the 20 grievances processed through the unions. (The reason for this is that Toyota workers soon learn that management expects such feedback; those workers who fail to meet a specified quota of suggestions can expect to be called in to make explanations—and offer apologies.)

As a student of the situation once remarked, British and American union members "worked for" their firms, while those on the Toyota assembly line "belonged to" theirs.

One of the goals of quality control circles is to achieve *Total Quality Control,* a concept developed by American managerial philosophers who introduced it to the Japanese after World War II. In 1954, Joseph Juran went to Japan to deliver a series of lectures on the subject. "Every member of the production team had to become involved in maintaining high standards," said Juran, "and not merely supervisors." The Japanese adapted Juran's concepts, refined them, and a quarter of a century later were amazed when Americans viewed them as some exotic flower of the Orient.

Similar to, but not quite the same as the more familiar "zero defects" programs introduced earlier in some American factories, total quality control places the responsibility for defects on assembly line workers, not inspectors and managers. In those factories where total quality control is strictly adhered to (and Toyota's are among them), a worker may ask for a shutdown of the line if he believes adjustments are needed to achieve the goal of no defects. Beyond that, he is required to consider the nature of the process and develop methods to perfect it.

Efficiency is rewarded, but not if the price is a higher rate of defects. Those who can demonstrate consistency and originality in such matters can hope to advance to foremanships and beyond. But this was not a native Japanese development; like Total Quality Control, it had roots in American managerial practice and thought. During the 1920s and since, assembly line workers at the Lincoln Electric Co. in Cleveland, Ohio, a major manufacturer of welding equipment, had the responsibility for zero defects, and their wages were based on such performance. Moreover, after a trial period, workers were guaranteed lifetime employment. James Lincoln attempted to spread this doctrine through talks, books, and articles. Visitors were welcome at the Lincoln facilities, and other businessmen were encouraged to try some of the techniques that worked so well there. What later had been thought Japanese developments of the post–World War II period had antecedents in midwestern America prior to 1941.

W. Edwards Deming brought the doctrine to Japan after the war. Beginning with a series of lectures in 1950, he spread the concept of quality control there for the next three decades. Japanese businessmen were so entranced by Deming's message that they instituted an annual prize in his name, now considered the highest award one of that country's industrialists can win.

In time, many Japanese businessmen came to view themselves as the inheritors of the industrial tradition, but the more perceptive among them understood the debt to American managerial philosophy and they also understood that they were doing a better job of realizing these concepts than were many American firms. As one of them told an American reporter, "You had so many good things. You must polish it up again."

The Japanese continued to seek inspiration from America, even after chalking up victories in a large number of contests with their counterparts in the United States. Whereas American scholars and businessmen would visit Japan to learn all they could about that country's economic miracle, hundreds of Japanese students poured into the best graduate business schools in the United States to imbibe knowledge from this country's top theorists. American and European concepts and practices provided the seeds that sprouted so impressively in Japanese soil.

Total Quality Control could not be achieved unless the corporation's suppliers also adhered to the concept. Whereas in the United States, suppliers whose parts shipments contained rejects could expect returns and cancellations of contracts unless the situation was remedied, in Japan, what might be considered an acceptable percentage of rejects might prompt an unannounced inspection tour by the purchasing corporation.

Managers and workers would be questioned about their practices, suggestions for improvement would be forthcoming, with the understanding being that unless conditions improved the contract would be cancelled.

The auto companies had yet another method of maintaining quality control on the part of suppliers. The companies would assist entrepreneurs wishing to enter the field of component production by taking equity positions in the new companies, purchase shares from existing manufacturers whose products were deemed acceptable, or establish partially owned subsidiaries. Toyota, for example, owns 9.8 percent of Hino Motor, 21.8 percent of Aichi Steel, 40.8 percent of Kanto Auto Works, 36.3 percent of Kyowa Leather Cloth, and 7.9 percent of Toyo Radiator, among other holdings. Nissan has large interests in Nissan Diesel, Nissan Shatsu, Nihon Radiator, Aichi Machine, and smaller interests in over twenty other suppliers. Large manufacturers even share ownerships. Toyota and Nissan both have substantial stockholdings in Kayaba Industry and Koito Manufacturing, Toyota and Mitsubishi share interests in Toyo Radiator, whereas among Press Kogyo's owners are Nissan and Isuzu. Needless to say, such practices would be illegal under American antitrust laws, and this is yet another example of how the Japanese government encourages industrial rationalization.

Large parts inventories are not required by firms practicing Total Quality Control, which led logically to another hallmark of the Japanese auto industry insofar as inventories were concerned. Simply stated, the Japanese maintain inventories at what for American companies would be considered perilously low levels. This practice has usually been translated into English by the inelegant, but highly descriptive term of "just-in-time production"; in Japan it is known as the "*kanban* system," after the small cards used to order components. It is one of the few totally Japanese contributions to the automobile-manufacturing process and as such has received much attention in the United States and Europe.

Kanban was conceptualized at Toyota in the 1950s by one of the corporation's executives, Ohno Taiichi, who observed that it had existed prior to that time, based upon common practice in other industries. "Normally you don't want workers or machines to be idle, so you keep producing parts whether you need them at the assembly stage or not," he said. "But if you do that in the just-in-time system, there is no place to stack them. If the workers have the materials to make parts but no place to stack them, they have to stop producing. When that happens, the supervisor knows he has too many people working on that production stage." To which Ichiro Maeda, a Toyo Kogyo executive, added, "If there is a large inventory and a machine breaks down, there is time to fix the machine and the problem is not reported to management. But with a low inventory, the machine gets urgent attention. The system helps workers and managers to see and adjust weak areas in the process."

The benefits from this practice are obvious, as are the potential problems. Small inventories mean that less capital is tied up in parts and storage facilities. Improvements can be introduced quickly, instead of waiting for the current inventory to be worked off. Furthermore, those who work under the *kanban* system are constantly aware of the fact that unless each part is acceptable, the entire process may have to be terminated, to await delivery of a new supply. And of course, the individuals responsible would have to answer for this to their superiors.

The discipline imposed by *kanban* can easily be imagined. Reject bins, so common in American factories, are much smaller and are found less frequently in Japanese factories. The savings are also great. Several American analysts have concluded that *kanban* alone is responsible for a $500 per car cost advantage over the Big Three, whereas other factors account for an additional $1,000 or so advantage.

American management consultants, most of them academics, visited and observed the automobile plants, and returned home to speak of clean assembly lines, uniformed and obviously efficient workers, and the Japanese élan. Some wrote articles in journals, but these had small circulations and were

COMPARATIVE COSTS FOR SMALL CARS,
GENERAL MOTORS AND NISSAN, 1981

PRODUCTIVITY/COST CATEGORY	GM	NISSAN
Labor Productivity, Employee Hours per Small Car	83	51
Costs per Small Car		
Labor*	$1,826	$ 593
Purchased components	3,405	2,858
Other manufacturing costs	730	350
Nonmanufacturing costs**	325	1,200
Total	$6,286	$ 5,001

*Average labor cost per hour in the United States, $20 per hour; in Japan, $11.28.
**Nonmanufacturing costs include those of ocean freight, selling, and administrative expenses.

SOURCE: Abernathy, Clark, and Kantrow, *Industrial Renaissance,* 61.

generally inaccessible. As has been noted, the mass circulation magazines and newspapers were more interested at that time in the German Economic Miracle than in anything happening in the Pacific. Still, the most prescient American scholars did not believe the Japanese were supermen.

Harvard professors William Abernathy and Kim Clark said as much in 1981 after an extensive tour of Japanese automobile factories:

> We had been half-prepared to find them [the Japanese automobile makers] using process technology far more advanced than anything available to their American counterparts. What we saw about us at every turn, however, was not newer technology but better management of the technology in place—not the exotic gimmickry of wide-eyed public expectation but a sober mastery of manufacturing.

Two years later, a Japanese journalist, generally considered somewhat to the left of center, wrote a scathing attack on the Japanese factory system. For several months he had worked on the Toyota assembly line and kept a diary that formed the basis

COMPARISON OF MANUFACTURING/STAMPING OPERATIONS IN JAPANESE AND AMERICAN AUTOMOBILE PLANTS

MANUFACTURING/STAMPING OPERATION	JAPAN	UNITED STATES
Parts stamped per hour	550	325
Manpower per press line	1	7–13
Time needed to change dies	5 mins	5 hrs
Time needed to build a small car	31 hrs	60 hrs
Total work force for average automobile plant	2,360	4,250

SOURCE: *The New York Times,* March 21, 1982.

of a book, the contents of which confused the growing army of American "Japan watchers."

In a few sentences he summarized an alternate view of just what it was that enabled Toyota to excel in automobile manufacturing. "The keynote of Toyota rationalization is the elimination of all waste," he wrote, noting that this resulted in substantial savings—especially in labor costs. The journalist scoffed at the notion that Toyota (and, by implication, other Japanese manufacturers) had any lessons to teach the West. On the contrary, he claimed the Japanese automakers had learned from the American and European turn-of-the-century corporations how to exploit workers. If he was to be believed—and there were those who didn't believe him—it would appear the Japanese had imitated the West in this respect, too.

> The rationalization is not so much to eliminate work as, more directly, to eliminate workers. For example, if 33 percent of "wasted motion" is eliminated from three workers, one worker becomes unnecessary. The history of Toyota rationalization is a history of the reduction of workers, and that's the secret of how Toyota shows no increase in employees while achieving its startling increases in production.

Of equal importance is an aspect of the Japanese economy that was often overlooked by novice onlookers during the

1960s, but that would come in for greater attention and exposure later, namely, comparative wage rates and economies realized from what usually is known as the *dual economy*.

That Japanese auto workers receive lower wages than their American counterparts has always been understood, although criteria are difficult to establish because social and economic structures differ. By some criteria, a Japanese assembly line worker of the mid-1960s received one-quarter the wages and benefits earned by Americans, but criteria that take into account bonuses, overtime, costs of living, and expectations put the figure at one-half. Whichever is accepted, one easily sees that the Japanese auto companies enjoy a great advantage in this sphere. It would seem that the big companies not only obtain better quality control operations from their workers but also drive their workers harder than the Americans did, getting as much or more productivity at a lower wage.

The dual economy refers to the fact that most Japanese enterprises are quite small by Western standards, and although Americans tend to concentrate on the giants, they sometimes ignore the fact that the large companies depend on the smaller ones to turn out components—and at extremely low prices with the same high quality demanded.

In 1960, firms with under 100 employees accounted for more than 58 percent of the Japanese labor force (compared with 28 percent for the United States). Most of these small businesses are managed by individuals who had not been able to find similar employment at one or another large enterprises, and they are staffed by laborers who are in the same position. These workers receive lower wages, aren't covered by lifetime employment contracts, aren't unionized, and work in constant fear either of dismissal for cause or the failure of the firm. (The failure rate in Japan during the 1950s and 1960s was much higher than the rate in the United States and most Western European countries.)

The implication was that Japanese productivity was purchased at the expense of worker exploitation and not any novel formulas that might be transplanted elsewhere.

Was this really the case? And if even part of this were true, might it not be impossible—given the nature of American society—ever to compete with the Japanese in autos? All of this further baffled Detroit.

The confusion and anxiety remained. How might one explain the apparent Japanese superiority in virtually every aspect of automobile manufacturing? Could Japanese techniques be adapted to the American scene? These questions, and others like them, would be heard frequently in the late 1970s and after.

---·9·---

The Japanese Stumble

Japan is plunging into the foreign car market here with two entries, Nissan's four-door Datsun and Toyota's somewhat larger Toyopet Crown. With over 50 foreign car makes already on sale here, the Japanese auto industry isn't likely to carve out a big slice of the U.S. market for itself. The Japanese companies, Nissan Automobile Co. and Toyota Motor Sales Co., feel that they have no other choice than making a stab at the small, second-car market here. Unlike Western European automakers, which in some cases can't keep up with local demand, the Japanese face an almost stagnant car market at home.

Business Week,
August 2, 1958

Such was the considered opinion of a presumably informed journalist at the time the Japanese Invasion was just beginning, and like many subsequent assertions about that country's automobile industry, it was an amalgam of fact and hearsay. Although the writer was correct in some of his observations, he erred in believing that the domestic market was listless, perhaps having come to that conclusion in the belief that the Japanese auto industry was undergoing the same cyclical malaise that plagued Detroit that year. In fact, demand for Datsuns, Toyotas, and other domestically produced cars was relatively strong, with 50,600 passenger cars turned out in 1958 against 47,000 the previous year. In 1959—when exports still accounted for a minor part of the output—production would reach 78,600 units. Still, by virtue of its low per capita income and tradition, Japan didn't seem destined to become a society based on auto transport; in the late 1950s, three-wheeled vehicles, powered by engines of 360 cc or less, were far more visible than were passenger cars, although, in retrospect, one could have seen that a change was coming. The reason for the invasion was obvious enough—or at least it seemed so at the time. By 1958, Japan had recovered from most of its wartime dislocations, and although still overlooked or ignored by the majority

JAPANESE PRODUCTION OF PASSENGER CARS
AND THREE-WHEELED VEHICLES, 1947–1959

YEAR	PASSENGER CARS	THREE-WHEELED VEHICLES
1947	110	7,432
1948	381	16,852
1949	1,070	26,727
1950	1,594	35,498
1951	3,611	43,802
1952	4,837	62,224
1953	8,789	97,484
1954	14,472	98,081
1955	20,268	87,904
1956	32,056	105,409
1957	47,121	114,937
1958	50,643	98,877
1959	78,598	158,042

SOURCE: Japan Automobile Manufacturers Association, *Motor Vehicle Statistics of Japan, 1981*, 1.

of Western observers, it had already begun to grow spectacularly. And a vital element in that growth was the export sector.

Japan was no different from other industrialized countries in seeking a favorable balance of trade and had more reasons than most to want one. Even then the country had set down strictures regarding the pattern of commerce. Japan would attempt to sell more than it purchased in Europe and the United States, particularly when it came to products like industrial equipment, steel, and consumer durables, and use the funds obtained therefrom to buy raw materials and petroleum from countries that exported them. Which is to say that Japan hoped to become an advanced industrial power, hardly an unusual ambition.

That British cliché, "export or die," has long been adhered to by all Western nations and countries in other parts of the world that have become Westernized. In the late 1950s, the United Kingdom exported 15 percent of its GNP, whereas Belgium sent one-third of its products to other countries. In contrast, Japan's exports came to a mere 9 percent of its GNP, and Japan was running a deficit in its foreign accounts. To Tokyo, a reversal of this vital statistic was imperative.

Japanese plans and strategies were hardly covert. In 1960, the government promulgated what amounted to a ten-year plan, indicating goals for economic development. It was anticipated that the GNP would expand by 7.8 percent annually, from $27.1 billion to $72.2 billion. In order to accomplish this, there would have to be a rapid and substantial increase in exports, to the point that Japan would have a favorable balance of trade. In 1956–1958, imports averaged $3.1 billion per annum, and exports only $2.7 billion; the targets for 1970 were $9.9 billion for imports and $10.3 billion for exports, thus achieving a positive balance. This would require an enormous increase in the export of finished goods, and the plan envisaged much of this being provided by such items as cars and trucks. For 1956–1958, Japan sold some $603 million worth of "machinery and transport" goods overseas; the target for 1970 was $3.5 billion, for a better than 14 percent per annum advance.

The performance of the Japanese economy far surpassed

the expectations of the most sanguine observers. Instead of the anticipated annual 7.8 percent growth rate, the economy expanded an average of 11.1 percent. But a price was paid for all this. Japan's inflation rate was 6.2 percent annually from 1960 to 1965, and 5.5 percent for 1965–1970. (In contrast, the American Consumer Price Index averaged an increase of 1.3 percent for the first half of the decade and 4.2 percent for the second.) Yet as a result of a badly undervalued yen—and a suspected government willingness to look aside as exporters lowered the prices of their goods to obtain market share—the prices of Japanese exports didn't rise. Exports soared, rising at an average annual rate of 17.5 percent during the decade (U.S. exports advanced by 7.7 percent per annum), spearheaded by automobiles. Japan's balance of trade with the United States in 1957 was still "unfavorable"; exports came to $601 million, whereas Japan purchased $1.3 billion worth of American goods. MITI and other Japanese bureaucracies involved with industrial development, finance, and foreign trade agreed that measures had to be taken to reverse the trade figures, although there was no clear consensus on how this was to be done. That overseas automobile sales might play a role in boosting Japan's exports seemed obvious enough. The Bank of Japan, which it will be recalled had a decade previously opposed the creation of a domestic industry, by now had altered its stand, and was prepared to join with MITI in supporting those companies— Nissan and Toyota, in particular—wishing to test the American waters. All had taken steps during the early 1950s to prepare for such a move.

That the United States would be the major target for the Japanese drive was by no means obvious. After all, the Datsuns and Toyotas were closer in size and power, as well as price, to the British, German, and French small cars than they were to the Fords and Chevys, and there might have been a ready market for them in Italy and Spain, as well. Yet the Japanese Big Two avoided Europe in favor of the United States for four basic reasons.

In the first place, the Americans had the lowest tariff on automobile imports in the world—at 7 percent in 1950, it was

PREDICTION AND PERFORMANCE FOR
THE JAPANESE ECONOMY IN THE 1960s

	(billions of dollars)	
CATEGORY	PREDICTION IN 1960	PERFORMANCE IN 1970
GNP	72.2	173.4
Exports	9.3	19.3
Imports	9.9	18.9
Machinery and transport exports	3.5	11.3

SOURCE: Hunsberger, *Japan in United States Foreign Policy*, 7 and *OEDC Industrial Policy of Japan*, 184, 193; *United Nations, Handbook of International Trade and Development Statistics*, 223, 243.

less than one-half that of European countries. Detroit had never found it necessary to attempt to keep out rivals in this fashion, feeling secure in the belief that Americans wouldn't purchase these cars, even if their prices were lower than domestic sedans. As indicated, the Beetle was deemed an aberration, and every other small car had failed in the American market. As for the luxury models—the Mercedes and the Rolls, for example—these really did not take sales from Cadillac and Lincoln and thus didn't seem worth the trouble of a lobbying campaign in Washington.

JAPANESE PASSENGER CAR PRODUCTION AND EXPORTS,
1960–1970

YEAR	PRODUCTION	EXPORTS
1960	165,094	7,013
1961	249,508	11,532
1962	268,784	16,011
1963	407,830	31,447
1964	579,660	66,965
1965	696,176	100,716
1966	877,656	153,090
1967	1,375,755	223,491
1968	2,055,821	406,250
1969	2,611,499	560,431
1970	3,178,708	725,586

SOURCE: *World Motor Vehicle Data* (1980), 43, 48.

MAJOR JAPANESE EXPORT PRODUCTS, 1960 and 1970*

1960		1970	
Steel	(9.6)	Steel	(14.7)
Cotton Textiles	(8.7)	Automobiles	(6.9)
Ships	(7.1)	Transistor Radios	(3.6)
Apparel	(5.4)	Synthetic Fibres	(3.2)
Transistor Radios	(3.6)	Optical Instruments	(2.6)
Toys	(2.2)	Apparel	(2.4)
Automobiles	(1.9)	Tape Recorders	(2.6)
Footware	(1.8)	Plastics	(2.2)
Ceramics	(1.7)	TV Sets	(2.0)

*Figures in parentheses indicate the share of each export item in the total value of Japanese exports.

SOURCE: Terutomo Ozawa, *Japan's Technological Challenge to the West*, 34.

Second, the very size of the American market tempted the foreigners. What matter if Toyota and Nissan gained 10 or even 20 percent of the Spanish purchases? One or two percent of domestic American sales would be far more valuable, and more to the point, obtainable.

Third, the Japanese must have been encouraged by the successes of VW and believed they had learned from the failures of other manufacturers. They were not entering the market as trailblazers, a role they tended to dislike and avoid. Rather, they could imitate the best and avoid the worst, a knack they had developed in other industries and would display often in the future.

Finally, the United States was closer than Europe, not only geographically, but also in terms of culture (or so the Japanese believed). The Japanese had felt a warm friendship, almost to the point of kinship, with Americans during the occupation, and believed that this sentiment was reciprocated. The companies' leaders shared this feeling, as did the government.

By now a great deal has been written regarding the Japanese government's role in coordinating business. Information and analyses regarding this subject are readily available, and the procedures are familiar. As has been indicated, in 1952

MITI and others decided to protect the domestic industry, and at the same time assist the major firms in case of an export drive later. High tariffs on foreign cars and parts were erected, and through rules, regulations, and red tape, American and European corporations whose products might compete with present and future Japanese ones were discouraged from establishing plants in Japan. They were even prevented from entering into joint ventures with Japanese companies, although the latter policy was to prove difficult to enforce, since many businessmen hoped to draw heavily upon European and American expertise and capital. MITI preferred to go it alone whenever possible, even though this might slow development.

When some large corporations defied MITI (and the automakers did so more often than any other industrial group), the agency compromised with what Americans of the late 1970s would come to know as "local content" laws, requiring a high percentage of components and raw material to be of domestic origin. Then MITI and those banks involved in financing the industry joined to urge the companies to develop new technologies, stressing domestic research and development. Finally, the Bank of Japan and successive governments were committed to an undervalued yen, which meant that the price of imported goods would be high, but the price of exports would be most attractive. This was geared to help all exporters, but in the 1960s, it did most for the automakers.

With all this, the Japanese cars of the early 1950s were technologically backward and managed to appear clumsy and fragile at the same time. Their low prices made them attractive to domestic purchasers, but they couldn't hope to appeal to many foreigners. Indeed, upper-class Japanese continued to prefer imports—especially from America, even if they were secondhand cars—to the Toyotas and Nissans that were more readily available.

MITI could hardly permit such a situation to continue, so in 1955 the ministry promulgated regulations designed to keep out as many imports as possible. Foreign cars purchased by Japanese had to have been in the country for at least a year, be more than two years old, and sold by an American who had not engaged in such a transaction for at least three years. In addition to all this, a separate government license was required for each sale. This meant that the Japanese would be limited to used foreign cars, whereas those Americans who had profited from importing cars and then reselling them to the Japanese were effectively blocked.

These were deemed temporary measures, to continue until Japan had consolidated its domestic market and made inroads overseas. So as to further aid the industry, MITI now engaged in what it was to do later on in consumer electronics and other areas where Japan started out at a disadvantage, namely, accept—with no little reluctance and with the clear understanding that the arrangement was temporary—the licensing from and entrance into joint ventures with foreigners that might expand domestic enterprise.

In this period, most Japanese automobile firms simply couldn't afford to pay for the kind of research and development that would enable them to catch up with, much less surpass, the Americans and the Europeans. They would compensate for this by licensing, imitating, and "borrowing," after making tours of Western installations, and any other method that seemed feasible. And the foreigners would be invited to Japan to manufacture, make a profit, but most of all, instruct the Japanese companies in their technologies. At a time when Europeans and Americans couldn't enter the Japanese market easily, the government guaranteed the remittance of all royalties—on condition that within five years at least 90 percent of the products and components turned out with the new methods be manufactured in Japan.

Just as Matsushita, Toshiba, and others were to benefit from early associations with Radio Corporation of America, Zenith, and General Electric, so the Japanese automobile companies did well in their cooperative efforts. In 1952, Nissan concluded an agreement with Austin to assemble 1,200 of its small trucks for sale in Japan over a five-year period. Isuzu engineered a deal with Rootes, under which a like amount of Hillman trucks would become available, and Hino had an arrangement with Renault to assemble 1,300 of that company's vehicles. It is not known whether any Japanese company approached Detroit's Big Three with a proposal, but in this period, the Americans showed little interest in the Japanese market. Mitsubishi did work in tandem with Willys, which was the only American firm to come to terms with the Japanese; thus, the Jeep came to Japan in the mid-1950s. Toyota, still the most independent of the automobile companies, held back, however, preferring to develop its own cars without foreign assistance.

As expected, this cooperation was short-lived. All the agreements were terminated by 1958, after which foreign companies were effectively barred from manufacturing passenger cars in Japan.

None of these contracts was meant to last longer than it took the Japanese companies to learn what they wanted from the foreigners, as the Europeans and Willys were soon to discover. The Isuzu-Rootes combine for Hillman trucks was the last to go, abrogated in 1964.

Concomitant with MITI's efforts to improve technology before attempting an export drive was a drive to consolidate the companies into three or four major groups, each to resemble General Motors. Nothing came of this in the 1950s, and in fact, additional companies entered the field soon after—Fuji, Toyo Kogyo, and Honda being the most important. MITI responded by rejecting several applications for the importation of foreign technology and capital. When this attempt to force the industry into consolidation failed, the ministry suggested that each company design a small car for the domestic market, with one being chosen for all to produce. Economies of scale being what they were, the price would be low, and eventually this car might become Japan's entry into foreign markets.

All the companies rejected the notion, and once again frustrated MITI's plans for rationalization. But the ministry didn't abandon the idea. It would be revived in the early 1960s with more success, and even now MITI feels that the industry would be better served with fewer entries. Thus, the situation in Japan regarding concentration is just the opposite of what it is in the United States, where the Justice Department is on guard against cooperation and, on occasion, companies that have been interested in mergers.

MITI also established a forum to share ideas, a body to lobby for tariffs, a place where financing might be arranged and later on, a governmental organization to assist in the export drive. But those who even now believe that "Japan Inc." dictated terms to the industry with its leaders meekly accepting advice and integrating efforts do not know that the companies had many clashes with MITI.

Initially, both the ministry and the industry thought the Japanese companies should concentrate on the domestic market, with exports a secondary consideration. But the automakers—again, Toyota and Nissan, in particular—had planned to expand overseas within a relatively short period, whereas MITI seemed to believe that such a move wouldn't come for many years. This was yet another difference between the businessmen and the bureaucrats, and another instance when the private sector's vision proved clearer than the ministry's.

The Japanese Invasion was informed by the European experience. Toyota and Nissan executives carefully studied the success of Volkswagen—and the reasons for the British, French, and Italian failures. Volkswagen had started out by offering an economy vehicle, which gave value for money. The reputation for quality came afterward. So it was that in the early 1950s, ownership of a Beetle signified penury or eccentricity, whereas by mid-decade, the car had been embraced by those who were impressed with quality, service, and originality. As shown, Nordhoff insisted on superior service operations, and Volkswagen of America developed a reputation for excellence that surpassed that of Detroit.

Some of the lessons were clear enough, having been dissected in both the popular and industry presses for several years, whereas others would come later on: enter the market by offering quality at a low price, maintain loyalty, and win new customers through dependability and service. There was yet another step VW hadn't taken but that was being considered even then: upgrade through the introduction of more luxurious and more expensive models to take advantage of an excellent reputation. The Beetle started out as a car that cost less than a Chevy or a Ford, but that was, in some respects, superior to either; by the mid-1960s, the 1500 Variant and the 1600 Fastback would be priced to compete with Mercurys and Buicks and were being targeted at some of the customers who were in the market for such higher-priced models.

These were the goals, but what did the Japanese have to offer in the late 1950s? The Nissan and Toyota sedans were undistinguished and dowdy, and their small pickup trucks, although popular in Japan and winning some acceptance in the Southeast Asia export markets, could not hope to win much of the U.S. market. Moreover, there remained the scars of World War II, which were bound to hinder sales.

Toyota and Nissan executives scouted the American market during the early 1950s, meeting with the same kind of reaction that had discouraged the Germans a few years earlier. Seisi Kato, a future chairman of the board of Toyota Motor Sales, but then a junior executive at the parent company, experienced this in 1952, when while sharing a taxi after a flight he sat next to an American who brushed him aside with a remark that two of his sons had died in the Pacific. "Whenever I see Japanese I feel like beating their brains out, whoever they are." Yet the Germans had overcome this, and that must have given the Japanese hope.

Toyota led the way, with Nissan close behind, and here, too, the German experience proved worth imitating. Just as Nordhoff had dispatched agents to survey the scene and report back, so did Taizo Ishida, who had recently become president of Toyota Motors, and Shotaro Kamiya, who headed Toyota Motor Sales. A three-man survey team arrived in the United States in August 1956, and after a nationwide tour, they decided that the southern California market would make the best beachhead. The reasons were obvious. California led the nation in percentage of foreign cars on the road. Not only was this area still a place in which the novel and the different were welcomed, but the proximity to Japan, the relatively large number of Japanese-Americans in the region, and the general familiarity with Japanese products would also work in Toyota's favor. California had been among the first states to embrace the VW; Toyota hoped for the same kind of reception for its Crown sedans.

Kato established the advance group in a Los Angeles hotel, while Kamiya shipped the first cars for the American market —two Toyopet Crown sedans—from Yokohama in late August 1957. Kato arranged for press coverage of the landing. Miss Japan was dispatched from Tokyo to the United States to place a wreath on the first Crown to be unloaded, and pictures of the event appeared in the local newspapers the next day.

Curious about the new car, several dealers contacted Kato regarding franchises. The Japanese were enthusiastic regarding possibilities, for from what they had seen it appeared that they might soon sell upward of 10,000 Crowns a year, with a network of dealerships throughout southern California. Kamiya dispatched his deputy, Tokutoru Kobayashi, to California in late October, and on the last day of the month he incorporated Toyota Motor Sales U.S.A., its first headquarters being a defunct automobile dealership office in Hollywood.

During the next few months, Kobayashi poured over the franchise applications, approving those that seemed promising, but in the end winding up with dealers who for the most part were underfinanced and understaffed. The typical Toyota dealer of this period tended to be a person who had been hoping for a VW franchise, was irritated by the wait, and was willing to settle for something else. Which is to say the very same kind of individual who was expected to purchase the Toyopet Crown—a frustrated, would-be VW owner.

Realizing the built-in problems of such an attitude, Kobayashi attempted to infuse these first dealers with enthusiasm and élan, brought over Japanese mechanics to train the Americans in service and repair, and in other ways, attempted to erect a system comparable to a successful VW operation. "Toyota impressed me from the start because they were building a big parts warehouse in Newark even before there were any dealers in the East," recalled one early applicant. "Toyota wasn't going to tell me to go see a big dealer over in Brooklyn if I wanted parts."

High optimism alternated with deep despair in southern California. The optimism remained for about a month, as dealers were signed up, orders were placed, and some of the showroom traffic in Hollywood was translated into sales to individuals willing and even eager to be the first Americans to drive a Japanese car in the United States. By January 1958, however, it appeared that Toyota had blundered badly and might have to abandon the American market for good.

The company's problems would have been familiar to the Italians, British, and French automakers who preceded it. Contrary to their original plans, Toyota had sold cars before service facilities were ready. This wouldn't have been too much of a problem, however, had it not been for the cars themselves. The Toyopet Crown had been considered a fine model of its type in Japan, where it was found to be a sturdy and dependable family vehicle, well suited to the narrow roads of the country in this period, where high speeds were not only discouraged but also usually impossible. Toyopets were used in Tokyo and other cities as taxis, where they were deemed most satisfactory urban vehicles.

In the United States, however, it fell between the Beetle and the American cars—larger than the former, smaller than the latter. The Toyopet didn't appeal strongly to those wanting small cars, yet it was more cramped than the first domestic compact. It was not unusual or "lovable" in any way, and at the same time it seemed somewhat tacky to a generation of Americans accustomed to thinking of Japanese goods as being inferior and still nursing the bitterness of the war. Then, too, the name was wrong. What did "Toyopet" suggest? It sounded like *toy* combined with *pet*, and neither had sales appeal.

The Crown offered neither quality or novelty, both of

which were offered by the VW. The car cost almost $2,300, which was $600 more than the Beetle and as much as a Chevy. Thus, it combined a high price tag with the appearance and size of an economy model. The Toyopet certainly was not a "quality" or "performance" car. On the contrary, for although it ran well enough in city traffic, the car fell apart on the open road, where Americans generally cruised at around twice the speeds for which it had been designed. One American executive jeeringly called the Toyopet "underpowered, overpriced, and built like a tank." Later on, Kamiya would concede this had been the wrong model to initiate the American assault and that Toyota should have started out with a smaller, less expensive car that might go up against the VW. Kato would sum up the Toyopet experience in his memoir a quarter of a century later:

> We were counting our chickens before they were hatched, to say the very least: when the Toyopet Crown was tried out in U.S. freeways at 80 mph, loud noises soon erupted and power dropped sharply. More trouble occurred before we logged even 2,000 miles. Although many people had praised the Crown as a "baby Cadillac," for example, our engines, designed for the narrow-road, low-speed driving of Japan in those days, could not even begin to handle the performance and endurance demands placed upon them. As our dreams sank out of sight like a ship with a giant hole in its bottom, we wrote to Tokyo that it was advisable to simply throw in the towel.

In 1958, Toyota Motors U.S.A. sold 288 cars in the United States, in 1959, 1,028. Then as the novelty wore off, so did the showroom traffic. Only 821 Toyopets were sold in 1960, and 576 in 1961, by which time franchises were being abandoned. When they covered the car at all, auto magazines predicted its disappearance from the American road. Advertisements for used Toyopets began to appear in Los Angeles and New York newspapers in early 1959, and it seemed, from this small sampling, that customer approval was low. So was the car's resale value, as might be expected for a model that not only seemed misbegotten, but might also soon be an orphan. Toyota's American beachhead hadn't expanded; in fact it was in danger of disappearing.

Rarely the pioneer, Nissan opted for a more conservative approach. In early 1957, the corporation commissioned Marubeni and Mitsubishi, two Japanese trading companies with some experience in the field, to study the American market. According to the contract, Marubeni was to survey the Pacific coast, Mitsubishi the Atlantic. Marubeni submitted a report that indicated some sales potential, and recommended that Nissan send some of its cars and trucks to the forthcoming Los Angeles show for imported vehicles. Nissan participated, the reaction to the Datsun sedans and trucks was favorable, and the company was encouraged to continue.

Nissan's experience did not differ much from Toyota's. Just as the latter company failed badly with its Toyopet Crown, so Nissan's first sedan, the Cedric, met with an indifferent reception. Americans who gave it a test drive generally found the Cedric overweight and underpowered, but not without promise. "This car is really quite good," concluded *Road and Track* after a test in the autumn of 1958. "With a few relatively simple changes it could go over. It is, even in its present form, better than most of the small British cars currently being sold in this country: not so fast, perhaps, but it should be more reliable and it has a nice solid feeling about it."

As had been the case with Toyota, Nissan received many applications from potential dealers, so many that the corporation was obliged to move more rapidly than was prudent. Instead of establishing an American subsidiary, Nissan opted to use Mitsubishi as its East Coast importer, and Marubeni would take care of the West Coast and be headquartered in California. Because neither trading company had any experience selling cars overseas, they sought large, well-entrenched American companies to handle the actual work. Thus, Mitsubishi entered into an arrangement with Luby Chevrolet of New York, which was granted an exclusive franchise for twenty-two eastern states, with the understanding that the new Luby Datsun Distributors would be held separate from the Chevrolet franchises. Similarly, Marubeni contracted with Woolverton Motors of North Hollywood to give its new subsidiary, Western Datsun Distributors, sole rights in eleven western and southwestern states.

Everything was in place by August 1958, by which time Luby and Western had established their first outlets and were taking orders. Although there was some interest in the economy Cedric, which sold for $1,799 POE, more attention was given the small truck, which appealed to Southern California farmers, especially those who were Oriental.

Nissan hadn't made as great a commitment as had Toyota to the American market, and its caution paid off. In the last four months of 1958, when the cars were hardly known, 83 Cedrics were purchased, almost all in California. The 1959 sales came to 1,131 sedans and 179 trucks, and the following year, 1,294 sedans and 346 trucks. Encouraged by this steady if not spectacular expansion, the parent organized "Nissan Motor Corporation in U.S.A." late that year, with Luby and Western the prime franchisees. At the time it appeared, Nissan had a better chance than Toyota had at developing an American following.

All this has to be kept in perspective, however. The Japanese had only a minuscule part of the American market. In 1961, when 378,542 foreign cars were sold in the United States, VW led the pack with 177,308, almost one-half the total. That year Nissan and Toyota between them sold 1,733 cars and 279 trucks. Contrast this with the increasingly unpopular Fiat, which with 11,839 sales had 3 percent of the market.

In 1961, the Japanese were behind not only the Germans but also the French, British, and Italians in the American market. Even the Swedes and Belgians had a larger share of sales.

But there was a difference between the fading Fiat and

other European automakers and the Japanese. Toyota and Nissan had made an important emotional as well as financial commitment to the American market, and they gave every indication of intending to remain. Important problems had to be addressed, however. Toyota would have to come up with vehicles more suited to American tastes, whereas Nissan faced problems of organization as well. Both companies still had to overcome the entrenched belief that Japanese products were inferior, not to mention the ingrained racism that had not plagued the Europeans, even the Germans. Could small yellow men *really* turn out cars as good if not better than those manufactured in Detroit and Wolfsburg? If the question wasn't often asked in 1960, it was because few believed it a serious one.

It would be going too far to say the Japanese were here to stay. Rather, they would remain if and when encouragement came from the marketplace. The outlook was hardly promising in the early 1960s. General Motors, Ford, and Chrysler had their compacts, the European invasion seemed to have been repulsed, VW had what was left, and precious little remained for the others. Most automobile industry experts expected the Americans to continue denying foreigners anything more than a token share of the market. Some said it was 5 percent and that when imports reached that level an American reaction in the form of new models would be triggered. Others said it had risen to 10 percent because of the heavy financing costs involved, as well as the conviction that even then a recapture would be possible.

From what quarter would the next challenge come? The betting was on Volvo and Saab, not on Toyota and Nissan. In 1961, the United Auto Workers sent a delegation overseas to study advanced techniques and quality control. It was sent to Sweden, not Japan.

The consensus was that the Japanese had stumbled. This didn't come as any great surprise. Given the record, the nature of the industry, and America's great supremacy, what else might have been anticipated?

10

The Beachhead

Foreigners have often stood in amazement at Japan's ability to swallow so many new ideas and institutions whole. They have dubbed her superficial, and questioned the permanence of her conversion to European methods. This is because they fail to realize two things—the innate strength of the Japanese character, and the continuous process of schooling which has enabled this particular race to face the new light without being blinded. . . . From the dawn of history to the present day, Japan, in her attitude toward foreign ideas—be they Chinese, medieval Portuguese, old-fashioned Dutch, nineteenth century European—has shown herself consistently teachable.

BASIL HALL CHAMBERLAIN,
1905

While President Kennedy was challenging the United States with the task of flight to the moon, Prime Minister Ikeda was publicly spurring Japan to double national income in a decade.

ALBERT KEIDEL,
1981

If ever there was an "American Decade," it would have had to be the 1950s, when throughout the world the United States not only was believed the most powerful country militarily and economically, but its artifacts and products were also emulated, if not overtly admired. Europeans and members of the Third World might rail against the nation's culture, but it was embraced by the masses. This was true for music and other popular arts, but was most obvious for what critics called "Yankee materialism." Which isn't to suggest that the desire for plentiful consumer goods was a particularly American notion. Rather, the American way of life, popularized in movies and magazines, re-reinforced and instructed European—and Japanese—yearnings.

That the Japanese embraced the externalities of American life with more enthusiasm and less criticism than any other people in the postwar world has been remarked on often and at length by most observers of the scene. This helps explain why such a people, in a relatively small crowded country where mass transport made more economic and social sense than most, craved automobiles. Much has been made of the Japanese need to export motor vehicles in order to obtain needed foreign currencies; insufficient attention has been paid to the domestic market for cars, without which the export boom wouldn't have been feasible.

Recognizing the benefits that might be realized by economies of scale, and having come to appreciate the possibilities of exports, the Japanese government embarked on a program to encourage the domestic industry. There was a sharp increase in highway construction, and the imposition of a requirement for strict biennial inspections, a measure that won the support of environmentalists concerned with air quality, but also discouraged Japanese motorists from keeping their cars for more than a few years.

In 1955, when Toyota and Nissan were planning the American invasion, Japanese automobile production was slightly more than 20,000 units, of which the grand total of 2 were exported. Almost all these cars were used in the cities, serving as taxis and rental cars, the need for which was obvious to anyone who was there in that period. By 1960, when the Japanese companies were making their initial inroads into the American market (exporting 7,000 cars), Japanese production was over 165,000, with an increasing number of them being purchased by Japanese consumers, often as replacements for old American cars left by the occupation forces. It was then that credit purchasing was introduced to the Japanese consumers. Until that time, the practice had been frowned on by both companies and customers and discouraged by the government. In 1960, mostly to stimulate the domestic industry, the Bank of Japan urged financial institutions and the car companies to experiment with offering credit to would-be buyers. Little came of it at first, but two years later, there was a discernible increase in the use of credit, and by 1966, three out of every four sedans were being bought on time, usually with 25 percent down and the balance paid out over 20 to 24 months. At the end of the decade, there was $1.6 billion in consumer credit loans outstanding, with cars accounting for $1.3 billion of it. Exports accounted for one out of every three cars produced by the mid-1970s, when the anticipated reaction against imports began and charges of dumping were being heard. And all the while domestic growth continued strong. In 1972, when Japanese companies exported 1.4 million cars, almost 6.3 million were sold in the home market, making Japan the second-largest car market in the world—just behind the United States.

JAPANESE PASSENGER CAR PRODUCTION BY COMPANY,
1950–1955

YEAR	TOYOTA	NISSAN	OTHERS	TOTAL
1950	463	865	266	1,594
1951	1,470	1,705	436	3,611
1952	1,857	2,376	510	4,743
1953	3,572	3,049	2,064	8,685
1954	4,235	4,650	5,465	14,350
1955	7,403	6,597	6,220	20,220

SOURCE: Duncan, *U.S.-Japan Automobile Diplomacy,* 144.

Similarly, the replacement rate for Japanese cars toward the end of the decade was second only to that of the United States. In 1960, only 1.2 percent of urban families owned an automobile. Five years later the amount had expanded to a fraction under 10 percent, and in 1971, one out of every four Japanese urban families had its own car.

In 1950, fewer than 55,000 cars were registered in Japan, against 40 million in the United States. Three decades later, there were 149 million cars on the American roads, and almost 25 million cars on Japanese roads.

Might the Japanese have developed an automobile industry without a strong export market? Certainly, for in fact, they did just that in the 1950s. The large Japanese companies entered the export market for private reasons, as well as to serve the national interest, but today the latter may have become more important than the former.

The American economy was vibrant and growing in the first half of the 1960s, and Detroit was ebullient, prosperous beyond anything anticipated even during the immediate postwar period. Domestic automobile sales came to 6.7 million units in the recovery year of 1962, the second best in history. The following year, 7.4 million were sold, followed by 7.5 million in 1964. Then, in 1965, a record 9.1 million cars were sold. A troubled Chrysler, which had $2.1 billion in sales and profits of a mere $11 million in 1960, posted revenues of $5.3 billion for 1965 and profits that year came to $233 million.

JAPANESE PASSENGER CAR PRODUCTION BY COMPANY,
1956–1960

YEAR	TOYOTA	NISSAN	OTHERS	TOTAL
1956	12,001	12,965	7,002	31,968
1957	19,885	18,786	8,374	47,045
1958	21,224	16,878	11,937	50,039
1959	30,235	26,753	16,499	73,487
1960	42,118	55,049	31,487	128,984

SOURCE: Duncan, *U.S.-Japan Automobile Diplomacy*, 144.

Although the recovery for Ford and GM wasn't as dramatic, it was most gratifying nonetheless. Ford's revenues went from $6.8 billion to $11.5 billion, and profits from $410 million to $703 million, and GM's revenues and net profits from $12.7 billion and $959 million to $20.7 billion and $2.1 billion. Only American Motors showed a decline in this euphoric half-decade, in both sales and earnings.

What accounted for this situation? A revival in the market for full-size cars that brought large profits for the companies, a seeming American victory over the foreigners in the compact area, and VW's slaughtering of rivals in the small imported market. Total sales of imports continued to decline in the late 1950s and early 1960s, not bottoming out until 1962, when 399,000 imports were sold, with Volkswagen accounting for 57 percent of the total—almost twice its market share in 1960.

What might the Japanese expect under such circumstances? The answer was quite a bit, given some good fortune in design, pricing, and marketing. This, in fact, was the case, as Toyota and Nissan had all three. In 1962 the two companies sold fewer than 3,000 cars between them in the American market. Toyota 1965 sales were 6,400, and although this was only half that for even so dismal a performer as Renault, it was far better than Peugeot. More important, in 1965 Toyota sold twice as many cars as it had the previous year, and its distributorship network was expanding rapidly.

Meanwhile, Nissan capitalized upon its early lead. Almost 18,000 Datsuns were sold in 1965, the sixth best showing by a foreign company, placing it above Renault, Simca, and Fiat, but behind Opel, the GM-controlled German manufacturer that still offered its products through the American distributors, who were yet to demonstrate any enthusiasm for the cars. At that, between them, Toyota and Nissan had only 3 percent of the market for imports.

Five years later, the two companies would sell 285,000 cars, and occupy second and third places behind a fading Volkswagen.

At first blush it might appear the reasons for the Japanese successes were the same as for the VW Beetle's acceptance several years before, namely, they turned out low-priced, economical, well-produced vehicles, which were serviced by an efficient organization. Only some of this was true. Toyota and Nissan certainly established smooth-running sales and service operations, and their cars were economical. But the prices for most models were above those for the Beetle, although Americans clearly didn't mind paying the difference. This was so because the Japanese had capitalized on a variation on themes developed in Wolfsburg and Detroit that was once again a clever compromise. Volkswagen led the way with small cars, and Detroit countered with compacts. Toyota and Nissan came up with sedans that were small compacts, combining the VW size with interiors, engineering, and appearances that would appeal to American drivers.

What the Japanese did, in effect, was design cars similar to those Detroit had talked about during the early 1940s—namely, the small economy model to suit the needs of postwar Americans. And as other Japanese firms in other industries would do during the rest of the decade, Toyota and Nissan demonstrated an ability to create unexciting, fairly conventional products that sold not only on price, but also on quality and recognizability.

In the late 1950s, as Nissan's sales first rose and then leveled off, company executives conferred with their American dealers to discover why this was happening. Fiat, Renault, and other foreign companies had had the same experience in the American market during the previous decade. Was it now Nissan's turn to be disappointed? The original strategy had seemed so obvious and sensible. Like Toyota, Nissan had exported its largest and most luxurious domestic model to the United States, believing that wealthy Americans wouldn't accept anything else. This was more the result of awe of and respect for potential purchasers than of anything resembling market analysis. Clearly, it had not been the right approach, and now the Japanese restudied the situation.

Two different suggestions were made. Some American distributors wanted Nissan to concentrate on manufacturing a lower-priced Japanese version of the VW Beetle, believing that success should breed imitation. Others saw no possibility of competing with the Beetle, and thought Nissan might upgrade its American offerings to compete against Volvo. This concept, logical though it seemed, meant that, if successful, Nissan might have a large share of a rather small and limited market, and this didn't appeal to the company.

In the end, Nissan decided to market versions of cars already being produced and sold in Japan. The company would offer the American purchaser a wide selection in body style, color scheme, and interior, this when the Beetle came in six colors and only as a two-door model. Moreover, Datsuns would soon be available with three- as well as four-speed transmissions, with automatics later.

The 200 series arrived in the United States in late 1959, led by the L 210 sedan, but also including a station wagon and a pickup truck. *Road and Track*, the respected journal of auto buffs, first reviewed this model in its May 1960 issue. "The Datsun is a product of the Nissan Motor Company, one of the oldest manufacturers of cars in Japan," it wrote in an understandably condescending review. "They have been building cars since the early Thirties and this experience, plus the fact that they have borrowed heavily from the designs of Austin of England, gives them more of an automotive background than one might otherwise believe possible. Their main product, the Datsun, closely resembles early postwar English cars and is a sturdy, if uninspired, performer." In fact, the Datsun was better designed and fabricated than the Austin, although a sluggish performer by American standards. It was a beginning, little more, but hardly auspicious.

The following year Nissan exported its 310 series, led by the four-door Bluebird sedan, which might be considered the first Japanese car with a meaningful appeal. "Whereas the car of several years ago had little to recommend it, the new car has much to offer," wrote *Road and Track* in early 1961. "The appearance of the Datsun Bluebird, as it now is called, is improved immeasurably. It no longer looks like an exact copy of some other car and the color schemes were apparently planned with the U.S. market in mind."

In 1961, Nissan brought over its SPL 212–213. This was a sports car competitively priced with the VW Karmann Ghia, but considerably more powerful. Like the other Datsuns of the period, it was available with many options and in a variety of colors.

Thus, Nissan really wasn't expecting to go head-on against VW. Rather, it was attempting to "re-invent" the small car in America, to suit the temper of the prosperous early 1960s as VW had for the mid-1950s. By then, the VW Beetle had become a fixture, much as had been the Ford Model Ts of the 1920s. But like the Ts, they had become outdated. Volkswagen was experimenting with larger Beetles and eventually automatic transmissions and the like. In time, new models would emerge from Wolfsburg, but by then they would arrive too late to catch up with the Japanese.

During the 1950s, VW had taken a page from Henry Ford's book; in the 1960s, Nissan would profit from the 1930s techniques and concepts of Alfred Sloan. Just as GM took an unbeatable lead over Ford in the 1930s, so the Japanese companies were to do the same in respect to VW in the 1960s.

Few Americans aware of international automobile developments during the early 1960s knew of the Japanese companies, and those who did might have expected Nissan to capitalize on whatever segment of the market might fall to companies from that country. As it turned out Toyota, not Nissan, was to become Japan's premier concern, not only in the overseas markets but at home as well. The reasons for this are clear today. Whatever advantages the Japanese developed in the home market, Toyota exploited to a greater extent than did its closest rival, and the same was true for the export area, especially in the United States. Starting again after a false start, Toyota was able to regroup and go on to develop a reputation unexcelled in postwar automobile history, becoming the premier exemplar of Japanese automaking for the better part of two decades.

Not even VW's earlier efforts compared with what Toyota was able to accomplish in the 1960s. The Germans had challenged Detroit in a narrow segment of the overall market. In contrast, Toyota did nothing less than oblige Detroit to consider accepting a new concept of the position of the automobile in Western society. The auto industry had originated on the European continent, primarily in Germany and France, but it had come of age in the United States, which, for more than a half a century had led the rest of the world. Protestations from Detroit to the contrary, Japan, led by Toyota, became the leader in what was no less than a reborn industry, as different from that of the 1950s as was the American enterprise of that era from the pre–World War II era.

Toyota's original approach hadn't differed markedly from Nissan's, in that it had come to the American market with what it considered its premier product, which as has been seen was the Toyopet Crown, a failure. And like Nissan, the corporation reconsidered its position and came up with a similar answer.

Toyota U.S.A. remained convinced that the essential rationale had been correct, that a frontal attack on the VW market was senseless, and that in any case, more sales could be made by appealing to traditional car buyers. "Especially difficult for the engineers to comprehend was what some of them called American '*creature comforts*,' the penchant for carpeting, soft upholstery, tinted glass, whitewall tires, and other embellishments," chided the author of an official Toyota U.S.A. history. "Those, too, were among the features that Toyota executives in the United States knew would help penetrate the huge American market." Moreover, such an approach in the low-priced sector gave Toyota a decided edge over the competition. "Other small imports were still homegrown models and utilitarian, but the Toyota group found that Americans would clearly welcome a touch of luxury in an economy car."

Toyota limped along in the early 1960s, maintaining a

skeleton organization in the United States and pleading with
its dealers for patience until a new, more acceptable model
could be turned out and shipped. In this period, the company's
sales effort was concentrated on the Land Cruiser, a utility
vehicle meant to appeal to owners of Jeeps and the like, and
these were sold not only through the original Toyota outlets
but also from virtually anyone who agreed to carry them, the
idea being not so much to make profits but to keep the Toyota
nameplate on the road.

The Land Cruiser was a mild success. Toyota U.S.A. had
sold 1,400 vehicles, most of them sedans, in 1959, which fell off
to 500 in 1960 and 400 in 1961. Slightly more than 1,000 Toyotas were purchased by Americans in 1962. Of these, 700 were
Land Cruisers, with small trucks accounting for most of the
rest; sedan sales came to a total of 87. For 1963, 1,100 vehicles
were sold, and again Land Cruisers accounted for the bulk of
the sales.

This was hardly substantial or encouraging. It appeared
that Toyota hadn't much hope of success in the American
sedan market, and that if any Japanese company had a chance
there, it would be Nissan.

Meanwhile Toyota designers rushed their new car to completion. Called the Corona, it was a standard small car that
resembled some of the Fiats of the period and was equally
unoriginal technologically. It wasn't even a new name, for
Toyota Coronas had appeared in 1952 as the corporation's response to the growing demand for taxis. Nor was the new
Corona produced primarily for the export market; work had
begun on it in 1959, both to upgrade the existing model and to
compete against Nissan's popular Bluebird.

The car, introduced in 1960, initially sold quite well domestically, leading Toyota to believe that in time it might join
the Land Cruiser in the American market as well. But within
a few months defects appeared, mostly mechanical, resulting
in apologies and embarrassed recalls. These were straightened
out by 1962, but the car's reputation remained low. Then, as
Toyota prepared to send the Corona to the United States, its

new Crown came down with a series of ailments, the most important being cracks in the frame. All efforts turned to correcting these problems, as Toyota's reputation for quality declined further and Nissan soared in the domestic market.

By then Toyota was badly damaged and in need of assistance. The company approached Ford seeking an arrangement for joint ventures, in part to obtain the American company's technology, but also to draw upon the American company's manufacturing and marketing expertise. Nothing came of this, however, and Toyota had to go it alone.

Toyota's problems were compounded by the failure of the Publica, an experience that illuminated the nature of the Japanese auto market of the period and offers a hint why Toyotas and Datsuns were later received so well in the United States.

Introduced late in 1960, the Publica was created as a response to MITI's long-held yearning for a "people's car," a small, low-priced, spartan sedan for the masses, designed and manufactured for individuals who in the past could afford nothing better than a three-wheeled vehicle. It was, in fact, a minicar, with few accessories and options, which kept to the target price of $1,100. The Publica was greeted by indifference and was soon removed from the market.

Seisi Kato, a Toyota executive involved with distribution, summed up the reasons for the failure in terms that would have been readily comprehensible in Detroit, indicating far more commonality between the auto buyers of Japan and the United States than might have been expected. "It was, if I can sum it up in a word, bland," wrote Kato.

> In those days, the idea of owning one's own car had always been not much more than a dream for the general public. Automobiles had always been beyond the reach of the common people in Japan, and thus when the "average citizen" finally found himself able to buy a car, it seemed he wanted one that would fit the image of that dream, even if he had to spend a little extra money. We learned that what he wanted in his car, in other words, was the same

element that had dominated Western automotive design for years: personality.

Which would seem to suggest that, in Kato's view, the Japanese auto buyer was closer to those Americans who liked Chevys and Fords than to Beetle enthusiasts. The kinds of small sedans preferred by the Japanese might be just the thing for the U.S. market. But Toyota seemed incapable of turning them out. During the early 1960s, the company found itself short of cash, having to rely more upon its banks than it might have preferred. In this period, too, attention had to be paid to the domestic market; the American invasion was of secondary importance, which provided Nissan with an even greater lead overseas.

The problems of the Crown were resolved by 1963, while the Publica underwent extensive revisions, most of which made it a more luxurious and more expensive car. As for the Corona, it was provided with a larger engine and a revamped electrical and fuel system, so that by mid-1964, all the bugs had been isolated and removed.

Now the car was ready to make its American debut, to be introduced to a people who had no idea of its early troubles and who, later on, would be convinced that Japanese automakers were infallible.

The Corona appeared at a most opportune time. The Big Three's early successes with the first group of compacts—Corvair, Falcon, and Valiant—had led them to believe that the Americans could throw back almost any foreign challenge that came along, if they were of a mind to do so.

But the Mustang was the only new car of this period that might draw sales away from the small foreign models. Chrysler's Barracuda and GM's Chevelle, introduced in 1965, didn't do as well; the former was a large sports car, the latter came close to full size. During the next two years, big, flashy, powerful new marques were the rage—Toronado, Charger, Camaro, Firebird, Eldorado, Cougar, AMX, and Javelin, while the once-compact Corvair, Falcon, and Valiant became larger. So by 1965, the Big Three were withdrawing from the small car field, leaving it to others.

Others, in those days, still meant VW, and, in turn, the Beetle. By now the car had a wide variety of improvements, from larger windows and better head and taillights and a somewhat plusher interior to a more powerful engine. As Nordhoff had promised, the car would change in an evolutionary rather than a revolutionary fashion, which was fine for those who still admired the design. And there were many who did. Volkswagen posted record sales of 384,000 units in 1965 and established a new record of 420,000 the following year.

Then in 1967, the company experienced its first decline in the American market, with sales dropping to 409,000 units. This proved short-lived, as the figure went above 500,000 in 1968 and remained there for the rest of the decade. By 1970, however (when VW sold 569,000 cars in the United States), it had become clear that the Beetle had peaked and was on the way down. Wolfsburg knew this, too, and had already started experimenting with a variety of alternatives, none of which captured the American imagination, but all the while planning a totally new car (to be known as the Rabbit) for which the advance word was that it was meant to be "the Beetle of the 1970s."

Thus, the Corona arrived in America at a most propitious time. Detroit was no longer concerned about small economy sedans, whereas the Beetle had become an old model, with nothing yet out of Wolfsburg to replace it. And in its Corona, Toyota was presenting Americans with a sedan that was both familiar and foreign, relatively powerful, but economical, low in cost, while almost luxurious in design, and sufficiently exotic to attract purchasers who, in other years, might have wanted Beetles. At the same time, it was conventional enough for those who liked Chevys and Fords.

The Corona had a front-mounted, 90-hp, water-cooled engine (compared with the VW 1300's rear-mounted, air-cooled 50-hp power plant). It weighed 2,183 pounds (against the VW's 1,722) and was 162 inches long (the Beetle was 2 inches shorter). The Corona sedan came with four doors and could seat a like number of passengers more comfortably than the Beetle. It offered a conventional jack and such novel features as a trouble light that plugged into an outlet in the glove compartment and a more complete tool kit than any other foreign sedan offered. This was a car that handled like a domestic model, but had most of the advantages of an import. It even had optional automatic transmission, which was far superior to that offered by VW.

The Corona listed for $1,890, which was $250 more than the VW 1300. Considering the extra features and size, it seemed good value for price. *Consumer Reports,* which by then had become a touchstone for potential purchasers of small imports, was impressed by what it tested. "The Corona's engine was quiet at all speeds, and the car managed to combine first-rate performance with fuel economy which was better than the VW's. Toyota dealer outlets, though they show uneven regional concentrations, are increasing at a rapid pace."

The magazine, long enthusiastic regarding the Beetle, by 1966 had conceded its day was ending. And automobile analysts wondered whether Nordhoff had made the same error Henry Ford had in the mid-1920s, when he insisted that the Model T could go on forever, and ignored the growing threat of the Chevy.

> The VW's trump cards are still playable: it costs less, its dollar depreciation is by far the lowest of this group, its frequency-of-repair record remains good, and its service outlets are the most extensive of the . . . cars. But as a competing small car, it is deficient in such basics as handling, acceleration, heating, defrosting and ventilation, luggage space and driver vision. In addition, its noise level is higher than that of its competitors and its wind sensitivity is too great.

To go along with its new car, Toyota developed an American-style advertising campaign, which began in early 1965. The messages, which appeared on television as well as in newspapers and magazines, were quite familiar. The Corona was an "exciting" car, the intimation being it offered power plus economy and luxury at "an affordable price." The Corona ads came out of the same tradition as those for the Big Three. In contrast, VW hadn't advertised at all during the 1950s, and when the company did so, it concentrated on the print media, with sophisticated, clever layouts and messages that stressed the Beetle's unchanging form and durability. Here too the VW appeared as an import, and was aimed at those who didn't want a Detroit product, while the Corona was developing an image of what amounted to an American car, which just happened to have been manufactured in Japan.

It worked. The economy was booming and, as already indicated, 1965 was to be a record year for automobile sales. By then, too, Japan's reputation for quality had been enhanced by their television sets, cameras, and other consumer items, so that car buyers were more receptive to the Corona than might have been the case earlier.

With all this, the Corona was hardly an overnight smash. For one thing, Toyota still had to develop its dealerships; the cars were available on the East and West coasts, but not in the Midwest, for example; nationwide, there were fewer than 400 showrooms, most of them quite small. Nissan had a sizable lead and a larger sales network, and in one of its new offerings, the 410, a four-door sedan that was both attractive and economical. In 1965, 6,400 Toyotas were purchased by Americans, slightly more than a third the number of Datsuns. Once again, these numbers must be considered in the light of the total market and the competition. Simca, now virtually ignored, sold twice as many cars in the United States that year as did Toyota, whereas AM, struggling to survive, reported sales of slightly less than a quarter of a million units. The following year, when both Toyota and Nissan expanded their bases, the Japanese shipped fewer than 57,000 cars to their American dealers, which was 25,000 fewer than did the British manufacturers.

A beachhead had been established. Nissan had performed reasonably well, and Toyota had recovered from a near-disaster. But their cars were still only regionally available and yet to demonstrate their appeal to the broad mass of Americans. Had Detroit appreciated their possibilities, the invasion might have been contained or even thrown back. At the time, however, the Datsuns and Toyotas were considered rivals to the Beetle, at best capable of gathering some of the sales from foreign-car enthusiasts looking for something a trifle different. The possibility that Coronas might appeal to Chevy and Ford owners seemed highly improbable in the early 1960s, and not only to the Americans. The Japanese themselves had no idea of how broad and deep their successes were to be.

11

Reshaping the Industry

Our philosophy of creating harmony between human and material elements guided Toyo Kogyo in designing the new Hofu plant.

TOYO KOGYO,
1983

We are not considering capital investment in the United States because we are incapable of producing or assembling our motor vehicles there, and conditions for production or assembly are not so favorable as in Japan.

K. KAWAMATA, chairman,
Nissan,
1970

The business literature of Japan is filled with descriptions of the very interesting firms that succeeded without strong government ties (for example, Sony and Honda), but there are not many to describe.

CHALMERS JOHNSON,
1982

By the mid-1960s, most Americans on either coast with any interest in automobiles had become aware of the Datsuns and Toyotas, and although neither received the interest accorded the Volvos, they appeared sensible, well-constructed, reasonably priced cars. Americans assumed that between them the two accounted for the entire Japanese industry, and some publications even believed that both nameplates came out of the same company. Such an error was understandable. To Americans of that time, who knew virtually nothing about Japan, the country still seemed a small island nation with a talented people, but nonetheless hardly an industrial power on the order of Great Britain, France, or West Germany.

That such wasn't the case would become evident later in the decade and in the early 1970s, when vehicles from other Japanese automakers started arriving in the United States. By then, anyone interested in knowing more about the subject might have learned that Japan had more viable auto companies than any nation on earth. It had been seen that the United States was incapable of supporting more than three major domestic companies plus one marginal one and that independents as large as a Studebaker, a Nash, a Packard, and a Hudson couldn't survive on sales of well in excess of 100,000 units a year. The Japanese demonstrated that viability was possible on far less revenues, in part because Japan possessed a different kind of industrial structure than the United States, one that would have been impossible here given the antitrust environment.

If one might categorize Toyota and Nissan as Japan's Big Two, then Toyo Kogyo, Mitsubishi, Fuji, Isuzu, Daihatsu Kogyo, Hino, Suzuki, and Honda (in descending order, as of 1965) might be considered the Little Eight. (The number had been nine the previous year; the reduction resulted from the disappearance of Prince.) That year, the Japanese industry produced 878,000 cars, of which 316,000 (36 percent) were Toyotas and 253,000 (29 percent) products of Nissan. Toyo Kogyo, the next largest company, turned out a mere 92,000 units (10 percent), and with 33,000 (4 percent), Isuzu was a viable concern.

There were limits to this, however. Suzuki and Honda, both newcomers to the industry, struggled along with a few thousand sales each, having staked out a limited part of the market for themselves. But Hino, which that year manufactured 22,000 vehicles, was in decline and was soon to disappear.

There were three basic reasons for this diversity. First, the Japanese firms had a much lower break-even point than the Americans had, and they could get by on fewer sales. Second, several of the smaller Japanese automakers had strong partners in the financial community to provide support when and if it was needed. None of this would have availed, however, were it not for the third reason—the Big Two chose to ignore an important part of the market, namely that for the micro-minis, cars powered by engines below 2,000 cc, which could carry two people rather uncomfortably. Profit margins on these vehicles were quite low, and given the strong domestic demand for larger cars, Toyota and Nissan could afford to remain out of the field. Thus, the Little Eight not only could survive, but actually prosper by addressing this market.

This would have important long-term consequences. The Big Two came to the United States with cars that, although conventionally sized by domestic standards, seemed small to Americans. But there was no market in the United States for the micro-minis. The Little Eight would eventually try to sell their cars in Europe and North America, but with little success until they came up with models at least as large as those turned out by the Big Two. This gave Toyota and Nissan an advantage that is only now being overcome.

Many critics of the American industry have claimed that lack of competition made the Big Three indolent and unreceptive to market forces. This wasn't as much a problem in Japan, however, and was another factor in the Toyota and Nissan successes—and the success of the companies following them into the American market. Yet it is something of a paradox. Under the guidance of MITI and other government agencies and bureaus, the Japanese companies were encouraged and prodded into coordinating efforts, especially when it came to industry structure and overseas marketing. Yet they competed fiercely domestically, with no sign of amalgamation other than that attempted in the 1960s.

As noted, several of the Little Eight had strong connections with major industrial groups, representing an expansion into a new field on their part. This was a time-honored Japanese business tradition. Excess capacity at a supplier might be alleviated by creating a customer for its wares, just as a prime manufacturer might establish suppliers in order to feed into its needs.

Such was the case with Toyo Kogyo, founded in 1920 as Toyo Cork Kogyo, which, as the name indicates, manufactured cork products. The firm diversified into machine tools late in the decade, at which time the name was changed to Toyo Kogyo. It was then that the old Sumitomo *zaibatsu*, centered on Sumitomo Heavy Industries, entered the picture, taking an interest in the firm, which, with Sumitomo financing, started manufacturing motorcycles as well as a light truck known as the Mazda. In 1940, Toyo Kogyo turned out its first passenger car under the Mazda nameplate. The two-door sedan was a clear copy of the Austin, not uncommon at a time when the Japanese imitated British designs. Its production was held up by the war, during which the corporation concentrated on trucks and construction equipment.

The Sumitomo influence continued after peace returned. Sumitomo Bank, Sumitomo Trust, and Sumitomo Fire and Marine Insurance each owned large blocks of shares. With their guidance and funding, the company created the prototype for midget economy cars, which were marketed in Japan in the 1950s. In the early 1960s, Toyo Kogyo, still strongly supported by Sumitomo, expanded into the small car field, competing directly with Toyota and Nissan. Toyo Kogyo's steel requirements were filled by Sumitomo Metal Industries, and components came in from other companies in the group. On the surface, Toyo Kogyo seemed a minor force in a major industry, but when viewed as part of the Sumitomo group, its true strength became evident.

Mitsubishi Motors was a creation of one of Japan's most powerful *zaibatsu,* which, as noted earlier, had experimented with motor vehicles through Mitsubishi Shipbuilding as early as 1918, and three years later had turned out the "Automo-go," which was produced through most of the decade. The *zaibatsu* was broken up into three separate companies after World War II, but they came together again in 1964 to form Mitsubishi Heavy Industries, which is Japan's largest manufacturer of heavy industrial equipment. Before then, Mitsubishi had formed Mitsubishi Motors Corp., whose small, well-constructed sedans had been so well received by the Japanese public that it was the country's fastest growing automobile company in the mid-1960s.

Fuji Heavy Industries and Daihatsu Kogyo concentrated on lightweight vehicles after the war. Fuji's original Subaru, the 360, was the smallest four-wheeler in Japan, weighing 886 pounds and powered by a 25-hp engine, whereas Daihatsu Kogyo started out in three-wheel vehicles and expanded into lightweights in the mid-1950s. Neither thought to compete with the Big Two during this period, but in 1960, Fuji introduced the "Star" line of automobiles, comparable in size with the Toyota and Nissan sedans. Still, these two were deemed the weakest of the Little Eight, the thinking being that in time one or both might be taken over by a larger firm.

It will be recalled that the predecessor of Isuzu Motors had arisen from a 1916 merger of the automotive interests of Tokyo Gas & Electric and Ishikawajima Shipbuilding, and that the entity, the Diesel Automobile Co., was third behind Toyota and Nissan in the late 1930s, when its name was changed. At the time, Isuzu was best known for its trucks, and as a major supplier to the military, it prospered during the war. Like the others, Isuzu was close to collapse toward the end of the fighting, but it re-formed in 1946, starting out as a repair operation and subsequently resuming production.

Isuzu had signed an agreement with Rootes, in 1953, to assemble Hillmans in Japan. Few were sold, but the experience encouraged the firm's leaders to develop sedans of their own. At that time, and even later, Isuzu considered trucks its major business and was one of Japan's leading developers of large engines. Isuzu combined truck and passenger car technologies to create the "Bellel" in 1961, the first diesel-powered sedan to go into production. Largely as a result of its truck business, Isuzu became a strong company in the mid-1960s, but passenger car sales were relatively stagnant, plateauing at the 30,000- to 40,000-unit level.

Disturbed by what it considered a needless proliferation of manufacturers and models, MITI urged Toyota and Nissan to each consider acquiring one or more of the Little Eight, or failing this, for the smaller companies to merge to form a third major entity. Pressures mounted late in the decade, when the Eisenhower Administration urged Japan to eliminate barriers to the importation of American goods. This bore fruit in 1960, when Japan announced the beginning of a trade liberalization program, and MITI became more concerned over the importation of foreign cars. It was then that Honda decided to enter the field, at a time and under circumstances that might have indicated there was little hope for success.

Honda was the most interesting of the Little Eight companies and the most atypical. Now the country's third largest auto company, Honda's phenomenal success belies the clichés that there are some essential, monolithic Japanese industrial techniques and values shared by all the large firms.

The son of a blacksmith, who was also a bicycle repairman, Soichiro Honda grew up in a rural village, barely finished high school, and was apprenticed as an auto repairman while still in his teens. His training completed, he opened his own repair shop, experimented with engines, and set up a facility to manufacture piston rings, some of which were sold to Toyota. During the late 1930s, it appeared he would become one of the thousands of small shops that supplied the large concerns.

Honda thrived as a parts manufacturer during the war, suffered through the last brutal months, and afterward tried to pick up the pieces of his business. He wasn't alone in perceiving the need for inexpensive transportation; Honda knew that the mass of Japanese couldn't afford cars, or even three-wheeled vehicles, and that fuel costs were bound to keep many out of that market. So he decided to manufacture a small engine that could be attached to a bicycle, an arrangement one finds to this day in Japan and parts of Europe.

The venture proved a huge success, with sales outrunning Honda's ability to turn out engines. Encouraged, he attempted a small motorcycle, which was also well received. The first model, known as the "Dream," appeared in 1949.

Requiring financing to get into full production, Honda formed a relationship with the Mitsubishi Bank not unlike those entered into by other budding industrial firms. Mitsubishi purchased shares in Honda Motor, and later, an additional equity position was taken by Mitsubishi Trust. Then both financial institutions helped guide the new corporation in its foray into the Japanese market, in which, at the time, there were more than twenty manufacturers.

A decade later, Honda was the largest motorcycle company in the world; the American Honda Motor Co. (headquartered in Los Angeles) had been organized and was about to enter the American market, where it would obtain a greater share in motorcycles than either Toyota or Nissan had in automobiles.

A small, highly voluble man, Soichiro Honda was the antithesis of what Westerners imagine Japanese tycoons to be. Well into his fifties, he was a prodigious womanizer and imbiber, and took few pains to disguise it. Honda loved to race automobiles and motorcycles, practiced a studied informality at work (rarely wearing dark suits, he preferred slacks and red shirts), and took pride in maintaining his independence from the business establishments. Never having attended college, and a self-categorized eccentric, Honda had no use for such institutions as *gakkubatsu* and related customs and traditions, preferring instead to innovate and develop them when needed. Americans who were bewildered trying to comprehend the Japanese business style had relatively little trouble understanding Honda, whose outlook resembled those found among executives in the Detroit Establishment more than those of his counterparts at Toyota and Nissan. American visitors often come away from a meeting with Honda remarking on how similar his personality and views are with those of Henry Ford II. Colleagues attest to his lack of self-consciousness and undisguised pride in a wild youth and middle age. In addition, Honda often has indicated a fine contempt, both for intellectuals and most of the Japanese business establishment, and an admiration for Americans.

This is not to suggest Honda refused to embrace the *kanban* system and other factory techniques and labor relations practices found throughout large Japanese manufacturing enterprises. Rather, he stressed individualism to an extent not found elsewhere in the industry and even encouraged his managers in this direction. At a time when directors and senior vice-presidents elsewhere were invariably in their fifties, Honda would elevate promising men in their late thirties to such posts. Nor was this approach limited to the executive suite. Honda often told men and women on the assembly line that as far as he was concerned they were working first for themselves, and second for the company. Along with such relatively young firms as Sony, Yoshida Zipper Company (YKK), Dai-Sei Supermarkets, and a handful of others organized in the postwar period, Honda seemed more American than Japanese in some of its attitudes. This seems to indicate that the Japanese edge in manufacturing isn't so much the result of organization or anything else reducible to theory, and thus capable of being exported, as it is to factors ingrained in that nation's culture.

Although concentrating its efforts on motorcycles, the

corporation did fund research in related areas. In 1958, Honda turned out its first electric generator, but more important, began work on automobiles.

Two years later, at a time when MITI was initiating its new drive to amalgamate several of the smaller companies into a third major concern and had introduced legislation into the Diet to forbid the creation of new automobile enterprises, Honda applied for permission to manufacture cars. Enlisting allies from the Department of Transportation and the Japanese Federation of Economic Organizations (the *Keidanren*), Honda was able to turn back MITI's attempt to restrict its development.

Honda had no immediate plans to enter the sedan or truck markets, which perhaps was one of the reasons the firm was able to sidestep MITI. Rather, its first product was a small sports car, the S 500, which was first marketed in 1962. A unique vehicle that united a chain drive with a small, but powerful engine, it was low in price and became popular with young Japanese. The S 500 soon took the lead in its limited segment of the market, elbowing aside such competitors as Fuji, Subaru, and the rival motorcycle manufacturer Suzuki. Other sports models followed, most of them well received, and in addition, the company manufactured a light truck. By mid-decade, Honda had become an established force within the industry, a number of whose leaders felt uncomfortable with such a maverick, but reasonably content to allow him leeway in the sports car area—which, it was assumed, he had entered on little more than a whim, to gratify his personal interests.

In 1966 Honda turned out 3,000 four-wheeled vehicles; Toyota was producing twice as many each week.

Meanwhile MITI proceeded with its program to restructure the industry. One faction in the ministry continued to favor the creation of two *keiretsu*, or industry groupings, revolving around Toyota and Nissan; another believed a third major constellation could be organized around Toyo Kogyo and/or Mitsubishi. As before, the companies themselves were unenthusiastic about this, each management group hoping to retain its independence and none eager to become subordinate to another hierarchy.

The companies won in the end, inflicting on MITI a rare defeat, but the industry was structured quite differently at the end of the 1960s from the way it had been at the beginning, this being the result of international as well as national pressures. All of Japan's smaller automobile companies but one was obliged to take in partners. The sole exception was Honda, which was adding to its reputation as an industry outsider.

The signal for the amalgamations to begin was given in May 1961, when MITI's Industrial Rationalization Council voiced its concern over weaknesses in the automobile industry and asked for an effort to create order and lessen competition, in the name of improving the product lines. Shortly thereafter, the ministry put together an industry-wide advisory committee that was chaired by Katsuji Katayama, who headed Nissan and was soon to be named to the top post at the Automobile Manufacturers Association, the industry's trade group. Represented, too, were the lead banks and several major producers of components. This committee was charged with devising plans for restructuring, which it was assumed would involve acceptance of one of the two basic approaches.

Underneath the traditional Japanese politeness and deferral a conflict was waged, with the auto companies signaling a willingness to accept compromises and piecemeal solutions and MITI insisting on radical restructuring. For four years the parties sparred with one another and then, in early 1964, a breakthrough was made.

For a while there had been talk of a merger between Prince, at the time the third largest Japanese factor in the manufacture of sedans and small trucks, with Toyo Kogyo, the new entity then becoming the magnet for others in the eventual creation of the third *keiretsu*.

That Prince would be acquired hadn't come as a surprise to industry insiders. The company was known for its advanced engineering, but it had a poor distribution network and, by

Japanese standards, inferior repair operations. Among its assets was a modern production facility staffed by a well-regarded labor force. To sweeten the deal it was known that the Japan Development Bank was willing to pave the way to a merger with a substantial long-term, low-interest loan. Toyo Kogyo balked at this, however, upon which MITI approached Toyota, thus reverting to the two-*keiretsu* rubric. Toyota, too, was uninterested, not only in this but in any merger. It was only then that Prince's and Nissan's banks entered into negotiations to bring the parties together. Nissan's reasons for agreeing weren't difficult to understand. Although there was a great deal of duplication of product, which would require years to rationalize, by taking Prince, Nissan would pass Toyota to become the largest Japanese manufacturer of vehicles.

The Nissan-Prince merger set off a series of convoluted and confusing arrangements. In August Toyota agreed—with no little reluctance—to take an equity interest, work in conjunction with, and then absorb the small, financially ailing Hino. Isuzu and Fuji also agreed to coordinate their efforts, although no purchases were made by either company of the other's shares.

There then followed a two-year hiatus in activity, which came to an end when the United States once again put pressure on Japan to ease trade restrictions and it appeared that the smaller companies wouldn't be able to make a go of it on their own. In early November 1967, Toyota and Daihatsu Kogyo announced a plan under which Toyota would purchase approximately 10 percent of Daihatsu's shares. The smaller company was to manufacture the lightweight, small vehicles for which it was known for Toyota, in addition to maintaining its own operations. Unlike the relationship between Nissan and Prince, Daihatsu wouldn't become an integral part of Toyota.

Now, attention was focused on Mitsubishi, Isuzu, and Toyo Kogyo, and rumors flew. There was talk of a Nissan–Toyo Kogyo merger, but nothing of consequence came of the discussions. Mitsubishi, now the logical candidate for the central company in a third *keiretsu*, initiated discussions with Isuzu; the latter was interested in a proposal because there had been little progress in its relationship with Fuji.

Kono Fumihiko, the president of Mitsubishi Heavy Industries, had long supported the MITI concept, and was willing to divest himself of Mitsubishi Motors, which could then be united with Isuzu and perhaps Fuji as well, from which would come a company approximately half the size of Nissan and smaller than Toyota, but certainly a strong competitor. This fell through, largely because of old rivalries and opposition from some of the banks. In the end, Mitsubishi Motors would be spun off from Mitsubishi Heavy Industries and then work in tandem with Isuzu on some projects. But MITI's grand design was never realized, and although doubtless disappointing to the bureaucracy, it may have been all to the good of the industry.

The smaller companies were becoming increasingly concerned about the growth of Toyota and Nissan. In 1967 these two accounted for 60 percent of the industry's production; two years later, they had expanded to take close to 64 percent, and indications were that this trend would continue.

For several years, Mitsubishi and other relatively small auto companies had monitored the Nissan and Toyota experience in the American market. That several of them would attempt to follow the Big Two there was taken for granted in Japan, and the time for this seemed to have arrived in the late 1960s. By then, however, they were busy protecting their flanks in the domestic market, and in any case, most lacked the wherewithal—and confidence—to take the plunge. This was the result of what must be considered a major miscalculation on the part of Mitsubishi, in particular, but of the others as well, in finding a solution.

Any thought that the Mitsubishi-Isuzu connection would become a third *keiretsu* had vanished by then when these two companies each found a different mate—ones hardly considered when MITI started its campaign. Mitsubishi and Isuzu were to become the junior partners of American Big Three companies, with the clear understanding that Detroit was operating from a position of strength while the Japanese hoped to overcome their weaknesses by allying themselves with the powerful Americans. Yet at the same time, the Americans weren't as confident of their superiority as they had been during the German Invasion, and several of the Japanese companies were beginning to suspect that they were in a better position than Detroit to fulfill the demands of a segment of the American market.

In order to understand why each party entered into its arrangement one must first understand that by then the Japanese beachhead had widened and deepened. As previously noted, Toyota and Datsun were in second and third places, respectively, in the American market, behind a fading VW, and in the following year, they would sell more cars between them than would the German corporation.

How long could this last? The Japanese automakers, along with executives in other export-oriented industries, had more confidence in Detroit's abilities to compete in its own market than the Americans had during the next two decades.

Moreover, the Japanese were puzzled over the American failure to erect trade barriers to keep all but a small number of Japanese cars out of the market. This was what Japan had done in the 1950s, and what was all but expected from countries whose industries were threatened. When and if protectionism triumphed, those Japanese firms with American partners might do better than would the independents. That such was the argument presented to MITI by those seeking joint ventures with the Americans was known at the time.

Nor was this all there was to it. Perceptions of Japanese goods and culture were rapidly being altered. Almost overnight that country's films, art, music, theater, and philosophy had become topics for study and admiration in fashionable urban and suburban salons, resembling nothing more than the fascination with things Japanese that had been one of the more interesting cultural phenomena at the turn of the century. There was an important difference in the 1960s, however. The

London, Paris, and New York literary sets of that earlier period had concentrated on Japanese culture, noting the differences between East and West, and indicating their preference for the former. Denizens of the counterculture in the late 1960s and early 1970s resembled them in reading books dealing with Zen Buddhism and in writing *haiku* poetry, but the mass of Americans were far more interested in the fact that Japanese companies managed to produce low-priced, high-quality goods. Businessmen throughout the country started to wonder how they might best respond to the Japanese challenge. Unlike the aesthetes of 1900, they didn't necessarily admire Japanese culture, but rather the knack the Japanese showed in turning out products invented and manufactured in the West.

Other matters concerned Americans more in these years than did Japanese imports, although these, too, served to enhance that country's image. The late 1960s were, after all, the period of Vietnam, and soon Watergate as well, when it became fashionable to consider America as what one writer called "a dead-end civilization." A reasonably large and certainly vocal segment of a people who, at one time, seemed convinced there was nothing beyond their capabilities now thought that there was little they could do right, in matters ranging from foreign policy to race relations to the manufacture of cars. Long a central artifact in American life, the automobile had come to symbolize this malaise. This suggests that confidence in the quality of Japanese goods was one reason for the boom in imports, but no less important was a widening conviction that American products were shoddy, and that the companies that turned them out were deeply flawed.

Cultural paranoia and self-hate have long been a hallmark of segments of American society. But this time the malaise was not imagined. Evidence of decline was there to be found, dissected, and acted upon.

Ralph Nader, a Harvard Law School graduate who, in the crusading spirit of the 1960s, engaged in the practice of public-interest advocacy, was the central figure in all this. An austere, seemingly humorless, certainly unrelenting individual, Nader would later be hailed by his admirers as impeccably honest and dedicated to the welfare of those who were underprivileged and exploited by big business, whereas his critics charged him with being a self-righteous, socialistically inclined, often ill-informed individual with pronounced vigilante tendencies. Later on it would appear there was some justice in both characterizations, but not in 1965 when, in the afterglow of the John Kennedy years, Nader seemed a young, altogether attractive St. George taking on the dragon that was General Motors. From that time on, attacks upon Detroit not only increased in scope but also became fashionable.

In 1964, when he was thirty-four years old, Nader moved to Washington to engage in lobbying activities for several public-service interests. There he latched onto the issue of automobile safety, long discussed in the capital, although little had ever been done about it. Nader soon concluded—with reason—that GM was the major roadblock to the introduction of forceful legislation in the field. After schooling himself in matters of technology, he became convinced that most of the cars driven by Americans were poorly designed, poorly constructed, and dangerous to both drivers and passengers.

His interests led Nader to the post of unpaid consultant to the Senate Subcommittee on Executive Reorganization whose chairman, Senator Abraham Ribicoff (D. Conn.), had long been concerned with automobile safety, and who, as governor of Connecticut, had supported laws and regulations imposing harsh penalties on speeders. With his support and encouragement, along with that of Senator Robert Kennedy (D. N. Y.), Nader participated in hearings on auto safety, drawing the admission from GM President John Roche that the company hadn't much interest in such matters.

Out of this came one of the great muckraking books of American history, *Unsafe at Any Speed.* Not a particularly well-written work, and given to overstatement, exaggeration, and hyperbole, it revealed Nader's biases in the opening sentence: "For over a century the automobile has brought death, injury and the most inestimable sorrow and deprivation to millions of people." "Nothing else?" one is bound to ask, wondering whether the author was referring to the Black Death or to a vehicle Americans and indeed most of the rest of the world considered vital to their well-being.

Initially the work received little attention, and might soon have been relegated to the remainder bins were it not for the fact that the Big Three chose to respond to the allegations and the publicity given the Ribicoff hearings. Nader had harsh things to say regarding each of them (American Motors came off relatively unscathed). "The Ford suspension arm, and the Chrysler steering wheel bracket are evidence of breakdown in production quality control," he stated. At the heart of the book is a scathing indictment of GM, mostly for having produced the Corvair, that rear-engine compact put out in 1960 in response to the Beetle threat and of which more than 200,000 had been sold in 1964. Nader all but accused GM of putting out a car it knew was tricky to steer and susceptible to rollovers, which leaked fumes into the passenger compartment.

Throughout the work are allegations of cost-cutting at the expense of safety and cosmetic artifices in place of sensible engineering. Nader also presented ideas on how safer and better cars might be produced. In so doing, he looked to neither Europe nor Japan—he would later claim the Beetle was the most unsafe car on the road and refused ever to be driven in one. Rather, Nader considered the best work in this area was taking place at private and university laboratories, especially a crash research unit at Cornell University, where designs for ultrasafe cars were being tested. Nader wasn't criticizing Detroit so that customers would turn to the Japanese, but rather was castigating automakers throughout the world, plutocrats who had little interest in the well-being of their customers. But it didn't come off that way; the implicit socialism and the unrealistic programs were overlooked in the sensationalism regarding the safety issue as it related to Detroit.

Little in the book was startling, which was one reason why Nader had difficulty having it published, settling in the end for a little-known house that couldn't afford to give it much publicity. But it did spark a series of lawsuits against GM, over 100 in all in which the plaintiffs asked for in excess of $40 million in damages. Panicked, GM put detectives on Nader's trail, attempting to discover unpleasant episodes in his past, to discredit the man and to block the lawsuits and any legislation he might have inspired. The detectives were directed to develop evidence that Nader was a homosexual and an anti-Semite, and engage in other aspects of what was supposed to be a classic smear. The plot was uncovered, resulting in embarrassed apologies from John Roche, dismissals at GM, and lawsuits from Nader against the company and the detectives, which he won and for which he received an out-of-court settlement of $425,000. Nader used this money to continue his work, part of which was a continued attack against the Corvair, which, because of the publicity, became a doomed car. Some 237,000 Corvairs were sold in 1965, in the following year, only 103,000. There followed a falloff to 27,000 in 1967, and the car was phased out in 1969. General Motors put out a press release to the effect that "It is our regular practice to review our products," but no one really believed it. Ralph Nader had almost single-handedly killed an American model—out of GM, no less. Such was the nature of the American auto industry in the late 1960s.

So a strong blow had been struck against the leading American car company. More would follow, against GM and the other members of the Big Three, and the result would be further damage to the reputation of the American automobile. Equally important, Detroit was put on notice that Washington would monitor its efforts far more carefully than had been the case thus far. This related not only to health and safety measures, but to quality as well. From this point onward, American automakers found themselves in an adversarial position vis-à-vis the federal government, at a time when cooperation in the face of the Japanese Invasion might have been a far wiser stance. Amazed at this short-sightedness, a Japanese auto executive later remarked that in his country "there would be no regulation until the government was sure the companies could meet the regulation." He added, however, that "by then there would be no loosening at all. It would be fixed."

Did the Japanese understand the implications of the Nader episode and the concomitant increase of interest in regulation? Were they sensitive to the antibusiness attitude of a portion of the American people—and of Congress—during the late 1960s?

This was a period when factory workers were protesting against "the American way" in a manner that had earlier characterized the New Left. A peculiarly American version of industrial sabotage was beginning to occur in auto factories. The general public learned of it through the slapdash nature of the cars they were being shown, and of which they took possession. Soon the newspapers and magazines were running stories about high worker absenteeism on Mondays and Fridays, the former to recover from weekend drinking bouts, the latter to begin them earlier. There was the sophisticated quest for the "Wednesday car," the idea being that only then was the entire work force in anything near full strength and decent shape to turn out autos, which, assuming all went well and with a modicum of luck, was close to what the Japanese manufactured every day of the week.

The phenomenon received a good deal of publicity when, in 1972, the workers at the GM plant in Lordstown, Ohio, went on strike, not over wages and hours, but rather conditions of employment. Complaining that the company cared nothing for their interests, and viewed workers as mere extensions of machines, they demanded a more humane workplace. The Department of Health, Education and Welfare investigated and concluded that "What the workers want most, as more than 100 studies in the past 20 years show, is to become masters of their immediate environment and to feel that they, themselves, are important. . . ." One worker, revealing his feelings to an investigative reporter, told her, "Some of the machines have written on them, 'Treat Me With Respect and I Will Give You Top Quality With Less Effort.' "

Publicity regarding recalls of automobiles to correct defects increased and almost invariably these were for American models, not Japanese or European.

Later, it would be charged that management blunders helped cause the decline of Detroit. Perhaps so, but the negativism, reformism, and general malaise of the period, combined with a willingness to accept lower-quality standards and at the same time insisting on higher wages and greater benefits, also must share the blame. Alienated workers and myopic management combined to bring about Detroit's decline.

Amazingly, the Japanese didn't fully appreciate what was happening—either that or they couldn't muster the self-confidence to take advantage of the opportunities that were being presented. From their point of view the American auto industry was as strong as ever. Business remained good in the second half of the 1960s; domestic sales came to 8.8 million units in 1969, and revenues to $19.3 billion, a new record.

Part of the reason that the Japanese respected American ingenuity derived from the initial failures of Nissan and Toyota, part from Detroit's towering reputation and the Big Three's vast resources, and part from the knowledge of how the Americans had turned back the foreign invasion earlier with their Corvairs, Falcons, and Valiants. By the late 1960s, it had become evident that the earlier experience was about to be repeated, with another Detroit counterattack against manufacturers of small cars.

Ford led the way in 1969 with the Maverick, a compact that was larger than the first Falcons. American Motors introduced its Gremlin the following year. Although powered by a conventional six-cylinder engine, this was a true small car, and its unusual shape—with a truncated rear—made it easily identifiable, the hope being that it would become the Beetle of the 1970s. Then, in 1971, GM came out with its Vega, a low-slung,

sporty car that had little in the way of originality to recommend it, and yet sold reasonably well. The Ford Pinto was a
more important vehicle. Like Ford's other "pony cars"—the
Mustang and the Maverick—it was a variation on a theme of
a car that wouldn't detract too much from the main line, but
still capture a portion of a market, which, although relatively
limited, could be quite profitable. In any event, both the Vega
and Pinto indicated that Detroit was once again taking aim at
the compact segment. Both cars were to be dismal failures,
mechanically unsound and poorly constructed. The Vega
would be dropped in 1977 and the Pinto three years later.

This, combined with the previously discussed concerns
regarding the power of Nissan and Toyota, both at home and
abroad, and fears that the United States would soon restrict the
importation of foreign vehicles, led the other Japanese firms to
seek American partners. On their part some of the American
automobile manufacturers were interested in cooperation, as
they were beginning to consider that price competition with
the Japanese would be difficult, given wage and other differen-
tials.

As expected Mitsubishi led the way. In September 1969,
Yoshizane Makita, Mitsubishi Motors' president and vice-
chairman at Heavy Industries, sharply criticized MITI's clear
preference for amalgamation of the industry into two groups.
"It is impossible for Mitsubishi to capitulate to Toyota and
Nissan," he said. "It was after that time that we resolved to join
with Chrysler."

Although many Japanese and American observers appreciated the possibility of joint ventures, it had been assumed
that the first to enter the field would be Ford or GM, as both
companies had been exploring the possibilities for several
years and of course had had some experience in Japan before
World War II. That Chrysler moved when and how it did had
more to do with problems there than with anything else, and
also a growing apprehension on the part of Mitsubishi that it
could not crack the American market without such a partner.

Chrysler was having nothing but trouble with its British

and French ventures, and even lacked the capital to put forth its own second-generation compact to go against Vega, Pinto, and Gremlin. Thus, the Americans were eager to make some kind of arrangement with a Japanese company whereby its small cars could be sold by Chrysler dealers.

In March 1970, Makita announced that there would be a joint venture between Chrysler and Mitsubishi Motors involving passenger cars, trucks, and other items. There followed the usual parrying for position, including participation by a reluctant MITI. The agreement was concluded the following May and approved by the Japanese government in June. Initially Chrysler was to purchase 15 percent of the shares of Mitsubishi Motors, with Mitsubishi Heavy Industries holding the rest, and in time, this interest was to expand to 35 percent. Mitsubishi was to have access to Chrysler technology and the American automobile market through having its cars offered by the third largest distributorship network, and Chrysler would offer a Mitsubishi sedan, called the Galant in Japan and to be known as the Colt in America, to its dealers.

Evidently Mitsubishi believed this was a sensible approach. Under the terms of the agreement, its cars might be assembled in Chrysler's overseas factories for sale in other markets, as well as the United States, and there was talk of investigating methods of achieving a degree of commonality of parts. The euphoria was badly damaged when Makita was informed by embarrassed Chrysler representatives that the corporation lacked the funds to purchase all the shares agreed upon. In time the money was paid, but Chrysler's credibility had suffered a severe blow, and Mitsubishi got a taste of what was to come.

Meanwhile Ford entered into discussions with Toyo Kogyo, the intention being to work out nothing more than technology sharing; the Americans were particularly interested in obtaining access to the Japanese company's research into the Wankel rotary engine. There was no thought of marketing Mazdas in the United States through Ford dealerships, much less a Ford absorption of Toyo Kogyo, which still remained firmly within the Sumitomo orbit.

MITI had no objections to this and, in fact, viewed the arrangement as yet another means of stilling Detroit's complaints regarding Japanese tariffs. In November 1970, it was revealed that Ford would be permitted to purchase 20 percent of Toyo Kogyo's stock and that, in the future, the two companies would engage in joint technological operations. Nine years later, Ford exchanged its ownership in its Japanese subsidiary (Ford Industries Co. Ltd. Japan) for additional Toyo Kogyo shares, bringing its equity interest to 25 percent. But Ford didn't get what it really wanted; the agreement specifically omitted Wankel technology from the arrangement.

The announcement of the Mitsubishi-Chrysler discussions sparked activity at Isuzu, which prior to that time had seen its future resting in cooperating with Mitsubishi in passenger car production. Shocked by this turn of events, but too small and weak to go it alone, Isuzu sought another partner, at first entering into an arrangement with Nissan to co-manufacture a small van, while seeking a more substantial partnership with another firm. On October 31, 1970, Isuzu disclosed it had found such a partner: General Motors.

The Mitsubishi-Chrysler agreement had not been expected, but it caused no great stir within the industry. Isuzu's announcement of its intention to join with GM was another matter entirely, both shocking and troubling the Japanese automobile fraternity.

Did this mean GM was planning a counterattack in the form of an invasion of the Japanese auto market? In 1970 such a move was deemed possible. Or would Isuzu become part of GM and, with massive infusion of American capital, manufacture a small car to be sold by American GM dealers as their answer to the Datsuns and Toyotas? This was an even more worrisome possibility. Few thought GM meant to have a relationship with Isuzu anything like that of Chrysler-Mitsubishi or Ford–Toyo Kogyo. For one thing, the proud American firm had always rejected joint ventures and, for another, who could imagine any meaningful relationship between GM and so minor a firm as Isuzu?

As it turned out GM was interested in obtaining access to some of Isuzu's work in pollution control, diesel engines, turbines, and small automatic transmissions and perhaps offering a small Japanese truck through its domestic dealerships. There were no plans to sell Isuzu sedans in the United States or to offer Chevys and Cadillacs through Isuzu. General Motors was to purchase shares in Isuzu, eventually achieving one-third ownership. Final arrangements were concluded in July 1971, which was shortly after Ford had signed its articles of agreement with Toyo Kogyo.

Other arrangements followed, the most important of which being a complex joint venture between GM, Isuzu, C. Itoh, and Kawasaki Heavy Industries for the manufacture of automatic transmissions and gas turbines. There were even rumors of a Ford purchase of Honda shares, after which that company's cars would be sold in the United States, although this wasn't likely, considering Honda's prized independence. By the early 1970s, however, it seemed destined to be the only independent company within the industry.

The second and most important phase of the Japanese Invasion was about to begin, and the industry was strikingly different from what it had been when the first Toyopets and Datsuns arrived a decade earlier.

Notwithstanding the new transnational arrangements, the most important change had been in attitude and perception. When the Germans arrived in the mid-1950s, Detroit had been confident; by the early 1970s, American supremacy had been challenged successfully. The Japanese had arrived to contest the Germans for control of the "economy" market.

12

Success in America

There is no question as to which car is most like U.S. cars—it is the Datsun, *with its familiar arrangement of components, its comparatively quiet running, its relatively soft ride, full equipment, and a level of quality that would put many U.S. cars to shame. It is, in fact, a gentleman's or lady's compact–compact, far from ignominious in behavior or appearance, economical, and pleasant to drive, with every appearance of being well put together. Like any other imported car, it should not be bought in the absence of reasonably accessible service. The* Datsun *is covered against "defects in materials and workmanship" for 12 months or 12,000 miles.*

Consumer Reports,
August 1965

PRODUCTION OF PASSENGER CARS BY MAJOR COUNTRY
1961, 1965, and 1969

	(in thousands)		
COUNTRY	1961	1965	1969
United States	5,543	9,306	8,224
West Germany	1,904	2,734	3,313
Japan	250	696	2,612
France	1,064	1,423	2,168
United Kingdom	1,004	1,722	1,717
Italy	694	1,104	1,477

SOURCE: *Japan: Its Motor Industry and Market,* 135.

Toward the end of the 1960s—a decade when there was a growing awareness in the United States and Western Europe of Japan's economic vitality—Toyota and Nissan appeared capable of performing what in the early postwar period would have seemed impossible: challenging Detroit. In comparison, every other country's industry appeared mature or stagnant; only Japan's was growing rapidly and there seemed to be no reason to expect this to change in the 1970s.

In 1961, Japan had been the seventh largest manufacturer of passenger cars in the world; eight years later, it was a strong third, two years later, it was second behind the United States, poised to make a run for the lead position.

As already indicated, most of this growth had been in the domestic market. In 1969, Japan exported 560,000 passenger cars, which placed it behind West Germany, the United Kingdom, France, and even Italy. Indeed, foreign sales of Japanese automobiles accounted for only one in nine of those produced, less than a third that of the Germans, who sent more than half their production overseas. Japan exported a smaller proportion of its passenger cars than any other country, except the United States—22 percent against France's 36 percent, the United Kingdom's 48 percent, and Sweden's 58 percent, for example.

Such figures, generally inaccessible and unknown to all but a handful of scholars and top-echelon industry figures, would have surprised American motorists who had witnessed the Japanese takeover of the import market. This was true because they continued to concentrate on exports to the United States. Toyotas and Datsuns were quite common on the streets of San Francisco and New York, but not in London and Paris.

And for the same reason as it had been at the start, Detroit didn't perceive the Japanese as real rivals and so hadn't lobbied for protection. Thus, the United States had erected few trade barriers insofar as cars were concerned. Moreover, the yen was undervalued relative to the dollar during most of the 1960s, so that the Japanese companies had an additional price advantage. So it was that North America accounted for more than half the Japanese automobile export market, whereas in 1969, all of Europe imported fewer than 63,000 Toyotas, Datsuns, and other Japanese models.

The Europeans recognized early the seriousness of the Japanese challenge and made it difficult for them to compete against their domestic models. France, the United Kingdom, and Germany, in particular, utilized tariffs to protect their national companies. As a result, more Japanese cars were exported to Finland in 1969 (18,065) than to these three countries combined (7,424). As recently as the first quarter of 1983 Japanese companies had only 9 percent of the European market, whereas GM and Ford companies there accounted for one out of every four sales, which was more than the second-place French Peugeot and Renault. Fiat, with 12 percent of European purchases, was ahead of the Japanese, although the Italian company had only minuscule representation in the United States.

European protectionism hardly bothered the Japanese companies, since in the late 1960s they were working overtime to meet domestic and American needs. Moreover, transport costs to Europe were high, especially since the Suez Canal was shut down. By then Toyota had a fleet of ten ships and Nissan six, each with a capacity of more than 1,000 vehicles, to carry their products to the West Coast. The Japanese firms were more interested in exporting to the Pacific Basin countries than to Europe at this time, and these markets also included Australia, South Africa, and possibly the Philippines.

That the Japanese Big Two had engineered one of the most dramatic turnabouts in automobile history—or in any industry—is well known today. They managed to accomplish this through a combination of industrial efficiency, intelligent marketing, good fortune, and the simple fact that they were able to offer Americans a superior product at low (even bargain) prices. As discussed, Detroit committed more than a few blunders along the way, but even so, the Japanese earned their victory; it hadn't been achieved through default. To crown their efforts, in 1972 Japan displaced Germany as the number one automobile exporter to the American market.

Although both Nissan and Toyota were successful in the American market, Toyota took the lead by 1968, due in large part to the nature of its product mix, an ability to rectify errors and learn from mistakes, and superior marketing techniques. In the beginning, however, Datsun captured the American imagination, for clear and obvious reasons.

Nissan had accomplished what it had set out to do, namely create and market what was, to all intents and purposes, a small American car, and had realized it better than could Detroit. More drivers would arrive at that conclusion in every year of the next eight. They would see Datsun distributorships expand throughout the country (their numbers would double in the next four years, and come to 640 by the end of the decade) and learn that the extended warranty was justified by excellent quality. These Datsuns seemed to combine aspects of the Beetle and the Chevy, and in so doing won an increasing share of the market.

Furthermore, Nissan displayed a sensitivity to the American market most European companies, VW included, lacked. The company produced a wide variety of cars for Japanese customers, ranging from minis to luxurious limousines and sent to the United States whichever of these seemed to make sense in any given year. Thus in the mid-1960s, the middle-range Bluebird, priced between the smallest Chevy and the VW, was a major seller. Then, as the Americans started stressing compacts, Nissan brought over the lower-priced (Sunny) PL 600 series, which proved even more popular. Flexibility in planning, integrity in manufacture, excellence in service, and shrewdness in pricing were the hallmarks at Nissan, and their increase in sales indicated that all this was recognized by the Americans.

Toyota started outpacing Datsun toward the end of the decade, with the key element and product being the Corolla, which was introduced in 1968 as a kind of "little brother" to the successful Corona.

As with the Nissan 600 series, the Corolla had been marketed in Japan for several years and was introduced to the American market in an attempt to retain a price advantage in the face of new competition from the American compacts. Its basic configuration, the 1200, was aimed directly at the VW Beetle, but in fact it took sales from Datsun as well. Perhaps without knowing exactly what they were doing, Toyota had found in the Corolla the 1970s equivalent of the late 1950s and early 1960s Beetle.

The Corolla of that period was a boxy, simple, surprisingly roomy car, which, as in the best of the Japanese sedans, combined an American feel with Japanese size and economy. Priced at $1,726 POE, it cost over $200 less than the Beetle and enjoyed a small price advantage over the Datsun 1200. Its engine, at 73 hp, was more powerful than those of either Datsun or VW, but did a shade better in fuel economy. In addition, it accelerated more rapidly and handled better in crosswinds. *Consumer Reports, Road & Track,* and other publications offering analysis of automobiles gave the Corolla high ratings for design and manufacture.

With the Corolla, Toyota had presented an economy car that was appointed and finished as well as many more expensive models. Just as the spartan simplicity of the Beetle had suited the American market of the mid-1950s, so this jewellike, but conventional sedan was most appealing to Americans who were losing faith in the worth of domestic cars, wanted reliability at a "sensible" price, and could not afford luxury models, but yearned for some luxury touches.

The Corolla had well-fitted seats and an imitation wood dashboard that somehow didn't seem cheap. Bumper guards came as standard equipment, as did handsome hubcaps, windshield washers, and later on, a rear-window defroster. It wasn't a Mercedes, to be sure, but the Corolla had a feel of quality and fit missing in even the VW. Indeed, this proved something of a problem and embarrassment for Toyota, for customers would enter the showrooms intending to look at a Corona and leave after having placed an order for its less expensive stablemate. The car even took on a personality of its own. During the late 1960s, protesters against the war in Vietnam tended to favor beat-up Beetles, whereas less activist drivers often could be found behind the wheels of well-tended Corollas. Of course such things should not be overstated, but the Corolla was becoming a badge of sorts, for all ages. Two decades earlier, older people felt uncomfortable in the noisy, cramped, unusual VW. A middle-aged man or woman who had learned to drive in a 1955 Plymouth had no trouble relating to the Corolla.

By 1973, the car accounted for close to half of Toyota's American sales, and the percentage increased throughout most of the rest of the decade. Largely due to the Corolla, Toyota passed VW as the import leader in the American market in 1975, having sold 278,000 units against VW's 268,000. Of this number, 151,000 were Corollas. Five years later, more than a quarter of a million of them would be sold in the United States, which came to one out of every ten sales in that category. Such was Toyota's victory over VW.

Aware of the situation and determined to maintain its position in the American market, VW developed two—or perhaps it would be more accurate to say one and one-half—new models, neither of which made much of an impact.

The first, the so-called Super Beetle, was introduced in

1971. An enlarged version of the familiar car, with such features as a curved windshield, the Super Beetle was four inches longer overall and 11 pounds heavier than the model it was supposed to supplant; it obtained the same number of miles per gallon—26 in simulated traffic tests—from a slightly more powerful engine. The Super Beetle cost only some $200 more than the original, but it was not a success.

The company expected more from its 411 model, a completely new car available with four doors and a plusher interior. The 411 was powered by an 85-hp, air-cooled engine against the Super Beetle's 46. It was 540 pounds heavier and 16 inches longer than the Super Beetle, but managed to get the same excellent mileage. Clearly the car was meant as an upgrade model; its list price of $3,382 was more than $900 more than that of the Super Beetle and more in line with American compact prices.

Would the American people pay this kind of money for such a car? The answer was no. The 411 was a conventional-looking sedan with nothing new to offer either the old VW owners or those who were interested in higher-priced models. Volkswagen could still boast of quality manufacture, but by then, so could the Japanese, and their cars seemed much more modern. One critic summed its problem up succinctly when remarking that 411 meant the model had four doors and was eleven years too late. Sales were sluggish—25,000 in 1971, and 33,000 the following year. With a fading Beetle, an unexciting Super Beetle, and the flawed 411, VW entered the mid-1970s in serious trouble in the American market. So the Japanese

SALES OF VOLKSWAGENS, TOYOTAS, AND DATSUNS
IN THE UNITED STATES, 1965 and 1974

	1965	1974
Volkswagen	322,941	336,257
Toyota	2,029	269,376
Datsun	10,315	245,273

SOURCE: *Ward's Automotive Yearbook, 1975,* 56.

victory over the Germans in the American market was complete in the early 1970s. But what, exactly, had been won? Detroit was about to bring along the next generation of compacts, which, as with the earlier ones, was expected to win back a share of sales from the imports, this at a time when the Japanese market, too, was showing signs of weakening. Washington was pressing Japan to liberalize its import restrictions against foreign cars, threatening tariffs unless this was done. Although, in retrospect, it might be realized that none of the American companies had much of a chance in that market, at the time it appeared otherwise.

In addition, the yen was finally becoming stronger, causing more worries in Japan, and the Japanese share of total American sales was declining. Detroit seemed to be bouncing back during the early 1970s, a development noted by Toyota and Nissan. The outlook for both companies was hardly grim, but the sky no longer was unclouded.

In the mid-1960s, each had been troubled by labor shortages; in 1971–1972, it seemed a glut might develop, obliging widespread retraining and possibly the first wave of dismissals since the end of the war. And to add to the humiliation and

SALES OF AMERICAN, JAPANESE, AND GERMAN CARS
IN THE U.S. MARKET, 1964–1973

| | (Sales) | | |
YEAR	AMERICAN	JAPANESE	GERMAN
1964	7,751,822	16,038	364,683
1965	9,305,561	25,538	376,950
1966	8,598,326	56,050	527,137
1967	7,436,764	70,304	472,360
1968	8,822,158	169,849	707,970
1969	8,223,715	260,005	642,157
1970	6,546,817	381,338	674,945
1971	8,584,592	703,672	770,807
1972	8,823,938	697,788	676,967
1973	9,657,647	624,805	677,465

SOURCE: *Automotive Trade Statistics*, I, 7; II, 4.

frustration, in 1973, Germany regained its old status as leading supplier of imports to the American automobile market.

The Big Two's problems in the American market were further compounded by the vitality of other Japanese firms. Americans who a few years earlier had assumed that Toyota and Nissan comprised the entire Japanese industry, now learned about the merits of the Fuji Heavy Industries' Subaru, Toyo Kogyo's Mazda, the Honda, and cars produced by Mitsubishi for sale by Chrysler. That some of these companies would have done well on their own is probable, but all were helped immeasurably by the pioneering work of Toyota and Datsun. In addition, they gained sales from those Americans who wanted a Japanese automobile and who chafed at waiting for those produced by the Big Two, so great was the demand by then. All enjoyed a measure of success, but the company that should have done best—Mitsubishi—had to wait another decade before its chance came.

In their early years in America, Honda and Subaru had experiences similar to those of the Big Two, which is to say they came in with the wrong kind of models and acquired poor reputations. The Mazda was another matter entirely; its success seemed assured, in large part because of the power plant in some of its models. This engine, based on what at the time seemed revolutionary principles, captured the imagination of a significant portion of the country's drivers, and for a season or two it appeared to be the most important automotive innovation since the development of automatic transmissions.

The engine, known as the Wankel, was based on a pre–World War II technology, developed by several French scientists, but named after Felix Wankel, a German who produced a working model in the early 1950s. It had been used in several German NSU sports cars in the late 1970s, which was when Toyo Kogyo licensed the technology, improved the design, and soon thereafter placed the engine in several of its own models.

The Wankel engine was a rotary, which is to say it contained a rotor that was propelled by explosions in three compartments, revolving in a circle instead of moving up and down as did the pistons in a conventional engine. The Wankel produced more horsepower per pound of engine weight than the most efficient engines in European, American, and Japanese cars, had fewer moving parts, and was less expensive to manufacture. It was smooth driving, providing tremendous acceleration; yet it was startlingly quiet. But there were problems. For one thing, the rotor seals wore out fairly rapidly and would have to be replaced frequently, and for another, the Wankel didn't get as many miles per gallon as did the engines used on other Japanese compact sedans. But they did better than the large eight-cylinder engines out of Detroit, and so in 1970–1971 were deemed competitive.

Mazda promised that the problems would soon be rectified; after all, this was a new technology, and given time—a few years at most—the Wankel would be superior to the piston engines in all respects.

Mazda entered the American market in late 1970 with no less than eight different models, the most important being the RX-2 coupe and the sedan, both Wankel-powered. Mazda Motors of America, which was initially established in Compton, California, had no idea of how the cars would be received, but it soon became clear demand would far outstrip supply.

After six months, American Mazda announced it would offer 80 distributorships, one stipulation being that all applicants would have to have a minimum of $650,000 in capital. Within a week, Mazda had 2,300 applications from auto men and others who recognized that this could be the biggest thing to hit the industry since the Beetle. Waiting lines for the car developed, unlike anything seen since that German model arrived and eager buyers were offering premiums of more than $2,000 for immediate delivery.

Detroit clasped the Wankel to its bosom, for here was a technology that might solve some of its problems. For years, the automakers had struggled to produce a large car with a small engine, a vehicle Americans would find conventionally sized, but relatively economical. The rotary promised to combine both qualities. Moreover, its simplicity could lead to significant savings, so that the Americans could keep their prices in line.

General Motors entered into a licensing arrangement with Toyo Kogyo, as John DeLorean predicted that by 1982 four out of every five domestic cars would be powered by the engine. Robert Templin of GM's product development group called the rotary "the only path we know to simultaneously improve fuel economy, vehicle performance, and emissions," and soon thereafter the corporation announced that the engine would be offered as an option in the 1974 Vega, while anticipating that two years later, from 200,000 to 500,000 GM cars would be equipped with Wankels.

Ford held back, with Henry Ford II pronouncing the engine as being of dubious value, but this was attributed to sour grapes resulting from his inability to obtain the technology when he was negotiating with Toyo Kogyo. Chrysler also seemed reluctant to license the technology, but partner Mitsubishi did, and the thinking was that Chrysler would get the information from that quarter. Other companies that made arrangements with Toyo Kogyo included Fiat, Volvo, and even Toyota and Nissan. Volkswagen earmarked $6 million a year for Wankel research, and Citroen worked with VW's Audi NSU subsidiary to develop a Wankel of its own. Rolls-Royce set up a team to study the rotary. Honda held back, claiming it had a superior engine that would defeat the Wankel, but talk in Tokyo was that the company was also working on its own version of the rotary.

Just how good was the Wankel-equipped Mazda? In April 1973, *Consumer Reports* wrote that "The experiences of several hundred of our readers who owned *Mazdas* of 1971 or 1972 vintage have been happy ones, judging by the results of our survey, sent out last spring." The article went on to say that the car racked up a better-than-average repair record. But not a Mazda RX-2 tested by *CR*. The engine burned oil at a rate of a quart every 875 miles, because of the need to lubricate the engine's seals, and such problems had still not been rectified.

The Mazda averaged 15 mpg, good by domestic standards, but far lower than the mileage available from Toyotas and Datsuns. This wasn't a major problem, however, since gasoline then cost about $0.36 a gallon.

The Mazda was an enormous success. For 1971, its first full year in America, sales came to more than 20,000, and the following year they shot up to 63,000, making it the number six import, behind the Big Two, VW, and captive cars of the American companies, but ahead of the likes of Volvo, Fiat, and Audi. Rotaries accounted for three out of every four Mazda sales, and the figure would have been higher had the company been able to keep up with the demand.

Subaru sold 24,000 cars that year, hardly spectacular but the figure showed a steady increase since its introduction in 1970. Or to be precise, re-introduction, for the company had made a tentative move the previous year when it brought the 360 to the United States. This minicar, which was quite successful in Japan, was a total flop in America. It couldn't go much above 50 mph, and certainly not against the wind. Acceleration was so poor as to be deemed dangerous, and several states banned the car from the highway. Not many were purchased, and the 360 quickly vanished from the scene.

The 360 was followed by conventionally sized sedans and coupes with several unusual mechanical features to appeal to a variety of drivers. For example, the car had a dual-radiator system, which eliminated the need for a fan, and so saved energy and power. Shoppers were surprised to find the spare tire mounted atop the engine, but they were even more intrigued by the power train and driving characteristics. The Subarus had front-wheel drives, which is to say the car was pulled by the front wheels rather than being pushed by the rear. Thus, handling was faster and more secure, the power loss of the conventional rear drive was eliminated, and the need for a "tunnel" that moved down the middle of cars that required drive shafts was obviated. Finally, Subaru had perfected a novel engine, known as the SEEC-T, which met the Environmental Protection Agency's pollution standards without complicated plumbing and could obtain up to 40 mpg at highway speeds.

The Subaru was not particularly popular, however, because the kind of dealer network required for a successful entry into the American market had not been created. Those who sought out the cars after learning of them by word of mouth discovered that Subarus were as dependable as the Corollas, and if slightly more expensive, had more power and more interesting features. Subaru's rise in driver affection would take several more years, however, and the car wouldn't come into its own until later in the decade when the company offered sports cars and four-wheel drive vehicles that found wider favor.

Mitsubishi's experience in the early 1970s was frustrating and disappointing. The Chrysler connection had been expected to bring the company enormous advantages in the form of a large sales and service organization and American know-how in marketing. Little of this occurred. Dodge dealerships offered the Colt and, later on, Plymouth outlets the Arrow, but insufficient attention was paid these cars, given their advantages and high quality. Automobile magazines were far more positive regarding their virtues than were many of the dealers who were supposed to present them in a favorable light. Potential customers reported having visited a Dodge dealer hoping to be shown a Colt, only to be shunted aside to a Dart, on which the salesman received a much higher commission. Mitsubishi must have known of this—the sales figures alone would have given them a hint of what was happening—but the Japanese firm could do little but protest and fume.

As indicated, the Colts and Arrows did better than Chrysler's French and British imports, the Simcas and Crickets, and in the second half of the decade, sales would rise sharply. Not because of Chrysler, however. Rather, in the aftermath of the 1973 oil shock, customers demanded to see and drive fuel-efficient cars, and lacking domestic compacts, Plymouth and Dodge dealers showed them the Arrows and Colts. In time, the Mitsubishi products would receive the plaudits they merited, but it came too late to do the company much good. The early 1970s must be regarded as lost years for Mitsubishi, a period when the company might have gotten off to a strong start, but was held back by its indifferent American partner. A strong fourth in the Japanese industry, Mitsubishi occupied the same slot in the American market, behind Toyota, Datsun, and Mazda, though ahead of Subaru and Honda. But the latter two companies then surged ahead, while Mitsubishi was close to being dead in the water.

Honda was an insignificant force in the American market during this period; as recently as 1971, it was behind such companies as Renault and Saab, and that year two and a half times as many Crickets were sold, without much effort, than were Hondas; all this would change later. More than Toyota and Datsun, Honda was to alter the nature of the import field.

Honda began with the hope of gaining a small segment of the market for minis—cars halfway between the Subaru 360s and the Corollas—and wound up establishing a new image for the Japanese cars, that of premium-priced quality rather than low-cost economy. That Toyota and Nissan would and could have done so on their own is quite probable, but the leadership was taken by Honda, which, as will be seen, played the role in the United States that Mazda was to have played.

Honda made its initial foray into overseas markets in 1966, when at the Paris and London auto shows it demonstrated a new sports car, the S800. The model was well received, with observers predicting that Honda would soon become a force in the market for small sports models and racing cars. This had little to do with marketing possibilities, or so went the argument, but rather the quirky personality of the founder, who was still enamored of racing. Moreover, a move in this direction would logically follow the company's established reputation in motorcycle racing. Finally, the move from a motorcycle to a sports car was more logical than one to a four-door sedan.

In discussing his sports cars, Soichiro Honda had remarked that "Driving a car is like sitting in the living room; driving a motorcycle is something like riding a horse—its driving and controlling something that is almost alive." A person with that attitude would hardly seem interested in the mass market.

Nonetheless, the following year Honda introduced a mini-car in Japan, and in 1968, when Japanese companies other than the Big Two were developing plans to enter the American market, Honda brought another new model, the N600, to Germany. This small car (with a 36.5-cc engine one-third the size of the VW's) had a top speed of 81 mph and was priced competitively with other models on the market. The N600 attracted a small, but expanding following, encouraging the company to explore the German market with other cars. In 1970, Honda introduced the 1350 there and in other parts of Europe. A cross between a sports car and a sedan, the 1350 was a relative failure, satisfying neither market. Yet Honda was establishing itself in Europe, apparently having decided to make less of an effort in the United States, as the competition there was quite fierce.

Meanwhile Honda engineers were developing a new engine the founder believed would take the play away from the Wankel. The compound vortex-controlled combustion engine (known more familiarly as the CVCC) was based on a dual-combustion chamber, in which the gasoline burned more completely and efficiently, the result being both greater fuel economy and fewer pollutants released into the air. Although the engine was designed to meet strict Japanese air quality standards, there can be no doubt Honda developed it with the American market in mind as well.

Honda first tested the American waters in May 1970, when it brought over the N600. Only 4,000 of the sedans were sold that year, and 12,000 the following. The small car, boxier, but not much bigger than the Subaru, wasn't considered much of a threat to the established imports, and was generally ignored by the auto magazines except for articles treating it as a freak. But the car was redesigned and equipped with an early version of the CVCC engine, while Honda concentrated on developing a dealership network.

The going was rough—there were only 215 outlets in early 1972—because in this period most of the attention was being lavished on the Mazda. True, the new Honda AN600 could get more than 30 mpg in local traffic and its new Hondamatic was generally conceded to be superior to most small car automatic transmissions, but its small size troubled even the purchasers of Beetles and Corollas. (The sedan was 15 inches shorter and, at 1,754 pounds, more than 300 pounds lighter than the Corolla.) It looked fragile, too, and driving one in highway traffic for the first time could be a frightening experience. But the CVCC engine met all the EPA's standards, and astute observers wondered whether a new, larger Honda equipped with that power plant might not become popular.

Detroit was far from being convinced, nor, for that matter, did it show much interest. All attention was on the Wankel, and although the CVCC's performance ratings were fine, it was, after all, really a modified piston engine. Even so late in the game, American engineers couldn't believe that foreigners could come up with significant modifications they hadn't thought of first. Detroit asserted that although the CVCC might be suitable for small cars, it would not work in larger ones. More to show up his critics than in the hope of licensing the technology, Soichiro Honda modified the eight-cylinder engine used on the Chevy Impala, which in mid-1973, passed the EPA standards. This did not impress the Americans, however.

In 1972, Honda introduced an entirely new model, a trifle larger than the AN600, and equipped it with a more powerful CVCC engine. Known as the Civic, it, too, met the EPA requirements and achieved 27 mpg in city driving and 39 mpg on the road. By then rumors had spread to the effect that Honda was preparing a bombshell for the mid-1970s: its own version of the Wankel, improved and more efficient than Mazda's. The company issued a prompt denial. "Honda CVCC have already shown their low emission capabilities without the need of add-on catalysts and afterburners; devices which rotary-type engines find necessary to use to even comply with current emission standards [much less the more stringent ones required in the future]."

Hondas enjoyed a moderate success in 1972, with 20,500 sedans sold. But this was hardly reason to rejoice. The company was still low on the import list, with fewer sales than Subaru, Colt, and, of course, Toyota, Datsun, and Mazda. In the CVCC engine and the Civic automobile, Honda had the technology that would alter the situation drastically the following year, when Japanese cars, in general, and the Honda, in particular, would be among the prime beneficiaries of the 1973 oil shock.

The Challenge Recognized

For every one percent of import penetration, there are 20,000 fewer jobs available in the U.S.

HENRY FORD II,
1971

Minicars, Mini-profits.

HENRY FORD II,
1972

What the hell do I want to go around the block to dinner in a Lincoln for? The big car as we know it is on its way out. That's gone forever. I'm a small-car man. I'm a promoter of small cars.

HENRY FORD II,
1973

I frankly don't see how we're going to meet foreign competition. We've only seen the beginning. We may become a service nation one day because our manufacturers could not compete with foreigners.

HENRY FORD II,
1974

During the first half of 1971, when for the first time in the twentieth century the United States ran a deficit in its balance of trade, American automakers demanded protection against imports, and given the ailing domestic economy, their complaints were heard in Washington. On August 15 President Nixon made an announcement that seemed to mark both the beginning of a new economic era domestically and the end of the postwar international finance and commercial dispensation. There was to be a ninety-day freeze on wages and prices along with tax cuts to stimulate the economy. The dollar was no longer to be convertible into gold. And Nixon temporarily placed a 10 percent surtax on all imports.

The new inconvertibility of the dollar caused its value to decline for most foreign currencies, which meant that Americans would find imported goods more expensive than their domestic equivalents. Add to this the surtax, and foreign manufactures became even less attractive, all of which was designed to end the trade deficit. Although it wasn't spoken of openly, everyone knew that this part of the program was aimed at the Japanese, and the Japanese car manufacturers, in particular.

Four months later, in a meeting held at the Smithsonian Institution, the leading trading countries signed an accord, under the terms of which currencies were revalued. The dollar was to decline by 7.89 percent, while the yen moved up by 16.88 percent and the mark by 13.57 percent. As part of this arrangement, the United States dropped its 10 percent surcharge. But price controls continued.

This was the first of two major international upheavals

that were to affect Detroit intimately and that, taken together, marked the beginning of a new age for world industry.

The sale of Japanese cars in the United States remained strong in 1971, largely because dealers were selling from stock. But they leveled off in 1972 and early 1973, and this was taken as a sign that the revaluation of the yen and the Nixon surtax had had their intended effect. The price advantage enjoyed by the foreigners had narrowed and, in some cases, disappeared. Now Detroit could more easily compete with the invaders. The Nixon program had provided the Americans with an invaluable opportunity to regain the initiative.

Yet the Big Three still evinced little interest in compacts, much less small cars. General Motors' Vega was recalled in the summer of 1972; the rear brakes were failure-prone and the wheels tended to spin off, while the body rusted almost as its woeful owner watched. Its highly touted aluminum engine started burning oil at 10,000 miles or so, and sales were slipping. As for Ford's Pinto, owners reported it was next to impossible to keep its front end aligned. The visibility was poor, the ride rough, and some drivers yearned for power steering, so tanklike was it to handle.

Americans seemed more involved with the Watergate scandal than anything coming out of Detroit. And there was

MANUFACTURERS' SUGGESTED RETAIL PRICES OF
SELECTED MODELS FOR IMPORTED AND
AMERICAN SUBCOMPACT PASSENGER CARS, 1971–1972

AUTOMOBILE	1971	1972	PRICE CHANGE (percent)
Toyota Corolla	$1,798	$1,953	8.79
Ford Pinto	1,919	1,960	2.14
Datsun 1200	1,736	1,976	13.82
VW Beetle	1,899	1,999	5.27
AMC Gremlin	1,999	2,121	1.10
Chevrolet Vega	2,090	2,060	−1.44
Mitsubishi Colt	1,924	2,095	8.89

SOURCE: *Automotive News* (February 7, 1972), 1.

that suppurating wound in Vietnam. Debate continued regarding the possibility of détente with the USSR and of curbing inflation on the home front. Enough one would think to keep the nation occupied.

Meanwhile the petroleum powers of the Middle East, the driving force behind the Organization of Petroleum Exporting Companies (OPEC), were restive. Few Americans had known what the initials OPEC stood for before the spring of 1973; by Christmas, no motorist would fail to recognize them as symbols of the greatest threat to his driving freedom since World War II.

It may be said to have begun on the first day of that year, when those companies with operations in OPEC nations came under a new order stating the conditions under which controlling interest in them might be obtained by the host nation. In May Iran withdrew from an arrangement whereby a consortium operated its petroleum industry. Then in June Libya nationalized some foreign assets and two months later took over its American-owned petroleum companies. In early October, shortly after the outbreak of a new Arab-Israeli war, Iraq nationalized the oil companies owned by Mobil, Exxon, and Shell.

And all the while OPEC was increasing the price of oil. A barrel of Arabian light crude, which had gone for $1.80 in August 1970, sold for $2.48 late in 1972, and $2.59 January 1, 1973. By August 1, 1973, OPEC oil was over $3.00 a barrel.

Much of this was reported in the print media, but casual and nonreaders, those who obtained their information regarding the world from television, might have been excused for not noting any of this; because of the Nixon wage-price freeze, the price of gasoline hardly changed. A gallon at the pump, with taxes, averaged slightly more than $0.36 in 1970 and actually declined fractionally during the next two years. Confronted with declining profit margins, refiners had little incentive to expand their American operations.

One might have discerned the beginnings of the price

increases during the summer of 1973, but even then American drivers were paying an average of under $0.39 a gallon. That fuel costs would have risen steadily and perhaps sharply as OPEC turned the screws seems indisputable. As it was, the Nixon freeze kept gasoline prices steady, creating a false sense of security, discouraging immediate conservation efforts, and assuring much more severe advances once controls were eased.

This was the backdrop for the gasoline crisis of 1973–1974. In large part as a result of bungling by several government agencies led by the Office of Emergency Preparedness, the Energy Policy Office, the Oil Policy Committee, the Federal Energy Office, and the Cost of Living Council, what might have been a period of stringency became one of national pain.

Spot shortages of gasoline appeared on the West Coast in early spring and worsened during the Memorial Day weekend. Prices started to rise, as OPEC applied the screws and an administration allocation program foundered. Amid talk of conspiracy, a permanent petroleum shortage, and an end to the age of the automobile, owners of vehicles lined up at gasoline stations to buy what they could. It was the petroleum equivalent of what an earlier generation had known as "runs on the bank." Had there been no "petro-panic" and no governmental intervention in the marketplace, the shortages might never have appeared. But they did, and troubled motorists sat in their cars for hours hoping to get $5 or $10 worth of gas. They formed car pools, used public transportation whenever possible, and cast critical glances at cars that gulped gasoline at the rate of a gallon every ten miles or so.

Gasoline prices rose steadily. In October the Arab nations placed an embargo against the United States because of its pro-Israel stance and, at the same time, announced production cutbacks and boosted the price of a barrel of petroleum to $5.12. By November—when Congress passed and President Nixon signed a measure that would have permitted rationing —the situation was close to pandemonium. There were reports of fistfights at service stations and even several murders when drivers tried to break into lines.

The OPEC price went to $11.65 a barrel January 1, 1974, having more than quadrupled in a year. Yet the price of gasoline in this period did not reflect this, having gone to an average of $0.43 a gallon from $0.37, hardly a drastic leap. The difficulties of 1973 weren't caused by fuel prices, but rather, availability. Prudent automobile owners knew that depreciation, repairs, and even insurance took larger bites of their transportation dollars than the increased cost of fuel did. Newspaper and television reports still noted that at $0.60 a gallon a person who put in 15,000 miles a year on a car that got 10 mpg would pay $450 more annually than would the owner of a subcompact rated at 20 mpg.

As expected, the price of gasoline jumped dramatically once controls were removed. Most economists concerned with such matters agreed that the price at the pump would go above $0.65, with some estimates of $0.80, and a handful warning of dollar-a-gallon gasoline.

The Nixon wage and price controls program ended in April, and the cost of fuel did rise, although not as much as had been feared. Still, the average price of a gallon of leaded gasoline in 1974 would come to $0.53 and would creep up steadily for the next four years.

The embargo would remain in place until March 18, 1974, by which time the lines had disappeared and the panic had ended. But the scars remained. Frank Ikard, President of the American Petroleum Institute, was one of many who voiced what by then had become the conventional wisdom. The oil shortage would last "as long as most of us will live," he warned. "We will have to adopt a whole new way of life," and Ikard predicted "The love affair of the American with the large automobile has come to an end." Or as another observer noted, "America discovered that miles-per-gallon was far more important than miles-per-hour."

The gasoline crunch of 1973–1974 had come at a time when the domestic automobile industry appeared strong. American production set a new record in the first three months of 1973, 20 percent over the same period in 1972. Talk in Detroit was of a better than 9 million car sales year, and such indeed was the case. The combined sales of American- and Canadian-built cars would come to 9.6 million units. In addition, 1.8 million imports were sold, a slight increase from 1972, and 15.3 percent of total sales. Domestic purchases of cars that year were 11.4 million, an all-time high—and one not likely to be broken in the foreseeable future.

This record had been made possible by a superlative first half. Sales declined in the second half, in large part because of the fuel situation, which had intensified inflationary pressures already in place. The Consumer Price Index rose by an acceptable 3.4 percent in 1972, but then soared to 8.8 percent in 1973. Moreover, the unemployment rate was rising, as the nation was about to undergo the bewildering experience of "stagflation."

All this crippled the domestic auto industry and cut into the sales of imports. Detroit found itself in an impossible situation. As the result of inflationary pressures, the companies had to increase the prices of their cars, while fewer buyers entered the showrooms, because of the recession and the fact that most of the models were gasoline gulpers.

In October and November of 1973, there came requests for and announcements of large price increases. Chrysler asked the Cost of Living Council for permission to raise the prices of its fleet by an average of $73 per unit and an additional $63 to cover the costs of a recent labor contract. General Motors said it would seek a 4 percent increase in the prices of its 1974 line. American Motors wanted an average of $150 more per unit, and Ford told the press it, too, would want an increase, although the figures hadn't been worked out. This in the face of a 12 percent falloff in car sales for October and 13 percent for November from the previous year's levels.

Ford President Lee Iacocca, considered the father of the Pinto, was pleased by continued sales of that small, though not especially fuel-efficient model, but noted that the car introduced in 1969 with a base price of $1,995 sold in late 1973 for

$2,225 and that even steeper boosts were on the way. Still, those seekers of small cars were able to purchase them at approximately the same prices as the Japanese imports and, in some cases, a few hundred dollars less. But the numbers did not tell the entire story. A stripped Vega or Gremlin—assuming it could be had—was not as well equipped as the basic Toyota Corolla or Datsun 510. Nor was it as carefully manufactured, or at least this was the presumption of an increasing number of buyers.

As was to be expected, Detroit laid off personnel and encouraged dealers to work off their inventory. In December–January alone, GM furloughed 70,000 assembly-line workers at 10 plants because of sluggish sales of medium-size and large cars. The layoffs—eventually 135,000 auto workers would find themselves on the unemployment line—affected virtually all parts of the economy, from firms that sold supplies to automakers to steel companies and down to travel agencies that booked vacations for auto workers.

Ever optimistic, GM Chairman Richard Gerstenberg predicted that 1974 car and truck sales would run only 8 to 12 percent below the 1973 level, making it a good, though hardly a banner year. The actual decline for the domestic industry would be 35 percent, or 6.3 million units, making this the most

LIST PRICES OF DOMESTIC AND IMPORTED SMALL CARS, 1973

MODEL	LIST PRICE
General Motors Vega	$2,146
American Motors Gremlin	$2,164
Dodge Colt	$2,204
Ford Pinto	$2,225
Toyota Corolla	$2,235
Volkswagen Super Beetle	$2,385
Datsun 510	$2,431
Toyota Corona	$2,511
Mazda RX2	$3,297

SOURCE: *Ward's Automotive Reports, 1973,* 82.

severe falloff since the Great Depression. And it would not be going too far to say that Detroit indeed had returned to Depression thinking and planning. Cold sweat was a common affliction in the boardrooms, where the seriousness of the situation was well recognized. For the first time since the industry began, auto company executives wondered whether their firms could remain strong in the face of so many onslaughts. The feasibility of steam-driven and electric cars was explored, as were conversion to alcohol, and chassis made of plastic and even wood laminates. And always there was the growing fear that because of the developing energy crisis, the Japanese would become the leading auto power in the world. Only a few years earlier it had appeared that Chrysler might purchase Mitsubishi. Now there were quite serious considerations that it might be well for Mitsubishi to absorb the ailing Chrysler, as the only cars that company seemed capable of moving in any volume were the economical and fuel-efficient Colts and Arrows.

Industry insiders appreciated the seriousness of the situation and the need for action. Although the sluggish economy had played a role in the sales falloff, this was no one-shot blow. There was clear and irrefutable evidence that the American auto-buying public was turning away from Detroit's products, demanding something different—preferably smaller, less expensive, better constructed, fuel-efficient cars.

Like the Toyotas and Datsuns.

The Japanese were also affected by the worldwide slump, although not as severely as the Americans. That country's automobile industry, now the world's second largest, turned out 7 million vehicles in 1973, up 13 percent over the previous year, and a new record. Sales started to decline in the third quarter, however, as Japan was struck by a fuel crisis. Gasoline prices rose, lines appeared at stations in Tokyo and other cities, and the government limited weekend and holiday driving. Then, in early 1974, the manufacturers increased the prices of their cars by an average of 10 to 12 percent, which also served to dampen sales.

Yet the individual companies fared well, in large part because of exports, which totaled over 2 million units, of which 1.5 were of passenger cars, with the United States accounting for the majority of shipments. This was not up to the numbers sold in the late 1960s, but by the end of the fuel crisis, the Japanese models were in stronger shape in the market than before it.

And with a new rising star. Some domestic observers were predicting that unless Toyota and Nissan changed their production and marketing strategies, Honda would be the leading automobile manufacturer and exporter by the end of the decade. In the aftermath of the oil shock, Honda's small, well-designed and -constructed, moderately priced cars won sales not only from the smaller Japanese companies, but the Big Two as well.

In 1973 327,000 Toyotas were sold in the United States. The Corolla remained the second most popular foreign sedan (behind the Beetle), but the sporty Celica was moving up rapidly. Datsun was in its accustomed third place, with 319,000 sales, its most popular model being the newly introduced PL 620, which replaced the somewhat drab PL 510. Then came Mazda, with 104,000 sales, twice that of the previous year. Almost all the Mazda sales were accounted for by the RX-2 and RX-3, both powered by Wankels. Placements weakened toward the end of 1974, however, as would-be purchasers were driven off by Mazda's relatively poor fuel economy.

Honda was in fifth place in the American market in 1973, with 39,000 sales; but the company had been learning about American requirements and was preparing a redesigned Civic for export. The car was scheduled for introduction in 1975, but Honda worked its design and production staffs overtime so as to get it to the United States earlier.

Of all the Japanese models Honda offered the most miles per gallon, and shortages of its minicars were reported in late 1973. Small even by Beetle and Corolla standards, it nonetheless appealed to Chevy and Ford drivers who listened hungrily to tales of it getting more than 40 mpg on the open road.

Moreover, its CVCC engine didn't require balky and expensive plumbing to meet EPA requirements and, unlike the models offered by the Japanese Big Two, it could run on leaded gasoline.

In late 1973 some American companies started talking of dropping their Wankel projects and replacing them with ones based on the CVCC engine. In fact, Honda was approached by Ford, with a proposed tie-up similar to that of Mitsubishi with Chrysler. According to one version of the plan, Hondas would be offered at Ford dealers, with a Ford nameplate, a suggestion that, if accepted—and assuming Honda could get sufficient cars to the United States—might have catapulted the company into the number one spot both domestically and in the United States within a few years. Honda rejected the overture, but did license its CVCC to Ford in 1973. Thus, Detroit continued to look to Japan for technology, but to another company.

Why did Honda opt to go it alone? For one thing, its own distributorships—there were 420 of them by 1973—were doing quite well, and the company was opening new ones at the rate of one every three days. Then too, the CVCC engine was a clear success not only in the United States, but also in Japan. The domestic market went into a slump in early 1974 because of the oil shock and a round of price increases led by Toyota and Nissan. Honda refused to increase its prices, while instituting a new advertising campaign stressing economy. The approach worked. That March, Toyota and Nissan sales were down 40 percent from the previous year, whereas Honda's were up by 76 percent. This advance was reflected in the American market too, as by late 1974, shortages of the popular three-door hatchback were reported, with increasing interest being shown the new two-door Civic.

Honda sold 39,000 cars in the United States in 1973. Led by the two-door Civic, it doubled this figure by 1975, redoubled it two years later, and redoubled it again by 1980, a year in which Honda sold 375,000 cars in the American market, almost three times as many as Subaru and twice as many as Mazda.

The reasons for this were clear. Honda combined high

quality with efficiency and economy, and as will be seen, its new models, especially the Accord and the Prelude, were well suited to the developing American market. And in the process the company was to oblige the Big Two to follow its marketing and even its design lead.

Honda was trailed by Subaru, whose Star Clipper was a small car even by Japanese standards, but also an economical one. Styled somewhat more along American lines than the Honda, it, too, reported better sales in the second half of the year, coming in at 38,000. And also like Honda, Subaru planned new models to capitalize on the growing American interest in fuel economy.

Dodge's captive Colt was next among the Japanese, with 35,000 placements, only 1,500 more than in the previous year. In part, this dismal showing was the result of pricing policies: Chrysler continued to insist on margins far out of line with those of the other Japanese imports, but in addition, the salesmen, accustomed to "loading" domestic models with options so as to enhance profits, attempted to do the same with their Colts, which raised their prices even higher. More to the point, however, was the growing reaction against Detroit, which to some had become the symbol of the national malaise, just as it had during the Sputnik era. Becoming increasingly discouraged, Mitsubishi executives now realized that they would have been better off on their own, and they began to explore how best they might obtain a divorce from Chrysler.

The fuel crisis ended in early 1974; Americans now could get all the gasoline they wanted, but at a price of around $0.60 a gallon for unleaded. The staflation continued, however, and although the Watergate crisis ended with President Nixon's resignation, there seemed little confidence that his successor, Gerald Ford, possessed the abilities to direct the nation's economic affairs. For 1974 as a whole, inflation came to a staggering and unprecedented 12.2 percent—half again that in 1973—and unemployment rose to 5.6 percent and continued to rise rapidly (to 8.85 percent in 1975, this a post–Great Depression record). Freed from the constraints of price controls, and responding to inflationary pressures, Detroit raised its prices. In 1974, GM and Ford put through six increases, and Chrysler ten. Cars cost approximately $500 more, on the average, that year than they had in 1973, and an additional $500 or so was tacked on in 1975.

Sales of domestic cars declined sharply in 1974–1975, going from 9.2 million in 1973 to 6.7 million in 1974, and then to 6.1 million for 1975, but the imports didn't do well either— 2.4 million sales in 1973, 2.6 million in 1974, and then down to 2.1 million in 1975, the worst showing in five years. The reason for the American decline was the double blow dealt the industry: fewer Americans had the wherewithal to purchase cars, and those who did were put off by the rapidly increasing prices. But the leveling off and then decline of imports was caused by an intriguing and important development, which was to repeat itself in the future: once the gasoline price leveled off and the shortages ended, Americans once again turned to larger cars.

By the summer of 1974, Ford found itself with a 96-day supply of Pintos, a car that had been in demand during the gas crunch. It was worse at GM, where there was a 110-day supply of Vegas. Chrysler had on hand a 105-day supply of Valiants; its imported Colt, for which there had been waiting lines only a few months earlier, was backlogged for 113 days, with Chrysler canceling orders to Mitsubishi.

But although the Big Three offered rebates on subcompacts, Ford was putting on double shifts at its Lincoln plant and was rationing eight-cylinder models to its dealers, as Henry Ford II petitioned the government to place a 10 percent tax on gasoline so as to encourage customers to buy small cars. "Although there has been some overestimation of the subcompact market, the company remains convinced the long-term outlook for small cars is bright," one Ford official said plaintively, while an engineer averred, "there would be no problem at all if people would just buy small cars." The leading Japanese companies—Toyota, Nissan, and Mazda—had the worst

SALES OF JAPANESE CARS IN THE UNITED STATES,
1973 and 1974

	(hundreds of thousands of units)	
MODEL	1973	1974
Toyota	327	269
Datsun	319	245
Mazda	119	70
Colt	36	43
Honda	39	41
Subaru	38	23

SOURCE: *Ward's Automotive Yearbook, 1974,* 27–39.

showings of all the Japanese automakers. The falloff at the Big Two was attributed to price increases caused by the stronger yen, as well as by the lack of new models. Mazda declined more than the others because of its low fuel economy and premium price; that once-spectacular performer was now troubled both at home and overseas, and instead of talk of expansion, there were rumors of bankruptcy. The rise in Colt sales was more the result of starting out from such a depressed base, a stronger push by Dodge dealers eager for any sales during the stagflation, and good reception in the first half of 1974 before the switch to bigger cars occurred. As indicated, Honda bucked the trend, with an increasingly high reputation for quality combined with a lower price. The Civic was one of the few successes of the time, an indication the company had not only established a strong base in the United States but was also well situated to increase both volume and market share. Governmental actions further compounded the industry's problems by causing Detroit to jump to false conclusions regarding its outlook. In 1975 Congress debated new legislation affecting the industry, which emerged as the Energy Policy and Conservation Act, and among its provisions was a requirement that the manufacturers have a corporate automobile fuel efficiency (CAFE) of 20 mpg by 1980. At the same time, pollution control policy was left unchanged, which not only would cause the prices of cars to rise, but also would penalize fuel economy.

Thus, Detroit was to downsize, either by producing and selling large numbers of very small and efficient cars (on which

PRODUCTION AND EXPORT SHARES FOR
JAPANESE AUTOMOBILE MANUFACTURERS, 1972–1974

	PRODUCTION			EXPORTS		
COMPANY	1972	1973	1974	1972	1973	1974
Toyota	33.2	32.6	32.3	36.6	34.9	32.7
Nissan	29.6	28.8	27.8	36.4	34.4	33.0
Toyo Kogyo	10.2	10.4	11.3	14.6	16.6	14.9
Mitsubishi	7.1	7.9	7.6	4.1	4.4	6.8
Honda	5.3	5.0	6.5	1.9	3.6	4.6
Daihatsu Kogyo	4.3	4.3	3.7	0.3	0.4	0.7
Fuji	2.9	2.9	2.5	1.8	2.1	1.9
Others	7.4	8.1	8.3	4.3	3.6	5.4

SOURCE: *Japan Yearbook, 1975,* 130.

profits were bound to be slim) to compensate for the gas-guzzling large cars (with their larger profit margins) or by shrinking their entire fleets. Moreover the "captive" imports—such as GM's Opel, Chrysler's Colt, and Ford's popular German-produced Capri—would not be included in the calculation of the CAFE.

The companies had known for years that regulations of this nature were on the way and had started planning for them. Generally speaking, Ford opted for the first strategy and stressed small, compact, "personal" cars, while GM decided to revamp its entire line, Cadillac included. American Motors remained dedicated to small cars and was given the greatest chance of making the CAFE, while Chrysler seemed paralyzed, unable to reach a decision.

Concurrent with the new policy regarding the creation of more fuel efficient cars was counterproductive activity to keep gasoline prices relatively low.

Believing that higher fuel costs would encourage conservation (and the purchases of small cars), President Ford attempted to develop the kind of policy that should have been put into place by Nixon in 1973. He ordered a $1 per barrel tariff on imported oil, to go into effect on February 1, 1975, which would be raised to $2 in June and $3 at some undetermined future date.

Largely because of the economic slowdown and conservation, oil imports did decline. But prices continued to rise, a tribute to OPEC's power and organization, leading to talk of conspiracies involving the petroleum companies, which were reporting huge profits. Public protests and demands for the alleviation of hardships caused by escalating fuel prices were difficult to withstand.

In response to them—and in part because of the coming presidential campaign of 1976—Congressional Democrats turned back the Ford surcharge. In late 1975, they sponsored and then managed to push through the legislature a measure that established a three-tier price structure, which, although cumbersome, did keep domestic petroleum prices down, and did as much for gasoline, whose cost barely changed in the next four years. This translated into fairly rigid controls on the price of domestic oil. Although the rest of the world was adjusting to paying more than $15 a barrel for its oil, Americans were enjoying $8 a barrel crude, and relatively stable gasoline prices that resulted from this.

The driving public and Detroit took this as a clear signal that the government would continue to keep gasoline prices down. Thus, Washington would all but guarantee there would be no repetition of the painful 1973–1974 increases. Of course, the CAFE requirements remained in place, and the companies would have to bring down their fleet averages. But individuals wanting to buy new cars weren't bound by CAFE strictures, and demonstrated their independence by opting once again for the larger models. It was as though the crisis had never taken place; big and intermediate cars remained the rage, and Detroit's lobbyists were in Washington attempting to extend if not repeal the CAFE requirements, although they were not certain what size cars to stress the following year.

What might have happened within the American automobile industry had the Nixon 1971 price freeze not included gasoline? And if Congress, four years later, hadn't acted to keep prices down, and the Ford surcharge had remained in place? The cost of automobile fuel would have risen, stimulating exploration and the search for alternate fuels along with conservation, and insofar as the short run was concerned, encourage motorists to purchase small and efficient cars. Detroit would have accelerated its development efforts, so that the Big Three and American Motors would not only have had downsized their fleets but have given high priorities to research and development along those lines.

As it was, the domestic companies embarked on their small car and downsizing programs more in response to government pressures than the pressures of the marketplace. In mid-decade there seemed little question but that the big, eight-cylinder gas-guzzlers were doomed and that, whether reluctantly or not, Detroit would have to enter the small car arena, with the foreign imports. Engineers and designers who, a few years earlier had been involved with cosmetic changes, were now instructed to develop cars with front-wheel drives, create new four-cylinder engines, and utilize new materials so as to hold down weight and thus improve fuel economy.

Paradoxically, one government program, CAFE, obliged the industry to manufacture and sell small cars whereas another, the controls program, discouraged Americans from purchasing those very models.

Nor was this the only indication of governmental short-sightedness. At a time when MITI was clearing the path for the Japanese companies and its counterparts in Europe were trying to do the same for their industries, the Federal Trade Commission fired a broadside at the industry. In 1976, a year after the passage of the Energy Policy and Conservation Act, the FTC initiated an antitrust probe of the automobile industry. This came at a time when Detroit was coming off a horrendous sales year and just recovering its momentum, and the Japanese challenge was strong and growing.

Confused federal policies notwithstanding, Detroit's mandate was to manufacture and market compact-to-small domestic cars that would compete with similar-size imports. Consumer decisions presumably would be made on the basis of initial cost, frequency of repairs, and the quality of manufacturing, servicing, and styling. The Japanese had the lead in most if not all of these areas. Their cars still carried lower price tags than comparable American models, because their hourly labor costs were lower and there were greater efficiencies in manufacturing. Moreover, even with the revaluation of the yen, the dollar was still overpriced in world markets and the situation was to worsen.

Virtually every magazine devoted to automobiles considered Japanese quality control and repair rate better than those of comparable American models. By the 1970s, Japanese dealership operations were at least as good as those of the Americans, and if there were not as many of them, there were enough in place to assure rapid service. The old familiar questions of the 1950s and early 1960s, which one magazine stated as "What if it breaks down in Dubuque?" were no longer being asked seriously. Not only were mechanics able to get parts rapidly, but drivers now also believed that one was more likely to have a breakdown in a Detroit product than a Japanese one. Finally, American drivers not only applauded the Japanese designs but also increasingly preferred them to those out of Detroit (which should have come as no surprise, since by then American companies were hiring Japanese designers, and Toyota and Datsun were hiring Americans to create cars for the American market).

As though to underline the quality differential, the American companies were obliged to recall a large number of models to correct defects. Such recalls had occurred in the past, but now they received wide publicity, especially from those who charged that Detroit was not only turning out shoddy products but unsafe ones as well. In the middle of the fuel crisis, Americans learned of no less than twenty-six separate safety-related investigations of domestically manufactured cars, and only eight involving the imports. The National Highway Traffic Safety Administration, dominated by reformers and often inspired by Ralph Nader's brand of consumerism, alleged that many of the defects were already known to the companies, the result of misplaced attempts to keep costs low. Thus, at a time when they were under a mandate to downsize and were faced with an increasingly strong Japanese challenge, Detroit was roundly criticized for a seeming inability to manufacture safe products.

Even so, the Americans appeared to believe they could not only hold onto their share of the market but expand it as well. Executives at the Big Three were counting on consumer loyalty, and they believed that owners of Chevys, Fords, and Plymouths would not turn to imports just to save a few dollars.

Then there was the matter of nationalism. World criticism of the United States during the Vietnam War was resented by large numbers of Americans. The oil shock had convinced them and others that the United States had become vulnerable to all kinds of foreign pressures, and this stimulated a xenophobia that hadn't been experienced in a generation. Along with a heightened yearning for isolationism came reactions against foreign goods, with the automobile one of the more important targets. Charges and allegations of "dumping," which is to say the sales of imports in the United States at below cost, were heard regularly and read about in newspapers and magazines. Articles and television programs on the contest for the American market became staple fare. As one commentator put it, "This has all the elements of war except the actual fighting." There were even territorial aspects to the contest. The Americans still dominated the Midwest and South, but the foreigners were strongest on both coasts; now each would mount intensive contests in the other's territory. *Ward's Automotive Reports,* the authoritative voice of the industry, reported this in early 1976, in an issue that took note of the fact that Toyota had finally passed VW as the leading import, that Datsun, too, had leaped ahead of the German company to take the number three post, and that Honda's sales had more than doubled, to go past the 100,000 mark. The magazine observed that Detroit had lost much over the years. The sales of imports had picked up in 1975, while those for domestic models still languished. *Ward's* called this "a beacon noticed by the Big Four for the first time, and one which will undoubtedly have a permanent effect on the course of the U.S. industry."

So the battle lines were finally drawn and the challenge accepted.

Imported cars have been an irritating, but generally ignored part of the U.S. auto market for years, like a boot nail working its way into the heel of the U.S. manufacturers. For a variety of reasons, 1975 became the year for U.S. car makers to sit and figure out just what was causing the pain.

III

Reinventing
the Automobile

14

The American Malaise

The average worker wants a job in which he does not have to put in much physical effort. Above all, he wants a job in which he does not have to think.

HENRY FORD II,
1970

We'd like to be like a supermarket. We don't know what kind of peas the customer will want. So we're going to have all kinds.

OSCAR LUNDIN, vice-chairman,
General Motors,
1975

People look upon their cars differently than they have in the past, generally in a more utilitarian way.

ROY CHAPIN, chairman,
American Motors,
1976

One thing is clear. If you want a small car that performs well and delivers good economy, the compromises Detroit is making with Pinto, Gremlin, and Vega won't do. They're okay on economy, but it takes a tighter package to do the job right.

Popular Science,
January 1976

The fun is gone. I wouldn't go into the automobile business again.

EDWARD COLE, chairman,
General Motors,
1974

That the American industry was in trouble seemed quite evident during the 1973 gas crunch. But for the rest of the decade, Detroit floundered about while the Japanese increased their share of the market. In those years, assorted American experts, both within and outside of the industry, sought to formulate a strategy to regain market share and lost status. Everything seemed to revolve around the responses to two complex and interrelated questions.

The first of these was how had the Japanese managed to win their great victory, and what might they do to solidify and expand upon it? Then, what was the nature of the American malaise, and how might it best be cured? The assumption here was that foreign successes wouldn't have been possible without some major miscalculations on the part of the Americans, and that given a proper response, the Big Three might yet regain their once-dominant position in the world automotive market.

As late as 1973–1974 Detroit had believed it would be able to satisfy its old customers with a concerted effort. The very idea that a middle-class, middle American might prefer a Honda or Toyota to a Chevy, Ford, or Plymouth was still alien to top executives in the mid-1970s. So even while shoppers in Seattle and Kansas City, New Orleans and Denver, were lining up for Corollas and Civics, GM, Ford, and Chrysler continued to assume they possessed the wherewithal and abilities to turn the tide in their direction.

The factors behind the Japanese manufacturing successes were dissected carefully in the late 1970s and have already been discussed (see Chapter 8: The Japanese Difference). At that point Detroit knew that given the manufacturing and marketing processes of the time, American firms had little chance to best Toyota, Nissan, and the others in the small economy market. The most practical solution would be for the Big Three to import these vehicles from their European and Japanese partners, slap on Chevy, Ford, and Plymouth nameplates, and accept low profits while trying to woo customers to the more expensive ornate higher-priced models. Meanwhile American designers would attempt to create a new generation of models —called "World Cars"—that would draw on expertise from several countries and appeal to extremely large audiences, so that important economies of scale could be realized.

It must be stressed, however, that in this period the Americans planned such an approach only for the low end of the scale. The suggestion that the Japanese could expand their market beyond economy and sports models wasn't taken too seriously. Yet the difficult markets of the post–gas-crunch period would change this too.

Higher automobile prices played an important role during these years. There were boosts up and down the line, for imports as well as domestic models, in the mid- and late-1970s. The term was yet to be coined, but large numbers of potential customers came down with *sticker shock* in 1973–1974, dumbfounded by the ticket for new cars after a three- or four-year absence from the showrooms. During the 1974 stagflation, would-be buyers came, looked, shook their heads, and left. And prices kept soaring. By the end of 1974, Pinto, which had risen from $1,995 in 1969 to $2,225 in early 1973, was being offered at $2,695. There were more such boosts to come.

The American driver who had purchased a low-priced Chevy in 1971 and who wanted to replace it seven years later would have learned that he would have to pay a great deal more money for the same kind of car. The 1971 basic Nova, considered a compact, listed at $2,870. It was 189 inches long, had a

111-inch wheelbase, weighed 3,095 pounds, and was powered by a 145-hp engine. The 1978 Chevelle Malibu, deemed an "economy compact," cost $4,297, was 193 inches overall with a 108-inch wheelbase, weighed 3,155 pounds, and had a 95-hp engine. The 1971 car was tested out at 18 mpg over a 300-mile trip; the Malibu did quite a bit better—almost 23 mpg. But was that worth the extra $1,427?

The response was that the price was not as high as it seemed. Inflation had cut sharply into the value of the dollar. Using the Consumer Price Index as a guide, $2,870 in 1971 dollars worked out to $4,592 in 1978, and so GM might have claimed the Malibu really cost less than the Nova and, in addition, was a superior car.

The price increases also reflected mandated antipollution and safety devices, which ran from seat and shoulder belts to emission controls of various kinds to the higher price of unleaded gasoline. Estimates vary, but Murray Weidenbaum, an economist with admittedly antiregulatory proclivities, thought that by 1978 there were approximately $666 in government-mandated safety and environmental equipment in the American car, the total bill for which came to $6.7 billion in higher car prices. Ralph Nader and his colleagues asserted this was a vast exaggeration, and they pressed for additional safety equipment, most notably airbags, which Weidenbaum and others claimed would tack on another $600 or so to the price of a car.

The reaction on the part of the customer was to hold on to the old car for a while longer, settle for a used model, or downgrade, and all these options were exercised. By 1980, the average American car was more than seven years old, older than at any time since the immediate post–World War II years; this statistic caused ripples throughout the economy, from oversupplies of copper and lead to cutbacks in the manufacture of rear-view mirrors and accessories. There was a nationwide shortage of auto mechanics, but auto salesmen were laid off. Dealers reported losses in the new car area, while profits picked up in repairs. Detroit became a major disaster area; the once-center of the nation's strongest industry was now deemed the capital of the "Rust Bowl."

The price of used cars shot up, as Americans suffering from sticker shock sought them out. Toward the end of the decade, rental cars coming off-lease, their drive trains guaranteed by the leaser, and available at approximately two-thirds the price of a new model, were sought after. Americans abandoned Chevy, Ford, and Plymouth dealers to buy their next cars from the likes of Hertz, Avis, National, and the others, and these companies, too, reported a larger share of volume from sales than had been the case in the past.

Dealers noted that customers were responding to sticker shock by downgrading sharply. Individuals who arrived at a GM dealership intending to purchase a large or medium-size Chevrolet wound up looking at the Vegas, which the dealers tried to load with accessories so as to boost profits, and then walked out, with a Datsun or a Toyota dealer the next stop. And there they would find cars that once were sold as economy models going for more than the American small cars. But they stayed and made their down payments. In 1963, Americans purchased foreign cars for reasons of economy; ten years later they purchased them because they were superior products.

One clear reflection of this were the relative changes within the product lines. The cost of a stripped Ford, for example, rose more slowly than most perceived, but at the same time, the company engaged in a daring strategy of loading Fords with extras and stretching the wheelbase, until the big sedans carrying the Elite, LTD, and Thunderbird nameplates competed with Oldsmobiles and Chryslers.

Ford took a different, but somewhat similar approach in 1975 with the Granada/Monarch. Frankly modeled after the Mercedes, with Ford even inviting comparisons, these cars were mid-range in price, which is to say fully equipped models might be purchased for around $5,000. The message was clear enough: You are paying more, but today's Granadas offer greater value.

The corporation hoped the narrow profit margins realized on the small cars would be compensated for by larger returns from the luxury models. The ploy failed, although the strategy would remain in place until the early 1980s. Meanwhile Ford deepened its commitment toward creating profitable small cars —the greatest challenge before the industry in the late 1970s.

As noted, under the terms of the Energy Policy and Conservation Act of 1975, auto manufacturers were obliged to have a CAFE of 20 mpg by 1980. This measure had been debated in a period when much attention was being paid to fuel economy. The buying climate had changed sharply by the time of its passage, however.

A large segment of the public hadn't been convinced its automotive future rested with small cars. The market shifted just when Detroit had its plans for conversion in place. After having entered into crash programs to manufacture Pintos, Vegas, Gremlins, Dodge Darts, and the like, American dealers found themselves with near-record supplies that were not easily moved.

The turning away from the subcompacts after the gas crunch pleased Detroit. Of some concern were the CAFE guidelines, which if not met would result in fines. The automakers asked for stretchouts, arguing they could hardly force Americans to buy cars they did not seem to want. When this failed, they indicated a preference for paying the fines rather than not selling cars. Which was to their advantage; Detroit earned more money on big cars than small, and buyers of the former tended to load them with highly profitable options. On the other hand, did this not mean that the small, relatively inexpensive cars would be in demand whenever gasoline was short and prices rose, only to become less desirable when the crisis passed? Obviously this question could not be answered in 1975.

This indeed was to be the case. Detroit was whipsawed by the market, just as it was tugged in various directions by Washington. During the next few years, consumer preferences would shift, leaving dealers alternately with oversupplies first of full-size cars and then of compacts. The companies were buffeted by these forces, which added another element of uncertainty. Profits declined sharply, as the cost of manufacturing autos increased, while prices had to be kept down in the face of a weak market. Meanwhile, enormous amounts of money were expended on research, development, and retooling for the next set of cars with which to recapture a share of the market. Customers switched from small to big and then back again, as desires for economy would alternate with those for power and comfort. The best statistical reflection of this may be found in the production figures for four-, six-, and eight-cylinder vehicles. The greater the tendency toward the fours, the more the craving for economy; the more the demand for eights, the greater desire for power.

A peak for the fours was reached in 1974—in the backwash of the gas crunch and stagflation—but demand then declined irregularly, whereas orders for eights showed a steady falloff after 1973. Generally, however, there was a revival of sixes, with purchasers of fours shifting upward and staying there in good years, and those with eights compromising with sixes.

Of the Big Three, Chrysler had gone furthest in the direction of smaller engines. In the corporation's 1978 fleet, 15 percent of the cars came with four-cylinder engines, 27 with six-cylinder, and 68 percent with eight-cylinder. At Ford, the mix was 13 percent, 25 percent, and 62 percent, respectively. General Motors was more inclined toward large engines than the others, with 8 percent, 21 percent, and 71 percent for the fours, sixes, and eights, respectively. Thus, Chrysler was better situated for the transition to smaller cars if that indeed was where Detroit was headed. Whether this was the path to be taken was one of the industry's major questions during the late 1970s.

All of this transpired while Detroit was studying the Japanese. Always the Japanese, who in the late 1970s seemed to be an ever-expanding force in the marketplace as Detroit's reputation continued to slide. The Big Three promised and even delivered some new models, widely heralded as the American response to the imports. These were smaller, more efficient,

FINANCIAL PERFORMANCE OF
AMERICAN AUTOMOBILE COMPANIES, 1970–1975

(millions of dollars)

General Motors

YEAR	NET SALES	NET INCOME
1970	18,752	609
1971	28,264	1,936
1972	30,435	2,163
1973	35,798	2,398
1974	31,550	950
1975	35,725	1,253

Ford

YEAR	NET SALES	NET INCOME
1970	14,980	516
1971	16,433	657
1972	20,194	870
1973	23,015	904
1974	23,621	361
1975	24,009	228

Chrysler

YEAR	NET SALES	NET INCOME
1970	7,000	(8)
1971	7,999	84
1972	9,759	221
1973	11,774	255
1974	10,971	(52)
1975	11,598	(282)

American Motors

YEAR	NET SALES	NET INCOME
1970	1,099	(56)
1971	1,233	6
1972	1,404	16
1973	1,739	45
1974	2,000	28
1975	2,282	(27)

SOURCE: *Standard & Poor's N.Y.S.E. Stock Reports.*

PRODUCTION OF FOUR-, SIX-, AND EIGHT-CYLINDER SEDANS IN THE UNITED STATES, 1970–1978

YEAR	FOUR	SIX	EIGHT
1970	2,300	974,000	6,610,000
1971	520,000	880,000	5,781,000
1972	851,800	970,000	7,201,000
1973	887,900	1,023,700	8,398,000
1974	1,058,800	1,558,800	5,719,100
1975	565,443	1,254,158	4,828,081
1976	869,266	1,762,965	5,813,129
1977	599,724	1,708,767	7,215,572
1978	939,611	2,211,509	6,102,612

SOURCE: *Ward's Automotive Yearbook, 1979,* 106.

and, in some cases, they even incorporated new technologies. But they were also priced higher than their Japanese counterparts, untried, and hindered by missteps.

Detroit's lead "economy cars" during the fuel crisis were, among the compacts, the GM Nova, the Ford Maverick, and the Chrysler Valiant; the three major subcompacts were the Chevy Vega, Ford Pinto, and the AM Gremlin. The Nova, which had a good reputation for reliability and economy, sold for a shade over $3,000 stripped, was 195 inches long, weighed 3,278 pounds, and got 16 mpg on a test drive. In terms of price, dimensions, and fuel economy, it was pretty standard for its group. As with the others, it was larger, more expensive, and less economical than its predecessors.

In later years, a number of critics would charge that Detroit had consistently enlarged its cars, added to their power, and boosted prices, while decreasing their fuel economy. But statistics indicate otherwise. Consider, for example, the following table, which compares the 1973 Valiant and its 1960 counterpart: the 1973 auto was a trifle larger and more powerful than was the model of thirteen years earlier, and certainly higher priced. Still, the cost rose more slowly than did the Consumer Price Index, and this more powerfully engined and roomier car obtained the same mileage from a gallon of gasoline. All in all, Detroit might have been forgiven its claims of having actually lowered the cost of driving during this time.

SELECTED STATISTICS FOR
THE 1960 AND 1973 VALIANTS

	1960	1973
Wheelbase	107 inches	108 inches
Length	184 inches	190 inches
Weight	2,790 pounds	3,121 pounds
Horsepower	101	105
Miles per gallon	18.5	18
Price	$2,379	$2,925

SOURCE: *Consumer Reports* (July 1960), 379; *ibid.* (March 1973), 199.

But there was a difference. These figures are for compacts, cars that were quite popular in the late 1950s and early 1960s. Since then, many Americans had graduated to mid-size and larger cars. Then, too, the tendency to load the domestic compacts with all kinds of options continued, so that, in practice, the Big Three products more often than not were far more costly and less economical than those of the early 1960s had been.

The American subcompacts were comparable to one another, offering decent value and performance insofar as the raw numbers were concerned. But they could not match the Japanese cars in price or performance, significant factors for a nation that was still concerned with future fuel shortages and in the middle of a recession. It should be kept in mind that these are statistical comparisons and do not take into account reputation, where the Japanese were quite a bit ahead of the

SELECTED STATISTICS FOR THE 1974 PINTO, VEGA, AND COROLLA

	PINTO	VEGA	COROLLA
Length	169 inches	175 inches	164 inches
Wheelbase	94 inches	97 inches	92 inches
Weight	2,451 pounds	2,542 pounds	1,836 pounds
Horsepower	80	75	65
Miles per gallon	26	25	32
Price	$2,442	$2,380	$2,109

SOURCE: *Consumer Reports* (February 1974), 161.

Americans. In 1960, potential customers did not know whether their foreign cars could be serviced adequately; by 1974, those who were looking at domestic cars were troubled over their relatively poor records for repairs, something that was not of major consequence for those who wanted Toyotas and Datsuns. The difference might also be seen in the way customers acted in the showroom. With the domestics, it was a constant struggle to get the best deal, to shave prices, and to compare the deals offered by several dealerships. With the Japanese, one accepted the price, knowing it wouldn't be shaved and would be within a few dollars of what might be quoted down the road. This difference, which had worked in favor of the Americans earlier, now made the sellers of Japanese cars seem somehow more reliable and honest.

All this had finally dawned on Detroit, which nervously readied the cars that were supposed to throw back the Japanese tide, just as their ancestors, the Corvair, Falcon, and Valiant, had done in the late 1950s. There was confidence in the air, then; however, the mood of the mid-1970s was one of trepidation.

This was because of the relative failures of the Pinto and Vega. Both cars had sold well, but by mid-decade their reputations were tarnished. *Consumer Reports* thought the Pinto's driver vision poor and its repair record below average, to which *The New York Times* added that the engine was balky and *Motor Trend* that the car as a whole was "disappointing." The Vega had "few strong or weak points," suggested *Consumer Reports*, whereas *Motor Trend* considered the car "rather humdrum." Neither car could come up to the Corolla or the Datsun B 210 in efficiency, construction, or value. Detroit knew that unless the next generation was a decided improvement, its market for low-priced cars might well be lost.

Detroit's response came in 1978, and initially from Ford, which by then had taken the lead in matters of styling innovation, usually because of Lee Iacocca's keen sense of the market. That year Ford introduced (or perhaps a more accurate term would be re-introduced) the Mustang II, a car that was meant to evoke memories of the 1964 sales hit. Although higher in price than the original, and with less standard equipment, the Mustang II was a faithful replica, a small car that offered economy combined with the appearance if not the handling of a sports car. Powered by a six-cylinder engine, the Mustang could be had with an eight for those interested in performance, and of course there was a wide variety of options from which to select, all intended to boost the profit margin.

A Mustang II, equipped with that larger engine, automatic transmission, and power options, cost around $4,500, almost $1,500 over the 1964 version. It weighed 3,269 pounds (more than 800 pounds heavier than the Pinto) and got around 13 mpg, which was hardly impressive. The comparison with the Pinto is apt, because there was a great deal of commonality of parts between the two cars, just as the original Mustang had borrowed heavily from the Falcon. This had become an Iacocca trademark; no one was more adept than he at squeezing the last drop out of a design.

All in all, the Mustang II was a typical Detroit product of the pre–gas-crunch period—heavily styled, loaded with extras, and less economical. And it bred the usual number of imitations. The following year saw a record number of introductions, with the Chevy Monza, Oldsmobile Starfire, and Buick Skyhawk derived from the Chevy Vega. None did well, and the Starfire and Skyhawk were dropped after one year. The Sunbird, the Pontiac version, appeared in 1976 and vanished two years later.

Initially, at least, Mustang II sold well. More than 385,000 of them went in 1974, almost one out of every twenty cars purchased that year. But there was a falloff to 188,000 in 1975 and again the following year. By 1977, when the Mustang II sold only 153,000, it had become evident that this kind of car was not likely to worry the Japanese.

Chrysler and GM made their big splashes in the post–gas-crunch scene in 1976 and, like Ford, tried to do it on the cheap.

That this would be the case is understandable; the stagflation years of 1974–1975 were disasters, with domestic production declining from 1973's 9.3 million to 7.3 million in 1974 and then to 6.7 million units in 1975. The Big Three offered rebates of up to $600 on their big cars, and all of them rushed to get compacts and subcompacts to the market. Even Cadillac entered the field with its Seville, a car that looked like an ungainly cross between a Mercedes and Rolls; 16,000 Sevilles were purchased in 1975, and 44,000 in 1976. So the incentive was there: small cars sold, big cars remained on the lots. What was lacking, however, was a clear appreciation of just what was needed in the small-car category.

Chrysler had a three-year plan, developed prior to the gas crunch and altered afterward, which was at the same time logical and affordable. For 1975 it would introduce the Plymouth Volare and Dodge Aspen, which would succeed the successful but aging Valiant and Dart. Two years later would come the Omni and the Horizon, true new-era subcompacts with front-wheel drive and transversely mounted engines. These cars strongly resembled the VW Rabbit, which in 1973 seemed a certain success, but was actually derived from a model created by Chrysler's French subsidiary, Simca. Attracting little attention at the time, the Omni/Horizon was to be one of the more important examples of the World-Car approach to design, creation, and marketing. In the past, GM and Ford had borrowed from their foreign companies, but never as much as Chrysler had, in this instance, for reasons of economy and to save time.

These cars were to be followed by restyled versions of the larger cars, thus giving Chrysler an entirely new line before the end of the decade. A sensible plan, which unfortunately was ineptly executed and ruined by circumstances over which the corporation had no control.

Simply stated, the Volare and Aspen were disasters, plagued by every imaginable problem. Like the Valiant/Dart, they were essentially the same model with different trim. Indeed, they were manufactured at the same factory, and by error the right side of some cars emerged as Volares and the left as Aspens, a typical blunder for those troubled vehicles. As the result of a design error, the carburetors caused stalling when accelerating during a slow turn—usually in traffic. This led to a recall. The brakes faded badly, another recall. There were reports of hoods flying up at high speed, yet another recall. The improperly galvanized fenders rusted, all at the same spot, a fourth recall, with owners on line outside of dealerships, comparing notes on myriads of other ailments. The recalls cost Chrysler $200 million—and much of its goodwill.

Yet the cars sold reasonably well in 1976/1977, largely because of the reputations of the Valiant and the Dart. Moreover it was the right-size car for the period, weighing 3,630 pounds and getting close to 20 mpg on a test drive. It was lower priced than its immediate competition—the Ford Granada and the Chevy Nova—and offered significantly better headroom and seating comfort. Indeed, the Volare outsold the Granada in 1977, and had it not been for the growing chorus of complaints, it might have gone on to become a popular success. But those criticisms mounted, with the Center for Auto Safety bestowing on the Volare/Aspen its 1977 "Lemon of the Year" award. As one Chrysler executive put it, "we pissed away a car." But it was more than that. This failure was the first of several that almost caused the corporation's total collapse.

Chrysler might have been able to withstand this fiasco had the Omni/Horizon been as successful as expected. Offered at a base price of $3,800, it was only slightly more expensive than the Corolla and was further advanced technically than that aging design. Weighing 2,230 pounds, with a 99-inch wheelbase, it had the interior dimensions of cars much longer and heavier, and its 75-hp engine was surprisingly powerful. The car delivered more than 30 mpg, putting it in the class of far smaller Japanese sedans against which it was supposed to compete.

Like the Volare/Aspen, it had been rushed to market, arriving in early 1978, almost a year and a half ahead of GM's next subcompact, the Chevette, while Ford was still relying on the aged Pinto and its German-manufactured import, the

Fiesta, another Rabbit look-alike that, although a sturdy car, was not available with the one option Americans tended to insist on: an automatic transmission. Within a year, there would be another gas crunch, and Americans would once again switch from large and intermediate-size cars to compacts and subcompacts, which might have resulted in lines at Dodge and Plymouth dealerships. Finally, the car got off to a good start. *Motor Trend* named the Omni/Horizon its "Car of the Year," an award Chrysler exploited to the hilt in its advertisements.

But this car, like the Volare/Horizon, suffered from design and manufacturing defects. There were five safety-related recalls in the first half year, ranging from cracks in the front suspension to misdirected fuel lines to carpet fasteners that penetrated the fuel tank. The most crushing blow, however, was the influential *Consumer Reports* verdict that the cars were "not acceptable," a rare designation, one given because of what the magazine claimed was the car's tendency to swerve when turned at high speeds, making it unsafe. Chrysler was on the ropes by late 1978. That year the Horizon and the Omni sold 188,000 units between them, a mere 2 percent of the market for domestic cars. Not only was this 86,000 fewer than Honda, which was third behind Toyota and Datsun for the Japanese, but below the by-now discredited Pinto.

General Motors introduced its new small car, the Chevette, in September 1975, amid the kind of ballyhoo attendant on such events that had been commonplace in the 1950s but not in the 1970s, when new nameplates had become more regular events. The claim was that this was "the right size at the right time," and the advertising stressed that "it's about time!"

The company did what it could to suggest the Chevette had been produced in response to a patriotic mandate. In effect, GM was saying that it had listened and then produced. Chairman Thomas Murphy called the Chevette "GM's first line of attack against the imports," the clear implication being that Americans who had claimed they wanted an economical subcompact now had one, and those who persisted in purchasing

Toyotas and Datsuns would have to justify their actions with some other, implicitly unsound arguments.

The Chevette wasn't a new, original, or particularly interesting car. It had been designed by GM's German subsidiary, Opel, for entry in that market and was also manufactured in Brazil. The car had been sold there and in Europe for several years and was brought to the United States only when the need for a small car became evident. The American version of the Chevette was little more than a miniaturized compact that lacked the virtues of the newer ones from overseas. For example, it had a front-mounted engine and, unlike the newer generation of Japanese and German cars (the Rabbit and the Subaru GF, in particular), a rear transmission, requiring a large hump that cut down on interior space and, in particular, made the rear passenger space quite cramped. The brakes were barely adequate. Originally designed to accommodate the Wankel, the Chevette was switched to a conventional four-cylinder engine after the gas crunch and was quickly deemed underpowered by the trade journals. Nonetheless it was—unlike the Pinto and Vega—a genuine subcompact, which, at 2,035 pounds, was almost 600 pounds lighter than the Vega and more than 100 pounds lighter than the Corolla. Despite its American touches, the Chevette would have been quite familiar in size and feel to Toyota and VW owners.

General Motors priced the stripped-down (and generally unavailable) Chevette at $2,900, which put it several hundred dollars below the price of the major Japanese economy cars. When similarly equipped, however, it came in at about the same price as the Honda Civic and Toyota Corolla. The Chevette delivered on its mileage claims; it got 29 mpg on a 190-mile test run, the same as the Corolla, but less than the Civic, and, backed by the Chevrolet organization, was considered capable of cutting deeply into their sales.

The general expectation was that the Chevette would cannibalize some sales from the Vega, but get most of its sales from individuals who otherwise would have purchased an import. If the price of success meant the demise of the Vega, then it would have been a low one indeed, since that model's appeal had faded badly, with only 208,000 of them sold in 1975, down from 369,000 in 1974 and close to 400,000 in 1973.

Although it cannot be said that the Chevette turned out to be a disaster it certainly was not a success, and over its run proved a financial failure, the talk in Detroit being that the Chevrolet Division lost $300 on each sale. Only 187,000 were purchased in 1976. As predicted, the Chevette cut into Vega sales (which came to 161,000 that year, and 78,000 the following, when it was discontinued) and 133,000 in 1977, when, in desperation, GM cut its price so as to make it more than $100 under that of a similarly equipped Corolla. Still, the Chevette managed to slow down, if not halt the move toward imports; one survey showed that almost one-third of those who purchased the car would have gone to a foreign make had it not been available.

The Chevette, then, was the stopper, but not the car with which GM expected to turn back the Japanese. Given the nature of the market and its sudden shifts, it had become evident that what was needed was a compact with subcompact economy, a car small on the outside and large on the inside, one that combined high gas mileage with the size Americans still wanted—which is to say, a seemingly impossible set of specifications. Furthermore, such cars would have to be sufficiently low in price to attract those who had been won over to the middle-of-the-line imports. This was the mandate GM gave its designers in 1976, with orders that such a car be manufactured for the 1978 model year.

The cars of the Mustang II, Volare, and Chevette era were to be transitional vehicles, to hold the market while Detroit retooled its thinking as well as its factories. The Omni/Horizon was the first of this new generation, and it didn't augur well for the others. In 1978, as before, GM was the key American player in the game, the one the others watched the most and from which industry leadership was expected. By then the corporation understood the dimensions of its problems and what was needed. The response was soon to come, in as solemn an atmosphere as the industry had known in the post–World War II period. "We are on a collision course," said Director of Organizational Research and Development Delmar Landen. "We have built institutions which were very effective in their time, but now there are increasing levels of aspirations and different value systems pressing against these institutions."

15

The Victory Secured

The cardinal rule of the new ballgame is change. Individuals, dealers, or companies that don't adjust to the new realities of this decade will just not survive in the industry.

M. PAUL TIPPITT JR., president,
American Motors,
1982

In the spring of 1979, as a result of the Iranian revolution that had begun the previous year, the price of petroleum shot up and its availability declined. Unlike the gas crunch and oil shock of six years earlier, this crisis hadn't come as a total surprise. Congress discussed a national rationing plan in May, while California was putting one of its own in place. Japan instituted Sunday gasoline station closings soon after, and such closings were debated throughout Europe as well.

The price of a gallon of gasoline reached $0.81 in early

June, as stations prepared to alter their pumps to accommodate sales at the $1.00 level expected before the summer was out. Controls were voted, but with the exception of alternate-day purchases and a brief flirtation with "gasohol" (a mixture of gasoline and alcohol), nothing more developed. The shortage was over by autumn, by which time fuel was over $1.10 a gallon, a rise of almost $0.40 in a year.

As might have been expected, the move toward fuel-efficient cars accelerated. American automobile manufacturers, who hadn't been able to move their small cars in 1978, were once again short of them. And in 1979/80 as in 1973/74, the foreigners—led by the Japanese—increased their share of the market. Thus, Detroit once again was whipsawed in the marketplace, and the auto industry was in disarray, with its leaders demoralized.

A few statistics are in order so as to better appreciate the condition of the American automobile industry and that of its Japanese competitors toward the end of the 1970s.

American and captive Canadian factories had turned out 7.3 million passenger cars in 1975, of which 6.7 million were sold domestically and 642,000 abroad. That year European and Japanese companies sold 1.3 million cars in the United States.

Production in 1980 came to over 7 million units, and 6.4 million of these were sold domestically, with exports accounting for the rest. More than 2.5 million cars were imported. Thus, General Motors, Ford, Chrysler, and American Motors sold some 300,000 fewer cars in 1980 than they had five years before, whereas 2.5 million Japanese and European models were purchased, an increase of almost 50 percent.

In 1950 imports had accounted for less than one-third of 1 percent of American car sales. Ten years later the figure had risen to 6 percent, and by 1970, it was up to slightly less than 24 percent. One out of every three cars sold in the United States in 1980 had been manufactured abroad, and their total value came to $16.6 billion, double that of 1975. More than $8.2

billion of that went to Japan; this was over twice the 1977 figure.

The Japanese sold 696,000 passenger cars in the United States in 1975; for 1980 the figure would come to a shade under 2 million. Japanese companies accounted for half the imports in 1975; in 1980 they were to take three out of every four sales. Toyota, Datsun, and Honda held the top three positions on the import list, followed by Volkswagen. Then came Mazda and Subaru. Of the top six imports for 1980, five were Japanese. But since more than half the VWs sold were assembled in Pennsylvania and should be considered American, that corporation really placed lower. Thus, all the top five imports came from Japan.

While the Japanese increased their total placements by a factor of more than two and a half, non-Japanese countries sold 117,000 fewer cars to Americans in 1980 than they had in 1975.

In 1980 the American companies turned out 6.4 million cars, 2.1 million fewer than the previous year and 3.4 million fewer than the record number sold in 1973, and it now seemed likely that that record would never be surpassed. They reported losses of $4.2 billion among them that year. Chrysler

SALES OF FOREIGN AUTOMOBILES IN THE UNITED STATES, 1975–1980

(thousands)

Year				Country				
	TOTAL	JAPAN	GER- MANY	ITALY	U.K.	SWEDEN	FRANCE	OTHER
1975	1,341	695	370	102	67	52	16	39
1976	1,712	1,129	350	83	77	37	22	14
1977	1,940	1,342	423	55	57	39	19	5
1978	2,192	1,563	416	70	54	56	29	4
1979	2,329	1,617	496	72	47	66	28	3
1980	2,521	1,992	339	47	33	61	47	2

SOURCE: *Automotive Trade Statistics, 1964–1980,* 4.

was close to illiquidity. Ford had passed its dividend with Wall Street believing that the corporation couldn't survive two more such years. As noted, the net working capital of the American auto industry declined by $11.9 billion in the four-year period ending in 1982, and in the same period, debt and liabilities increased by $12.2 billion. Detroit certainly wasn't bankrupt, but it was closer to bankruptcy than at any time since the Great Depression.

The Japanese produced 7 million cars in 1980. The American figure came to 7.2 million, but exclusive of captive Canadian factories, 6.4 million. When trucks and buses are included, the combined U.S.-Canadian total came to 9.4 million, and the Japanese total, 11 million. That country could then claim to be the world's leading automobile manufacturer.

The lead was expanded in 1981, when American factories, exclusive of Canada, produced 6.3 million cars and those of Japan, 7 million.

Of the top ten motor vehicle manufacturers in 1980, four were Japanese, two American, two French, one Italian, and one German. Of course, these figures don't include those from American overseas subsidiaries, which were substantial and a source of future strength. But the national decline could be seen in the relative position of Chrysler, now ranked four-

PROFITS AND (LOSSES)* FOR
AMERICAN AUTOMOBILE MANUFACTURERS, 1978–1981

| | (millions of dollars) | | | |
COMPANY	1978	1979	1980	1981
American Motors	24.1	68.1	(155.4)	(136.6)
Chrysler	(204.6)	(1,097.0)	(1,710.0)	(475.6)
Ford	1,588.9	1,169.3	(1,545.0)	(1,060.0)
General Motors	3,408.0	2,892.7	(762.5)	333.4
Total	4,816.4	3,033.1	(4,172.9)	(1,338.8)

*Loss figures are in parentheses.

SOURCE: American Motors, Chrysler, Ford, and General Motors, *Annual Reports*, 1981.

WORLD MOTOR VEHICLE PRODUCTION, 1977–1981

Country	(millions) Year				
	1977	1978	1979	1980	1981
United States*	10.4	10.3	9.4	7.2	7.0
Japan	5.4	6.0	6.2	7.0	7.0
West Germany	3.8	3.9	3.9	3.5	3.6
France	3.1	3.1	3.2	2.9	2.6
United Kingdom	1.3	1.2	1.1	0.9	0.9

*Includes Canada.

SOURCE: *Ward's Automotive Yearbooks, 1977–1981.*

teenth worldwide, producing fewer passenger cars not only than Honda and GM's German Opel operations, but also the USSR's Lada works. Chrysler was the world's most rapidly shrinking auto firm and Honda its fastest expanding one in 1980.

Such were the dimensions of the Japanese success, which by 1980 was more complete than any reasonable person—on either side of the Pacific—might have believed possible a decade earlier. That Toyota and Nissan could ever have bested

THE TOP TEN WORLD MOTOR VEHICLE MANUFACTURERS, 1980

COMPANY	COUNTRY	(millions)		
		CARS	TRUCKS	TOTAL
General Motors	United States	4.1	0.7	4.8
Toyota	Japan	2.3	1.0	3.3
Nissan	Japan	1.9	0.7	2.3
Ford	United States	1.3	0.6	1.9
Renault	France	1.5	0.2	1.7
Peugeot	France	1.4	0.2	1.6
Volkswagen	Germany	1.2	0.1	1.3
Fiat	Italy	1.2	0.1	1.3
Toyo Kogyo	Japan	0.7	0.4	1.1
Mitsubishi	Japan	0.7	0.4	1.1

SOURCE: *Ward's Automotive Yearbook, 1981*, 91.

VW would have been thought improbable in 1970; in 1980 both companies surpassed Ford. A handful thought they might reach even GM's level before mid-decade.

Some of the same individuals predicted that the industry was about to undergo a worldwide shakeout, with many companies going under while others merged. The list of likely survivors from such an ordeal usually included GM, Ford, Toyota, Nissan, Honda, Renault, Fiat, and British Leyland. But there were those who believed Ford might not make it—at least as an independent factor in the American market. Indeed, during contract negotiations in 1982 Ford hinted that unless the United Auto Workers proved more cooperative in the future the company might close down its domestic plants, expand overseas, and import cars produced there for its American market. And British Leyland could survive only with large-scale government help, which was thought to be unlikely, given the policies of the Conservative regime of Margaret Thatcher.

A world in which Japan was the largest and most profitable manufacturer of motor vehicles, in which there was only one company in America and two in Europe? With Ford somewhere in between? Not likely, and more than a trifle overstated, perhaps, but from the vantage point of 1980 not impossible either.

By then, too, the handful of authentic independent industry scholars had been augmented by scores of instant experts prepared to explain how this startling reversal of fortunes had come about. Although analyses differed, most were pretty much the same. On the Japanese side, there were the high level of worksmanship, lower wages, trade restrictions, the lack of unionization, the advantages of a homogeneous society, the dollar-yen relationship, and the uncanny ability of MITI to make the correct move at the propitious moment.

Meanwhile, so the argument ran, the Americans committed managerial blunders, turned out inferior products, failed to respond to market forces, and suffered from worker dissatisfaction, low productivity, and high wages.

The news out of Detroit was almost unqualifiedly bad. General Motors was obliged to admit it had sold Oldsmobiles and Buicks with Chevy engines; the corporation's claim that this was a widespread practice and had no negative implications didn't sit well with those customers who had paid a premium price for what they believed to be a top-of-the-line power plant. Ford was hit with lawsuits deriving from the Pinto's flawed gasoline tank; errors that would have cost a few dollars per car to prevent, resulted in the fiery deaths of several drivers and passengers whose Pintos were involved in rear-end collisions. Chrysler's reputation for quality control continued to slide. Firestone Tire & Rubber was forced to recall a run of its radial tires, which all but threw the corporation into insolvency and further ruined its reputation, this while an increasing number of Americans were insisting on Japanese and French tires.

Although most of these factors played a role in the rise of the Japanese auto industry and in Detroit's slide, it was more complicated than that. The relative levels of inflation in both countries should have been taken into consideration, for example; the more rapidly rising prices in the United States forced costs upward at a higher rate than was the case in Japan. Furthermore, the differential in the prices of American and Japanese steel, copper, plastics, and many other products utilized in cars, gave Toyota et al. a head start over Detroit. Finally, federal and state regulations forced Detroit to make substantial and important changes in design, which added to the prices of its products. Although it was true that Japan also established norms, there was a spirit of cooperation in that country unmatched in the United States, where regulators often took an adversary stance and the automakers did what they could to avoid and even evade such controls.

All this gave the Japanese significant advantages in the American market. How far and in which direction they would go remained key questions. Japan dominated the subcompact category and was strong in compacts, but there was no guarantee that these models would remain as important as they had appeared to be in the aftermath of the 1973 gas crunch. Indeed, as was seen, Americans turned strongly to larger and less economical cars once the memories of the gas crunch faded and fuel prices stabilized.

The Japanese faced limited challenges, but challenges nonetheless, from European companies who were encouraged by the declining reputations of American cars. Volvo underwent a revival, while BMW became the standard in its field. As will be seen, the French reentered the market through the purchase of a controlling interest in American Motors. The most dramatic renewal, however, was at VW.

Volkswagen made an effort to upgrade in these years, as the Beetle was phased out and a variety of new, higher-priced models, led by the Rabbit, Dasher, and Scirocco, made their debuts to mixed receptions.

The Rabbit was designed to be efficient and economical. It resembled two boxes mounted one behind the other, the first to house the engine and other mechanical components, the second the passengers. The car had a water-cooled, transversely mounted four-cylinder engine with a front-wheel drive and was greeted as a higher-priced, but worthy successor to the Beetle. But it seemed to have developed a variety of mechanical problems, including oil leaks, and was subject to several embarrassing recalls. Volkswagen managed to straighten things out, but not before its reputation for quality had been seriously damaged.

The corporation did manage a limited recovery. The combination of fears regarding American tariffs and quotas on foreign cars, plus a strong Deutschmark, encouraged VW to build an assembly plant in Pennsylvania, which started turning out Rabbits in 1978. By then most of the mechanical defects had been corrected, the company's credibility was restored, and Americans had adjusted to the new price levels. Most important in VW's fortunes, however, was the introduction of a diesel-powered Rabbit in late 1977.

The diesel wasn't a new engine, of course, having been available in passenger cars from Mercedes-Benz for many years, whereas other Europeans offered them in limited quantities. In addition, most of America's large trucks were powered by diesels. Attractive for their simplicity of construction, rugged performance, excellent mileage, and the lower cost of diesel fuel, this engine appealed to Americans seeking such characteristics at a time when fuel prices were soaring. Those fearful of future shortages and possible rationing reasoned that the trucking lobby would make certain that diesel fuel was not only available but also low priced.

Few drivers could afford a Mercedes, the quintessential luxury car, but uncertainty about the price and availability of gas led several manufacturers to try to market a lower-priced diesel model. General Motors rushed diesel-powered Oldsmobiles and Cadillacs to market, but they were flops; their engines turned out to be deeply flawed, and this further eroded the American reputation for reliability.

Not so the VW diesel, which, after a few bugs were ironed out, proved both reliable and efficient and cost only $195 more than the gasoline-fueled model. Since the diesel-equipped Rabbit got 43 mpg, it was a true bargain. VW's director of diesel research Peter Hofbauer reported that the corporation was testing an engine capable of getting 60 mpg from a Rabbit-size car. For three years the diesel seemed the engine of the future, evoking enthusiasm reminiscent of that given the Wankel in the early years of the decade. And the diesel Rabbit was the best buy in the category.

The American plant started turning them out in 1978, by which time dealers had waiting lists for diesels, which, if not quite as long as those for Beetles in the mid-1950s were still impressive. By then, nearly a third of all Rabbits sold in the United States were diesel, and many more would have been taken had they been available. The company was in the midst of a turnabout, with sales rising by 26 percent in 1977 to 263,-000, reversing a seven-year decline.

Despite this recovery, VW was in no position to challenge the Japanese, whose lead was in any case too great and whose position was quite secure. For one thing the corporation lacked

PRICE RANGES OF SELECTED DOMESTIC AND IMPORTED SEDANS, 1965-1978

(dollars)

Year	Model			
	FORD	BUICK	TOYOTA	VOLKSWAGEN
1965	2,020–4,953	2,343–4,440	1,616–3,495	1,595–2,765
1966	2,060–4,879	2,348–4,424	1,760–3,430	1,585–2,595
1967	2,118–4,825	2,411–4,469	1,760–3,430	1,639–2,955
1968	2,252–4,924	2,513–4,615	1,870–3,585	1,699–2,499
1969	1,995–4,964	2,562–4,701	1,686–3,583	1,799–2,775
1970	1,995–5,182	2,685–4,854	1,727–3,583	1,839–2,875
1971	1,919–5,516	2,847–5,253	1,798–3,810	1,845–3,122
1972	1,960–5,293	2,925–5,149	1,956–4,199	1,999–3,329
1973	2,021–5,577	2,605–5,221	1,998–4,335	2,199–3,825
1974	2,442–6,799	2,875–5,748	2,199–5,043	2,625–4,440
1975	2,919–7,701	3,234–6,516	2,711–6,138	2,895–4,850
1976	2,895–7,790	3,435–6,852	2,789–6,480	3,499–5,545
1977	3,077–7,990	3,642–7,358	2,788–6,799	3,499–5,629
1978	2,995–10,143	3,706–8,087	4,102–7,604	4,220–6,540

SOURCE: *Automotive Trade Statistics, 1964–1980,* 65–68.

the resources for a major push, and for another the Rabbit and other models weren't as attractive as the Toyota and Nissan lines. More to the point, VW was in fact and generally perceived as being an American company. It was plagued by low profit margins, necessitated by domestic wage rates and pressures to keep prices down so as to compete with the Japanese, as well as the growing sentiment that foreigners manufacture cars better than do Americans. One saying of the time was that there were some things Fritz could do far better than Frank, implying that the Germans were superior and more skilled and dedicated workers. This belief was reinforced when it was learned that VW Manufacturing Company of America was having trouble with several of its domestic suppliers, whose quality control failed to meet German standards. (The lesson wasn't lost on the Japanese, who monitored the VW experience carefully, intending to learn as much from it as they could for when they made their move to manufacture passenger cars in the United States.)

Ironically VW, which had done so much in the 1950s to develop the idea that Germans were hard-working, intelligent, and sticklers for quality, found the concept had come back to haunt them. Just as the Beetle may have suffered earlier for having been a foreign product, so the Rabbit had problems because would-be purchasers knew that it was put together by American rather than European or Japanese workers. In the process VW had become a more limited company in the American market, competing more with firms like Volvo than across the board with Toyota and Nissan.

The Japanese Big Two continued their cautious policies during the last years of the decade. They explored the possibilities of the sports car and cars for the "youth" market, knowing that higher profit margins could be had from these vehicles than from small sedans and wanting to solidify positions there against the time when they might have to cut back on sales due to American restrictions. Toyota, whose Celica and sports version of the Corolla were big hits, led the way. More important than these ventures, however, was an interesting double action that transpired in the late 1970s. While Detroit was downsizing, the Japanese were upgrading.

That the Japanese would upgrade had been predicted by students of that country's industrial scene, and for that matter by American manufacturers who had experienced being run down by the Japanese bulldozer. Earlier, in such fields as textiles, steel, cameras, and varieties of consumer electronics, Japanese firms would come in with inexpensive products, accepting little or no profits, in the hope of obtaining market share. Then, when several American competitors were forced from the scene and the remaining competitors were demoralized, the Japanese would simultaneously upgrade their products and raise prices. So it would be that the reputation would pass through three stages: from low priced to good value to high quality.

Such an approach wasn't realistic in the early 1970s. The Big Three were simply too well entrenched in the upper reaches of the sedan market; the American driver, who enjoyed his big four-door Oldsmobile or Chrysler and who used it for long trips, carrying four passengers and a trunk full of baggage, wasn't interested in a Corolla or a Datsun B-210. The Japanese might contest the Europeans for a share of the sports car market, and so they did, but in this period the chances of significantly improving the small economy sedan image seemed remote.

Then came the oil shock, the well-publicized recalls and flaws in American sedans, and the startling price boosts for Big Three cars. These allowed the Japanese companies to capitalize on their models' fuel economy and reputation for worksmanship and to use both to bring in more luxurious products.

The problem of upsizing was also resolved in this period. It was thought originally that the Japanese might have to bring in sedans comparable in dimensions and power to the ones Americans had long enjoyed. But because of a variety of market and governmental factors, Detroit was downsizing, in effect, coming in with specifications not much different from those of Japanese luxury cars manufactured for domestic consumption. Thus, the Japanese wouldn't have to create wholly new models, but rather bring to the United States cars already in production or about to be introduced. Now a slightly larger Toyota would compete against a much smaller Buick. Moreover, the Big Three would have to spend billions of dollars on research, designs, and new machinery, whereas the Japanese were spared many of these costs. The Americans would have to fight on the Japanese turf, and at a disadvantage.

Toyota and Datsun took the lead. Toyota introduced the Cressida to the American market in 1978. This car, whose $8,279 price placed it in low end of the luxury class, came fully equipped, and its fine appointments surprised motorists who hadn't known the Japanese were capable of turning out such a model. The Cressida was 185 inches long overall, with a 104-inch wheelbase, which were 5 and 6 inches, respectively, shorter than the smallest Mercedes, and at 2,816 pounds more than 800 pounds heavier than the Corolla. It was powered by a six-cylinder, 108-hp engine, so there wasn't the appreciable power loss from air-conditioner use that bothered some Toyota owners. The Cressida offered the price of the Toyota and the luxury of the Mercedes. Although the Japanese didn't say as much, it represented the initial step in upgrading, which would be followed by others, the most important of which would be the redesign of the Corona, which was given a higher price tag and targeted at an upgraded audience.

Datsun's 810 sedan (soon to be renamed the Maxima) was in the same class as the Cressida, with similar specifications and price. Like the Toyota entry, it was marketed to two kinds of audiences: owners of B-210s and 510s who were interested in upgrading and those accustomed to driving Buicks, Mercurys, and Chryslers who were interested in purchasing a Japanese car, but who had found that the smaller models didn't meet their size, luxury, and status requirements.

Neither the Cressida nor the Maxima made much of an impact initially, and the Japanese didn't push them particularly hard. But by 1982, they had developed a following, and there was talk that the two companies soon would bring over their top-of-the-line cars, Toyota's Century and Nissan's President, costing upward of $17,000 each, which would compete with Mercedes, Jaguar, BMW, and the like for the high-status segment of the market. But even without these cars Toyota and Datsun had a full line to go against GM and Ford and one that was more complete than Chrysler's. Thus, the dream of the post–World War II American independents for a fourth major corporation that would compete head-to-head against GM and Ford was on the verge of realization—but by two Japanese companies. By 1979 the sedan price range for Toyota went from $3,748 for the two-door Corolla to $8,879 for the Cressida station wagon; at Datsun, the B-210 two-door went for $3,899 and the Maxima wagon for $8,529.

Although Toyota and Nissan retained their top and follow-up positions in the import category they did face challenges from Subaru, Mazda, and especially Honda, all of which were growing more rapidly, while Mitsubishi was negotiating to free itself from Chrysler and mounting a marketing effort on its own.

By the late 1970s automobiles manufactured by these companies were no longer exotic, models accepted somewhat reluctantly when purchasers wished to avoid waiting lines at Toyota and Datsun or because of some novel, desirable mechanical or design feature.

Mitsubishi's increasingly tense relationship with Chrysler led to chronic rumors that a corporate divorce was on the way, or at the very least, that Mitsubishi would negotiate for a degree of freedom in marketing its own cars in the United States. Such talk had substance. Chrysler's introduction of its Omni/Horizon in 1978 removed some of the incentive for dealers to push the Colt and the Arrow. Furthermore, after 1980 the captive imports no longer would count when it came to calculating a company's CAFE, which meant that Ford would have to reconsider importing its Fiesta and Capri as would Chrysler its Mitsubishi products.

It was known that Chrysler was in financial difficulties, although few realized just how serious the situation had become, but in any event, Mitsubishi was in a good position to make a cash offer for some if not all its freedom. Chrysler was reluctant to negotiate, however. Although the Colt and Arrow sedans may have been made redundant by the Omni/Horizon, some of the Mitsubishi sports models were doing well. In the Colt Champ, Plymouth dealers had a low-priced, high-quality,

SALES OF JAPANESE CARS, 1974–1978					
	1974	1975	1976	1977	1978
Toyota	269,376	322,553	396,723	576,728	536,682
Datsun	245,273	331,203	350,403	488,217	432,700
Honda	41,719	102,389	150,929	223,633	274,876
Subaru	22,980	41,591	48,928	80,826	103,274
Mazda	75,079	69,384	41,179	56,193	80,017
Mitsubishi	42,925	60,356	78,972	118,024	76,210

SOURCE: *Ward's Automotive Yearbook, 1978,* 104.

fuel-efficient vehicle better than anything Chrysler had in its future. Moreover, the Americans had some success with Mitsubishi small trucks, and Chrysler negotiated an arrangement to purchase 200,000 four-cylinder engines from Mitsubishi for the Omni/Horizon, with Mitsubishi responding by purchasing some automatic transmissions from Chrysler. Still, the Japanese persisted, awaiting the time when they could break loose from what they considered a most unfortunate arrangement.

Subaru had a unique niche of its own by 1976. Although the company's sedans and station wagons sold well, Subaru's best-known feature was its four-wheel drive, available on most models and quite popular in the snowbelt. American Motors also had a four-wheel-drive vehicle that was not as economical to buy and own. In the early 1980s, these vehicles accounted for half of the company's sales.

That Subaru didn't do even better wasn't due to any deficiencies in the offerings. Rather, it could be attributed to its parent Fuji Heavy Industries' initial and continuing unwillingness to fund a dealership development program in the face of stiff competition from other Japanese companies. Subarus were often taken on by Volkswagen dealers, who had been left without a low-priced model after the Beetle was discontinued, hardly the kind of arrangement from which to challenge Toyota and Datsun. Fuji's reluctance to make a major financial commitment was evidenced by its establishment, in 1968, of Subaru of America as a publicly owned corporation. Fuji retained 48.7 percent of the shares and sold the rest, mostly to Americans.

In 1975–1976, Mazda came close not only to losing its place in the American market but also to going bankrupt at home. The reason was the Wankel, the once-heralded engine that was a prime victim of the gas crunch. Domestic sales were cut in half in 1974 and shipments to the United States were down by a third, with almost all the losses attributed to the Wankel-powered RX series. American observers of the Japanese scene monitored the situation carefully, because one of the purported weaknesses of the Japanese industrial structure was the inability to absorb failure, as a result of guaranteed employment and the bonus system. "They have a bicycle economy," said one critic. "It goes along fine so long as forward movement is maintained, but goes on its side should it have to stop."

This was not so at Toyo Kogyo, however. The corporation's lead bank, Sumitomo, provided fresh capital and helped restructure management, while the labor force was cut by 10,000 through attrition and the payment of bonuses to workers willing to accept early retirement. Production was shifted from the RXs to piston-driven cars and one of them, sent to the United States in 1976 as the Mizer, managed to halt the collapse. The company introduced a two-door hatchback economy model the following year. Known as the GLC (Great Little Car), it was priced at $3,245, which was more than $600 below the least expensive Datsun and slightly more than $100 over the bottom-of-the-line Corolla. Thus, Mazda, whose early cars had appealed to middle-income purchasers, repositioned itself in the lower end of the price spectrum.

Toyo Kogyo, meanwhile, worked to refine the Wankel, and a totally redesigned rotary was placed in its sports car, the RX-7. A speedy machine with a startling pickup, the RX-7 was priced at $6,365, substantially below the Datsun 280Z to which it was often compared, and it soon gained a following. Mazda would not fulfill its earlier promise of challenging the Big Two, but it did survive, itself no mean accomplishment considering the problems it had to overcome.

Once more Honda proved the maverick of the group. At a time when the other Japanese companies were fighting the idea of manufacturing cars in the United States, Honda agreed to produce motorcycles here, starting in 1979 in a plant near Columbus, Ohio. Honda even demonstrated an unexpected willingness to talk with United Automobile Workers representatives. Earlier, the corporation had gambled and won in refusing to consider the Wankel when others were convinced it was the engine of the future. In the mid-1970s, when Toyota and Nissan were heading in the direction of becoming full-line companies in the American market, Honda elected to pin all of its hopes on a single model, the Accord, and once again was successful. The Accord was not only a huge sales success, but its design and mechanical components were also imitated, by the Americans as well as the Japanese.

Part of the reason for this was the kind of company Soichiro Honda had created; as has been shown, he was highly idiosyncratic, taking a positive delight in confounding the conventional wisdom in a country and industry where such things simply were not done. Then too, while the other Japanese companies were manufacturing cars for the domestic market and sending some of them abroad, Honda deliberately set out to make Americans, not the Japanese, his leading customers. In 1977, when Toyota and Nissan were sending a third of their production to the United States, Honda sent over half his. Thus, Honda had to be extremely sensitive to American emissions legislation, marketing problems, the dollar-yen ratio—in fact, everything that might affect the marketability of his cars, including the image of the Japanese industry in the American press.

The Accord arrived in the United States in 1976. Larger than the Civic (a 94-inch wheelbase, 2,018 pounds versus an 87-inch wheelbase, 1,665 pounds) and more expensive ($4,145 versus $2,779), its dimensions approximated those of the Toyota Corolla and Datsun B-210, while costing several hundred dollars more, as much in fact as a Rabbit diesel. Within a year, it had become the most wanted imported sedan, with waiting lists and would-be buyers offering premiums to dealers who would put them at the top of the list. Two years later, in 1978, the Accord was the second-best selling import behind the Corolla and would have been the leader had Honda been able to manufacture and ship more cars.

The Accord was highly praised in all the automobile magazines, and *Consumer Reports* called it "one of the best subcompacts we have ever tested." Although the price was high, it was for a sedan that was more fully equipped than most. In fact, Honda advertised that "the list of standard equipment starts where most lists end." Thus, the basic model arrived with a five-speed transmission, FM/AM radio, interval windshield wiper, rear windshield wiper, side- as well as rear-window defrosters, radial tires, and a tachometer, which meant that in terms of value the Accord was on par with the other Japanese imports. Like them too, it was fuel efficient (26 mpg) and initially didn't require unleaded gasoline, because it was equipped with a CVCC engine.

Early on some analysts predicted the Accord would find favor with owners of Honda motorcycles, but such wasn't the case. Rather, surveys indicate that Honda purchasers weren't much different from those who under ordinary circumstances would have purchased Toyotas and Datsuns, which is to say the Accord was taking sales from the Corolla and the B-210.

The factors that brought the Accord success—which spilled over to the Civic, because those disappointed in not being able to purchase the former often settled for the smaller car—were difficult to determine. It wasn't an unusual car like the early VW. Nor did it possess that combination of low price, high value, good quality, and American feel that contributed to the Corolla's popularity. Part of the reason might have been that many Americans wanted to own the latest model from Japan and more than a few might have been lured by its extras.

The basic factors behind the Accord's performance, however, seem to have been that it was perceived as a luxury car, while sporting a medium-range price tag in a time of continuing sticker shock. The price rose steadily—by 1979 the Accord was selling for over $6,000, while the Civic listed at $4,100. But so did the weight, which shot up to 2,200 pounds while all the other dimensions grew as well. Contrary to practice, Honda enlarged his key model, added more amenities, boosted his prices, and in the process transformed this car into one that competed against the Cressida and Maxima for the higher reaches of the Japanese import market, and with great success.

In 1978, too, Honda brought over its sports car, the Prelude, which at $6,445 proved quite competitive, taking sales from the Celica among others. During that recession year, when all other Japanese auto companies suffered domestic sales declines and the Big Two had troubles selling their cars to Americans who suddenly turned to the mid-size vehicles, Honda increased its exports to the United States by 23 percent.

That 500,000 Civics, Accords, and Preludes could have been sold in 1979 had they been available was obvious. Whether through good fortune or design, Honda had created and marketed what was to become the standard of excellence and value for the early 1980s.

As the 1980s wore on, it became evident that the Accord suited the times admirably. Customers whose last cars had cost $3,000 to $4,000 and who now had to go to five digit figures for automobiles had no intention of trading them in every few years. Demands for high quality and durability became more insistent than ever, and as will be seen, were heeded by auto-makers throughout the world. At the same time, the whipsawing caused by alternating fuel shortages and glut resulted in a compromise size for standard sedans—which happened to be that of the Accord. The family auto of the future would have to accommodate four adults with a reasonable degree of comfort, have such amenities as air conditioning and all the latest electronic gadgets, be trouble-free, and get around 30 mpg. That pretty well described the Accord. Although it would be going too far to suggest that this car led the way in the transformation, it might be claimed that it became the symbol of the move and the standard against which the others would be measured.

This, too, was something to be pondered in Detroit during its period of reappraisal and reform.

---————— ·16· —————---

The American Response

Japan still holds the competitive edge in the small car field, owing to our past experience and generally superior technology. But the U.S. auto industry has the technological sophistication and financial resources to close this gap if it wants to. Detroit seems determined to do just that and, frankly, we are worried.

YOSHIKI YAMASAKI, chairman,
Toyo Kogyo,
1981

For us, the confidence of the consumer is the whole ballgame.

"PETE" ESTES, president,
General Motors,
1980

We will be coming up with new products. I predict they will be highly sophisticated, very technologically oriented. We won't be making hula hoops.

ROGER SMITH, chairman
General Motors,
1982

In the autumn of 1979, General Motors Chairman Thomas Murphy announced the development of a five-year, $40 billion plan, at the end of which the corporation's line of cars would be completely revamped. With understandable hyperbole, he called it "the most ambitious product and facility improvement program ever undertaken by any corporation in the world at any time in history."

Murphy made it appear that this was the first shot in a new battle. Detroit had finally learned its lesson and knew what had to be done. General Motors would take whatever actions were necessary to regain market share lost to the Japanese during the 1970s. The struggle wouldn't be over with the completion of the five-year plan, but would rather be an ongoing one, lasting perhaps for decades.

Soon thereafter, Ford and American Motors announced they too would restyle their entire lines. Although still in danger of bankruptcy, Chrysler had already signaled its intention to transform itself into a different kind of company, one which in hewing to a narrower line would be highly effective in its markets.

The total bill for the rest of the industry would come to approximately another $40 billion. Such were the chips required to turn Detroit around.

That such a sum could be raised seemed plausible, although in the process, GM and Ford would have to expand their long-term indebtedness to the point of having to accept lower credit ratings. As its price for remaining in the game, AM had to play the role of a subsidiary of a foreign-owned corporation. Chrysler would survive, although this would remain in doubt for another two years and would be accomplished by selling its profitable defense business to General Dynamics, drawing upon government loans, renegotiating contracts with the United Auto Workers, abandoning most foreign markets, and implementing a harsh program of economy and cutbacks.

All understood what would be required. The American companies would have to turn out well-designed, trouble-free, efficient cars to sell at prices competitive with those of the imports. They would have to convince the public that Detroit was as capable of manufacturing cars with these qualities as were the Japanese. Government assistance would be needed, especially to keep imports from taking an even larger share of the market than they already had. Union leaders and the rank and file would have to cooperate, too, in holding wages and benefits down while increasing productivity.

Which is to say that the problems facing the Americans in the early 1980s weren't much different from those the Japanese had to overcome twenty years earlier. In 1965, domestic customers found it hard to believe a Toyota or a Datsun possessed the quality and reliability they had known in Chevys and Fords. In 1980, the car shoppers weren't convinced an Oldsmobile could match the Honda Accord or even whether the Cadillac was as fine a car as the Maxima and the Cressida.

Although all four companies had the same goal, each adopted a different strategy for the struggle, approaches that suited their traditions, circumstances, and assets.

General Motors remained the largest and most powerful automobile company, not only in the United States, but the world. With 1979 sales of $66.3 billion, it was also the biggest industrial enterprise, with operations on all continents. In 1979 1.7 million cars came from its overseas plants alone, almost as many as turned out by Nissan. Four times larger than Toyota and more than ten times larger than Honda, there was little wonder the Japanese felt that GM could crush them if things fell into place for it.

Yet GM had glaring weaknesses. If giants can destroy all in their path, they also move slowly. For all the reforms initiated by Sloan and refined by his successors, GM was a cumbersome beast. True, division chiefs competed with one another, knowing the one with the best record stood a good chance of advancing to the top at executive headquarters in Detroit, but this often led to inefficiencies and duplications of effort. This wasn't too serious a problem during flush times, but GM had to support that enormous capital-spending program in the early 1980s, which meant that more than ever the board's major task would be to gather and allocate resources among competing claimants. General Motors went to the capital markets repeatedly in order to finance the projects, and it showed on the balance sheet. The corporation's long-term debt in 1979 was $880 million, and its working capital that year came to $6.7 billion; by 1981, at which time Chairman Roger Smith was obliged to announce that part of the spending program would be deferred so as to build up reserves, the long-term debt had risen to over $4 billion and the working capital was down to $1.2 billion. Such was the price of competition in the automobile industry in the 1980s.

General Motors pinned its hopes on a well-thought-out, essentially conservative plan that took its strengths into account. The corporation knew that the Japanese inroads in the past half decade had been made at the expense of Ford and Chrysler; throughout this period, GM's share of the market had fluctuated around the 42- to 48-percent level. Thus, although domestic buyers may have turned toward Toyota, Datsun, Honda, and the others, it was not because they had rejected GM, where customer loyalty remained strong. In this respect, as well as others, GM was in a more advantageous position than the two other Big Three companies.

Under Smith's guidance, GM developed a two-pronged strategy. In the first place, the entire line would be downsized, the large two-ton cars of the earlier era being replaced by small- to medium-size models. Not only was there to be a series of small Chevys, but also a four-cylinder Cadillac, to be known as the Cimarron, would be offered. A Honda look-alike priced competitively with that import, the Cimarron was correctly viewed as a gamble and even an admission that Cadillac was threatened by the Japanese cars.

The second prong involved mechanization of the factory, elements of which were frankly adapted from Japanese models. By late 1981, the corporation had 1,200 robots either already installed or on order, performing such tasks as painting, inspecting, assembling, and die-casting. Two years later the GM robot work force came to 2,000 (against half as many at Ford) and the corporation boasted that within a year its factories would be more automated than most factories in Japan.

Not only did robots replace labor with capital—a technique pioneered by Ford and Sloan between the wars—but they also allowed the corporation to bypass legally the Environmental Protection Agency's regulations regarding the workplace. All the companies were interested in robotics, but none as much as GM—again, because the corporation had the requisite capital. Smith then proceeded along the line of backward integration, this time in alliance with a Japanese corporation, Fujitsu, the parent of Fujitsu Fanuc, a major manufacturer of industrial robots. Out of their cooperation came GM Fanuc, to be based in the United States, and from which, in 1984, came robots not only for GM, but the entire automobile industry as well.

Ford's strategy was quite different, and also derived from its position in the late 1970s. With a far more extensive—and profitable—overseas commitment but less capital, and always suffering from a lack of mid-price cars to go against GM, Ford opted for a global approach, with piecemeal alterations then and more significant ones to come. Dictated by necessity and resources, this approach was also taken with an eye toward squeezing as much profit as possible from large cars before they were forced from the road.

Knowing that GM was downsizing rapidly, Ford opted to concentrate initially on the small, relatively fuel efficient cars already on hand, such as the Pinto and Mustang, to which would soon be added the Fairmont/Zephyr, and to use them to compensate for the long, heavy, expensive, and highly profitable Versailles, Lincolns, and Mark VIs, hoping to sell the latter to Cadillac owners unhappy with the smaller models. Then, as CAFE requirement dictated, Ford, too, would turn out smaller versions of the luxury cars, but only after making one last effort for profits from the older behemoths.

Except for finances Ford was better situated than GM to enter the new era. By 1980, one-third each of Ford's cars came with a four-, six-, or eight-cylinder engine. In contrast, only one of every four GM cars had a four-cylinder engine, with two-thirds powered by eight cylinders. Lee Iacocca's knack for turning out small cars with relatively high price tags and profit margins paid off, even though, as will be seen, Iacocca himself was no longer on the scene to gain credit for his accomplishments.

Ford eliminated its dividend in 1981 to preserve capital and also floated new bond issues, with balance sheet results similar to those of GM. In 1979–1981, Ford's long-term debt rose from $1.3 billion to $2.7 billion and its working capital declined to a bare $236 million from $2.3 billion; and in 1982 it would come in at a frightening negative $1.6 billion, because of mounting deficits and heavy capital spending.

Ford used this money to create several new cars, drawing upon its European experience and designs. Parts would be manufactured in those countries where costs were low, and the same models would be fabricated in facilities on all continents. Thus among the domestic corporations, Ford pioneered in the creation of World Cars.

Ford wasn't alone in this, just as GM had not had a monopoly on robotics. Ford was the American leader in multinational cooperation as a result of its position and assets when the changeover began. The corporation couldn't afford the high capital investments an extensive commitment to robots would have required, and so it hoped to cut costs by manufacturing or purchasing components in low labor cost areas and through economies of scale made possible by offering a limited number of cars worldwide.

At least Ford had the luxury of evaluating resources and coming up with a strategy. Resources were minuscule at AM, and that corporation had to take assistance where it could be found. Historically the most marginal and chancy of the American manufacturers, AM had revenues of $3.1 billion in

1979, so it was hardly a midget by industry standards. Yet it was bigger than Fuji Heavy Industries and only slightly smaller than Toyo Kogyo, which indicated that viability in Japan was possible with fewer sales and also with the smaller profit margins realized by AM.

Given a better credit rating, AM might have opted for the routes taken by GM and Ford, namely borrowing heavily and using the money, together with cash flow, to restructure the product line. This not being feasible, the corporation cast about for a savior.

What domestic corporation with responsible leadership would have been interested? Although its AM General division, which manufactured vehicles for the military, was quite profitable, the rest of the company showed little promise. Its cars, led by the soon-to-be discontinued Gremlin and the Spirit, were indifferently received, and sales were on a downward slope, having declined from 255,000 in 1977 to 160,000 in 1979 (less than 2 percent of the market), when its losses came to $156 million. Almost to a unit, AM dealers were undercapitalized, demoralized, and obliged to add one or more of the less popular imports to their lines merely to survive. American Motors might have gone under years earlier had it not been for a large volume of sales in the corporation's home base of Kenosha, Wisconsin, mostly to individuals hoping to save the jobs of their friends and relatives.

Yet AM was not without assets. It did have an organization and something of a following. Among its leaders were individuals who understood the domestic market and who, given more in the way of capital, might become more aggressive marketers. There was also a dedication to small cars that went back to the time of George Mason and George Romney. Although only a quarter of the line was powered by four-cylinder engines, more Spirits, the company's most popular car, sold with that power plant than with six cylinders.

Renault was interested in obtaining a controlling interest in AM, for good and obvious reasons. The $13 billion corporation was France's leading auto manufacturer and fifth on the world list (behind VW, but ahead of Peugeot and Fiat). That Renault generally reported deficits wasn't as consequential as might ordinarily have been the case, because it had been nationalized and received substantial governmental subsidies. Renault's mission was to throw back the Japanese invaders in the domestic market (with aid in the form of high tariffs and related legislation) and expand sales so as to provide jobs for French workers.

Even before nationalization, Renault had had ambitions to expand meaningfully into the North American market. The corporation had blundered there during the 1950s, at a time when given the proper cars and service facilities it might have enjoyed far greater successes than it did. Now Renault was prepared to make a new start, and a merger with AM would provide them with a ready-made dealership operation and organization, to which would be added cars already on the European market.

Renault knew Congress was considering legislation to restrict imports; if this passed, the Japanese and others would have to erect facilities in the United States. Indeed, Honda already had plans to do just that. By merging with AM, Renault would be able to manufacture its cars in Kenosha, bypassing whatever tariffs and regulations that might be put in place in the 1980s.

It was, then, an excellent fit. The combination of the AM organization and Renault's cars might allow both corporations to achieve the success in the United States neither could have had on its own.

The relationship began in 1979, when the two corporations signed an agreement. American Motors became the exclusive North American importer and distributor of Renault cars, while the French corporation would market AM products in France and several other countries. This was followed by direct purchases of approximately $500 million in AM securities, which gave Renault a half interest in the corporation. American Motors' chairman, Gerald Meyers, resigned in 1982 to be succeeded by President Paul Tippett, Jr., who then named Renault's Jose Dedeurwaerder President and Chief Operating Officer. Other Renault personnel took their places in the corporation and on the board, as the first modern trans-Atlantic entry was born.

American Motors was thus saved. In the immediate future it would be the manufacturer and distributor of French automobiles, although later on, when new cars were to be created, AM designers would play a role. A variant upon the Ford theme, this arrangement was to create another version of the World Car. In the process, however, AM became, for all intents and purposes, a Renault subsidiary.

The saga of Chrysler illustrates both the industry's malaise and its ability to recover and become solvent. It also provided the industry with a new charismatic leader, the most important person to emerge from the industry since George Romney.

Chrysler's fall from grace wasn't sudden, nor were its financial difficulties in the late 1970s unknown. In 1976, in attempting to revive its reputation and increase sales, Chrysler had offered an extended warranty, and one official had joked that the cars would be guaranteed "for 12,000 miles or until the company goes out of business." Chrysler's deficit then was $282 million. It would earn $453 million during the next two years, but in 1978 it lost $205 million. Unable to move its big cars during the 1973 gas crunch and caught with insufficient medium-size and large models when customers turned to them in mid-decade, plagued with recalls and poor quality control, Chrysler had replaced AM as the industry's nominee for auto corporation most likely to go under.

As losses mounted early in 1979, there was talk of a merger with Ford, which unless it transpired would result in the layoff of perhaps as many as 100,000 workers with a like number joining them as the ripples spread. Chairman John Riccardo and President Gene Cafiero had lost the confidence of Wall Street; they were unable to raise funds to keep the corporation afloat and had failed in their early attempts to obtain government help.

Meanwhile, Lee Iacocca had been fired as president by Henry Ford II and was seeking employment elsewhere in the industry. Soon thereafter he entered into negotiations with Chrysler, and in late 1978, he agreed to come on as president, with the understanding that there would be a promotion to chairman and CEO within a year.

Whether or not Iacocca or anyone else could save Chrysler seemed doubtful at the time, but the essential strategy for recovery and future development was in place when he arrived. Riccardo and Cafiero had made a major commitment to downsizing with the Omni/Horizon, which would be followed by the "K-cars" (the Reliant/Aries), which were to replace the Volare/Aspen; if all went well, they would be true World Cars and Chrysler's major product for the early 1980s. By 1980, 40 percent of Chrysler's fleet would be equipped with four-cylinder engines and only 20 percent with eight-cylinder; under the Riccardo-Cafiero plan, more than half of production by 1982 would have been of four-cylinder cars with front-mounted transmissions.

Iacocca's initial contributions were in the areas of sales and publicity. He managed to restore credibility to both the corporation and its cars, in a way that perhaps no one else might have done. He then streamlined operations, cutting Chrysler's break-even point to a sustainable level. In the process he became a national figure, who by 1983 was even being talked about as a possible presidential candidate.

Yet it isn't clear that Detroit would have been badly wounded by a Chrysler bankruptcy. Given the blessings of the Justice Department, Ford might have come in and taken over operations without a significant loss of jobs. The product lines of the two companies would have complemented one another, enabling Ford to divert human and financial assets into more productive enterprises. Such a solution would have saved Chrysler's products and jobs and created a more viable Ford.

Finally, the wisdom of government guarantees to save any company was and is questionable.

The salvaging of Chrysler required an unusual mix of government, labor, and management cooperation, together with the bending of rules by financial institutions and suppliers. The result was the most dramatic bailout in American business history.

Iacocca's agreement with Chrysler was that he would be in full charge of operations, while Riccardo concentrated on obtaining loan guarantees and placating the corporation's suppliers, but realistically, the government would not have cooperated without pressures from organized labor, and the vendors would have refused to make concessions were it not for concrete results in the factories and salesrooms. From the first, then, Iacocca and United Auto Workers President Douglas Fraser were the keys to the corporation's survival.

Federal loan guarantees of $1.5 billion were granted in late 1979, the government receiving warrants to purchase 14.4 million shares of Chrysler common at $13 a share, as a "sweetener" few seriously expected would be exercised. Later on the Canadian government added $100 million to the total, in the hope of saving jobs in Canada. The union allowed concessions that amounted to $5,000 per hourly worker, making Chrysler the lowest-cost North American auto manufacturer. Further cuts plus a wage freeze followed, with Chrysler inviting Fraser to take a seat on the board; this, too, was unprecedented.

Meanwhile, Iacocca instituted a program of plant closings and by the end of 1980 had cut the work force by more than 30 percent, with the UAW's approval. French automaker Peugeot-Citroen, which in 1978 had exchanged its shares for Chrysler's operations in that country, made the corporation a $100 million loan secured by that stock. The twenty-odd banks that held more than $4 billion of Chrysler's paper agreed to a loan restructuring, while suppliers granted close to $40 million in concessions.

Never before had any American corporation received so massive an infusion of funds and credits along with other assistance. MITI and other Japanese agencies had not done anything consequential to aid Toyo Kogyo when it was close to failure. Those who earlier had spoken of Japan Inc.'s aid to that nation's auto industry might later have reflected that, with the Chrysler program, the United States had made a commitment of major consequence, reversing long-standing policies that had ensured competition and prevented combinations.

All this took place in an atmosphere of near-panic. Unemployment was rising throughout the industry and this, combined with federal anti-inflation policies, exacerbated what might otherwise have been a mild economic decline, turning it into the worst of the post–World War II recessions. By August 1980, one-fourth of the industry labor force—more than a quarter of a million auto workers—had been laid off. All the companies were obliged to cut back, with Chrysler alone permanently shuttering ten plants. During the next three years approximately 3,000 dealers would go out of business. Some 650,000 jobs in steel, rubber, glass, machinery, suppliers, and other fields would be threatened. Newspapers reminded readers that one-fifth of the GNP was directly or indirectly derived from automobiles. A pall fell over Detroit, as some commentators, knowing fully what they were saying, indicated that the Japanese had inflicted upon Detroit the equivalent of another Pearl Harbor. As unfair and exaggerated as this was, it remains to be noted that at the end of 1981, imports had 27 percent of the market, almost twice as much as a decade earlier. The connection between the two developments was obvious, as was the need to rejuvenate the American industry by almost any means. Pressures from the Detroit Establishment intensified, as did those from the unions.

The American response of the early 1980s took two forms. The first came from the industry, producing new lines of cars; the second from government, limiting foreign imports. In both cases, there was a resemblance to Japanese practices, but too much should not be made of this. Although Detroit studied Japanese methods, the approaches used were more American than anything else, and the actions of Congress in the foreign trade field resulted from domestic pressure, not any desire to emulate MITI.

The turnabout began in 1979–1982, when each of the Big Three introduced what turned out to be the initial wave of domestically manufactured models of the new dispensation. Not all of them reflected the new strategies—which is to say they didn't have transversely mounted, four-cylinder engines or front-wheel drives, the symbols of the changeover. Most were designed more to halt the inroads made by imports than anything else. In other words, they were to keep the enemy at bay until the second wave would be ready. Lee Iacocca intimated as much in June 1980, when he told a reporter, "Today, we are caught a bit short of our planned-for products and capacity [to make small cars]. As a result we face a serious permanent erosion in our dealer networks, market shares and customer loyalties."

The first-wave vehicles were the Omni/Horizon and Reliant/Aries (Chrysler), Fairmont/Zephyr and Escort/Lynx (Ford), and the Citation/Phoenix/Omega/Skylark (GM). The Omni/Horizon, which has already been discussed, was a relative failure; although arriving before the others, it was unable to capture a significant portion of the market. Yet it was a near-perfect "Econobox," with most of the features Americans were supposed to prefer in imports—including European and Japanese parts. Originally, Chrysler had hoped these models would not only draw sales from the Japanese, but also make inroads among former customers who had been won over to GM and Ford. The first of the front-wheel drive, four-cylinder models, its failure troubled not only Chrysler, but the others as well. Still, as Chrysler went to great pains to stress, these weren't designed as "company savers." That role was to be filled by the aforementioned Reliant/Aries, the K-cars.

The first Reliants and Aries left the factory in June 1980. There was a drama in the event rarely found in Detroit, and also a sign of the American industry's desperation. Chrysler already was drawing upon its government loan guarantees, knowing that without the new line these wouldn't have been available and that if the public rejected the line, the loans would go into default. Two months earlier, Ford had refused Chrysler's final overtures toward a merger, so it was clear Chrysler was on its own. Iacocca got all the mileage out of the event that he could. "This is the beginning of the re-industrialization of America," he proclaimed, to the applause—and relief —of admiring executives and workers.

The Reliant/Aries bore a family resemblance to the Volare/Aspen, but with a 100-inch wheelbase and a weight of 2,342 pounds versus a 109-inch wheelbase and a weight of 3,250 pounds, it was much smaller. Also new was the transversely mounted engine, manufactured by Mitsubishi. Base-priced at $5,880, it was competitive with comparably equipped Fords and Chevys.

Both cars were instant successes. More than 10,000 Reliants were sold in October, the first month they were available, and the figure was up to 13,000 by December. Encouraged, Iacocca gambled on providing dealers with models loaded with expensive options, hoping to obtain greater profits per unit. He drew back when consumer resistance developed, however, after which sales picked up once again. For the model year, Chrysler turned out 229,000 Valiants and 181,000 Aries. For the time being, at least, Chrysler was saved, while Iacocca's reputation advanced. In the celebration was forgotten the fact that it wasn't he, but rather Riccardo and Cafiero who had authorized production of the Reliant/Aries. Iacocca had rescued the company, but had yet to demonstrate an ability to create the kind of models that could take the corporation beyond the mid-1980s.

General Motors' X-cars were the most ballyhooed of the front-wheel-drive generation, the long-anticipated response to the Japanese challenge from the industry giant and the entries that, more than the Reliant/Aries, were supposed to break new ground for Detroit. The result of a project that required a capital investment of $2.7 billion, it was to be the first step in the restructuring of the entire GM line. The Chevy Citation was to replace the Nova, and at the time of its introduction in April 1979, was being publicized as America's response to the Toyotas and Datsuns.

The Xs seemed small to those accustomed to purchasing and driving American vehicles, but almost standard insofar as interior dimensions were concerned. They weighed around 2,600 pounds (800 pounds less than the full-size Chevy Impala) on a 105-inch wheelbase (the Impala's was 116). A front-wheel-driven car available with either a transversely mounted four-cylinder or a new V-6 engine, dealers found that orders for the large engine outran those for the smaller by six to four.

The Citation wasn't a particularly fuel-efficient model, but the four did get around 22 mpg, which was better than the Nova, and the cars were priced competitively with several of the imports, the four-door Citation listing at $6,404 FOB Detroit.

Compare this with the Toyota Corona, which by 1980 had moved into the mid-price range, ahead of the new Tercel Starlet and the repositioned Corolla, but behind the Celica and the Cressida. This car had a 99-inch wheelbase and weighed 2,500 pounds, coming in under the Citation. But the interior dimensions were approximately the same, whereas the POE price was $6,269, or somewhat lower than the Citation. The advertised fuel economy was approximately the same for both cars. The Corona, however, was a tested model and and one with a reputation for quality, whereas American cars were notorious for developing bugs in their first year. And so it was for the Citation group. After an early burst of enthusiasm, showroom traffic slowed down. Disgruntled owners complained that the four-cylinder models were underpowered and sluggish. There were difficulties with the transmissions and reports of balky carburetors and body leaks.

With all of this, however, the Xs did sell, largely because of the gas crunch of 1979, when Americans rushed to purchase the relatively small, fuel-efficient cars, at a time when Chrysler was having trouble with its Omni/Horizon, and the Reliant/Valiant was yet to come. As will be seen, Ford's Fairmont/

Zephyr was not a true new-wave vehicle, and the company's reputation had been harmed by lawsuits originating from the Pinto's design failures.

More than 300,000 Citations were taken in 1979, whereas the X-cars as a group provided 554,000 of GM's sales, slightly less than 7 percent of the industry's total, which was considered reasonably good for an introduction year. Gratified, Chevrolet predicted that by the early 1980s more than half a million Citations alone would be purchased. (Toyota's total American sales for 1979 were 639,000.) But it hardly represented an engineering or manufacturing triumph; there were four recalls in 1980 alone, resulting from brake, suspension, fuel system, and transmission flaws.

Nonetheless, there was a mood of optimism at headquarters; in April 1979, Pontiac General Manager Robert Stempel told a reporter that "These days, it's exciting to be at GM." The strategy was unrolling nicely. The Chevette, still America's best-selling model—451,000 purchased in 1980—was to be replaced by a front-wheel-drive mini, perhaps manufactured by Isuzu, in two to three years. By then, the Citation would have become the Chevrolet Division's basic compact, to be joined by a new, yet-to-be named model (known as the "J"-car), which was somewhat smaller, but more luxurious—the aforementioned Honda Accord look-alike. The top-of-the-line Malibu, Impala, and Caprice were all to be downsized and upgraded, and similar models would come out of the Pontiac, Buick, and Oldsmobile divisions.

In 1980 the corporation's attention was riveted on the quite satisfactory sales record established by the Citation group. During that recession year, 572,000 X-cars were sold, despite continued criticisms from the automotive press and the leaking of a GM internal memo outlining deficiencies and indifferent reviews. There were eight more recalls during 1981–1983, and in the summer of 1983, the federal government levied a fine of $4 million against the corporation and demanded it recall 1.1 million X-cars sold in 1980 to repair a brake defect. Further, the government alleged that GM had known of these problems before the car was released, and knowingly provided the Highway Traffic and Safety Administration with false information regarding the models. General Motors denied the charges and indicated it would contest them in court. But the damage had been done, and the X-cars seemed doomed.

The Citation and its stablemates had been created and advertised more for Americans who were ready to accept downsizing, but still wanted domestic products, than for owners of Japanese cars; these were not World Cars, turned out to sell in Europe as well as in the domestic market. If the designs were new the approach wasn't; they were presented in the belief that Americans who were considering imports would remain loyal once they realized that Detroit had reinvented the car in its old tradition, and not anything truly new or imitative of imports. Ever the most conservative of the Big Three (and profiting greatly as a result), and geared to middle-class, middle Americans, GM still wasn't prepared to abandon the kinds of cars that had served it so well before the early 1970s. Pioneering would be left to those who had to do so or fall to the wayside, like Chrysler and Ford.

The Fairmont/Zephyr, which was Ford's replacement for the aging Maverick/Comet, was a typical compromise vehicle. It was small (106-inch wheelbase, 2,720 pounds), low priced (around $6,000, fully equipped), and available with a four-cylinder engine that got 25 mpg. But it had a rear transmission, thus requiring the transverse hump, which in so small a car meant that it had to be considered a four-passenger vehicle. Like the Omni/Horizon, the Fairmont/Zephyr boasted European components, but it wasn't considered a World Car. Rather, like the Citation, it was designed strictly for the American market. Backed by the strong Ford organization, it sold well—442,000 units in 1979, 380,000 in the 1980 recession year—but by late 1980 it was no secret that it was supposed to hold the market for the World Car being prepared for introduction the following year.

This would be Ford's Escort/Lynx, which despite its transitional role, was that corporation's "make-or-break" vehicle.

Had it failed, Ford might well have been obliged to sell major divisions, institute significant economies, and transform itself into quite a different entity from what it was, namely the second largest factor in the world industry. Given an ill-received Escort/Lynx, Ford might have slipped behind both Toyota and Nissan. As it was, Escort/Lynx was a smashing sales success, the first important step not only in Ford's recovery, but also in that of the entire industry.

Introduced for the 1981 model year in October 1980, the Escort was an instant success, with 285,000 sold, while another 91,000 Mercury Lynxes were taken. Except for the new downsized Granada, it was the sole bright spot for the Ford division. Unlike GM, Ford had no backup car like the Chevette; the discredited Pinto was being phased out, with nothing to take its place. Mustang and Fairmont sales were down sharply; as noted, both those cars were overdue for replacement, as were the Thunderbird and the LTD. Ford was already preparing new models for introduction in the 1983 model year, but until then it had to rely on the Escort.

The car was everything the Horizon and Citation attempted to be, while also possessing attributes of its own. It was a product of European design, but contributions were made by the Americans as well. Like the Chrysler and GM entries, it had the by-now mandatory transversely mounted, four-cylinder engine and front-wheel drive. There were some complaints that it was underpowered, but this was compensated for by excellent fuel economy. Moreover, the Escort listed for substantially less than the Citation and was even competitive on a price basis with the Corolla and Datsun 210.

But there was a problem, which Ford executives freely conceded. With all its success, the Escort/Lynx wasn't a moneymaker. When it would turn around couldn't be predicted, but Ford could survive until then by drawing upon its still substantial European profits. The corporation clearly was using the Escort/Lynx to grab market share, the idea being that once established, the price could be raised and profits made. This was one lesson the Americans had learned from the Japanese and were applying in their own market.

COMPARISON OF 1981 TWO-DOOR CITATION, RELIANT, AND ESCORT

	CITATION	RELIANT	ESCORT
Wheelbase	104.9 inches	99.6 inches	94.2 inches
Overall length	176.4 inches	176.0 inches	169.3 inches
Overall width	68.3 inches	68.6 inches	65.9 inches
Overall height	53.5 inches	52.3 inches	53.3 inches
Weight	2,480 pounds	2,342 pounds	2,021 pounds
Engine horsepower	84	84	65
Miles per gallon	22	25	28
Base price	$6,270	$5,880	$5,158

SOURCE: *Ward's Automotive Yearbook, 1981*, 218, 221.

Taken as a whole, these models represented the greatest overhaul in automobile marketing in history, as illustrated by two statistics. The average 1983 American car got 24.6 mpg, whereas the figure in 1977 had been 18.7. American cars outperformed imports in all but one of the seventeen weight and model categories in which they competed. Thus by early 1984, it had become evident to all who knew the statistics that, on the whole, American cars were the most fuel efficient in the world. The trouble was that few outside the industry knew this, and most Americans had an entirely different perception. Moreover, this economy came at a time when Americans were demanding larger and more powerful cars and appeared to be relatively disinterested in fuel economy.

The beginnings of government aid to salvage jobs could be seen in the late 1970s, when unemployment in the automobile and supplier industries became a concern of Congress, with measures to limit imports being introduced by Congressmen representing areas in which autos were manufactured. In February 1981, Senators John Danforth (D. Mo.) and Lloyd Bentsen (D. Tex.) cosponsored legislation to place a 1.6 million unit quota on the importation of foreign cars, and despite some embarrassment when it was learned that Danforth owned two Mercedes, and Bentsen one, the measure won strong support in the upper house.

Led by Toyota, several Japanese auto companies mounted

campaigns to demonstrate that, in some respects, the United States actually benefited from the importation of automobiles. Did the imports take jobs from Americans? Of course, but the automobile import business directly employed more than 150,-000 Americans. Toyota U.S.A. alone accounted for 36,000 of them, whereas in 1981 the corporation spent $1.7 billion on payrolls, supplies, and taxes. In 1981, the corporation placed orders with American suppliers for $189 million worth of goods, mostly headlights, antipollution devices, and seat fabrics. The figure for 1979 had come to $98 million and would advance steadily throughout the decade. Moreover, the money Americans spent on Japanese automobiles was used to purchase products and services from the United States. Japan was second only to Canada as a trading partner, and the largest importer of American farm products.

To this, congressional, industry, and labor spokesmen responded that far fewer jobs had been created than were lost, and that although in 1980 Japan had imported $12.5 billion worth of American goods, its exports to the United States stood at $20.8 billion.

Protestations to the contrary, the Japanese knew that restrictions were coming; during the past decade, many European and Latin American countries had acted to curb auto imports, the Europeans tending to do so with tariffs, the others through "domestic content laws," requiring a set percentage of parts for cars to have been manufactured locally. Now the United States was considering both. The Japanese were being urged to manufacture (or at the very least assemble) more of their cars in the United States, thus following VW's lead, or face the probability that stiff tariffs would be imposed. There was a third alternative: the Japanese might voluntarily limit their exports to the United States, thus obviating the need for legislation bound to harm relations between the two countries.

The Japanese tended to argue for time and patience. Local content laws wouldn't be necessary, they said, for domestic purchases were rising without them. Their spokesmen asserted that by purchasing Japanese cars, American consumers were signaling a preference for small sedans, not imports, and that once Detroit turned out reduced-size vehicles in volume, the percentage of the market taken by Japanese cars would shrink. "Imports have been drawn in to fill the *temporary* gap between domestic production and consumer demand for small cars," Nissan Vice-President Yasuhiko Suzuki told an American audience in January 1981. "This is not a case of Japanese push, but American pull." Nor was there any need to urge the Japanese to establish fabrication and manufacturing facilities in the United States. That, too, was taking place; led by Honda, all the major concerns were in the process of erecting plants, creating partnerships, or exploring means whereby joint ventures could be expanded. Finally, the Japanese observed the revival taking place in Detroit and predicted that a resurgent GM, Ford, and Chrysler would soon recapture an important portion of the market share they had lost in the 1970s, making all such talk irrelevant.

Matters came to a head in March 1981, when Japan's Foreign Minister Masayoshi Ito arrived in Washington for trade discussions centering on automobiles. The Americans were divided on the subject, with Secretary of State Alexander Haig and Treasury Secretary Donald Regan opposing tariffs and related restrictions and Transportation Secretary Drew Lewis and Commerce Secretary Malcolm Baldrige insisting that they were necessary if Detroit were ever to recover and that without tariffs and other restrictions there would be a chronic recession.

In the end, President Reagan opted for voluntary restraints, so indicating to Ito, who nonetheless continued in his attempts to avert all forms of restriction. "The agreement that came from the meeting" said the foreign minister, "is firstly that a major objective is to preserve the principle of free trade. As to the specifics of what methods might be followed in pursuance of this objective, there will continue to be discussions between the two sides."

This was not sufficient, Chairman of the Senate Finance Committee Bob Dole (R. Kans.) told a group of visiting Japanese legislators in mid-April. Dole scheduled hearings on trade restriction measures, and Danforth suggested that an even lower quota than 1.6 million units be considered. This came on the heels of a warning by Germany's Economics Minister, Count Otto Lambsdorff, that any form of American agreement that held down imports might lead to similar European programs aimed at the Japanese and, thus, could trigger a trade war that might have disastrous consequences.

The Japanese bowed on April 19, at which time MITI head Rokusuke Tanaka proposed to U.S. Trade Representative Bill Brock that imports be held to 1.68 million units per annum for a two-year period (equal to the average number of Japanese vehicles exported to the United States in 1979/80, which came to 22 percent of the market); this was a 7.7 percent reduction from the 1.82 million cars sold the previous year. There were clauses permitting increases should the domestic industry revive, as well as a clause providing for a third year of restraint should both parties agree. This was what both parties accepted, the announcement being made on May 1. "We automakers understood that our U.S. counterparts needed time to meet changes in the marketplace," said Toyo Kogyo's General Manager Hitoshi Nakashima. "And when the government decided to impose the self-restraint program on a temporary basis, we cooperated." The clear implication was that in his view the program was to be considered temporary, to be ended once Detroit had recovered.

Thus, Washington cooperated with Detroit to help revive the American automobile industry, or to be more precise, to give the companies some breathing room while they reorganized and put out more acceptable cars. Such an approach, had it been taken five years earlier, when Japanese cars were considered excellent economy models, might have stemmed the advance, but it was the wrong approach for the early 1980s, by which time the imports were winning a sizable share of the market for higher-priced vehicles. What was needed in addition to the unit count was some provision on total value, but this was missing from the agreement. Instead of shipping three Corollas, for example, Toyota might send over one Cressida, and obtain the same profit therefrom. The 1981 settlement meant that, in the future, the Japanese would shift from the low-priced end of the spectrum to the higher-priced one. In the mid-1970s, Toyota, Datsun, and the rest challenged Chevy, Ford, and Plymouth; now they would try to gain market share from Chrysler, Lincoln, Olds, and even Cadillac.

Those Americans who understood the situation observed that the shift in strategy had begun before Congress considered protection, and that under the circumstances, Detroit obtained all that might have been expected, because without the agreement the Japanese might have defeated Detroit across the line.

That the Japanese products had become the class of the market was further signaled by an announcement made later in the month. Iacocca agreed to free Mitsubishi from its agreement to market its cars through Chrysler dealerships. Those models already being sold in America would continue under the old arrangement, however, and Chrysler would have the right to select one other car or truck from the Mitsubishi line. In addition, Mitsubishi would supply engines for several Chrysler small cars. The Japanese company then announced the formation of an American subsidiary and told reporters its dealerships would open for business in the autumn of 1982. That there was no shortage of Americans seeking franchises was only to have been expected. In the weeks that followed Mitsubishi indicated that its inability to sell versions of the Colt, Arrow, and Sapporo sports car would not constitute a serious problem. The Japanese company intended to concentrate on the middle and upper ranges of the market, leaving the lower one to Chrysler.

In 1971, when the Chrysler-Mitsubishi union had been created, it had seemed that the Americans were powerful and the Japanese relatively weak. Ten years later, only a rare Chrysler dealer would have refused to exchange his franchise for one from Mitsubishi. Chrysler's future was still in doubt; Mitsubishi's could not have been brighter.

17

The Shape of
Things to Come

*There have been and always will be many opportunities to fail in
the automobile industry. The circumstances of the ever-changing
market and ever-changing product are capable of breaking any
business organization if that organization is unprepared for
change—indeed, in my opinion, if it had not provided procedures
for anticipating change.*

ALFRED SLOAN, JR.,
1964

*These professors [a survey team commissioned to study possible
labor-management cooperation] aren't going into any GM plant.
If they are interested in participative management, we are not.
We have paid the damnedest wages and benefits to keep the workers
and the unions out of management's prerogatives. There is no
other justification for the high wages. Participation is a lot of
economic crap.*

LOUIS SEATON, director of
labor relations, General Motors,
1968

Fifteen years ago I knew that every union officer was a real dyed-in-the-wool son of a bitch. And I'm also sure that those same people I'm talking about knew that I was a first-class bastard. We bred our industrial relations people to conflict. We chose them for their ability to "fix those bastards." Now this is slowly changing.
ALFRED WARREN, director of
personnel development, General Motors,
1982

Depending on how one measures and defines such things, insurance, banking, agriculture, housing, or transportation is the world's largest industry. Clearly the first two are involved with financial services, while agriculture and housing are so nebulous as to be best understood as constellations of industries. Similarly, transportation includes railroads and airlines, along with automobiles, and by some calculations, even shoes and horses.

Putting all this aside, one can say that automaking in its various manifestations and support industries—steel, tires, batteries, service stations, and, of course, petroleum—has been the largest manufacturing industry in the world for the past half century or more. Perhaps it will be different in the early twenty-first century, when data-processing in its many permutations takes over. But for our generation, and our times, transportation is paramount, and the auto is its central product.

Let us assume that such is the case, an assumption easily supportable by statistics and the testimony of one's senses. If this is so, then what happened to the world industry in the mid-1980s? And in particular, in the United States, a country whose modern era has been built around the automobile, where every boy was supposed to have been born with an innate ability to tinker and every girl with a yearning to sit behind the wheel of a snappy sports car, one of whose most durable if contentious heros is Henry Ford, where John DeLorean could rise and fall on the front pages depending on the success or failure of a new vehicle, and where Lee Iacocca could be seriously discussed as a presidential hopeful because he helped save a nearly bankrupt automaker?

And if we assume this to be the case, what might be considered the most important industrial development of the late 1970s and early 1980s? Simply this: the average price of a new automobile in 1979 was $6,900, and by 1983 it was $9,900. A 1982 Hertz Corp. study claimed the average cost of owning and operating a new compact was $0.47 per mile, twice what it had been in 1979. General Motors Acceptance Corp. reported that the average length of a new car loan had gone to 48 months, up from 36 months in 1976. The price of the familiar four-door, six-passenger sedan had risen beyond the ability of many Americans to purchase. Look at it another way: a relatively modest sedan cost more in 1983 than did a three-bedroom house in 1953.

Put aside all thoughts of Japanese versus American manufacturing techniques, treatment of labor, and concepts of management. Sticker shock and reverberations arising therefrom were central to the industry's development and the strategies developed and implemented in the early 1980s. And the shocks came fast and hard in this period. At GM, for example, there was an average $149 increase in January 1981, followed by $351 in April and $617 on the new 1982 models in August. This seemed to have become part of GM's strategy in the post–gas-crunch period. The corporation would introduce a new line at low prices—often so low as to result in losses. Then, if and when the cars sold well, the prices would be increased, often substantially. Noting the phenomenon with the X-cars, *Automotive News* wrote: "They are GM's best selling models and the corporation has boosted them accordingly. In less than a year, the new front-wheel drive compacts have jumped an average of $954 or 19.98 percent over their introductory stickers."

Industry critics charged GM with having instituted predatory pricing policies; defenders shot back that maximization of total profit was not only necessary to finance the changeover but an established capitalist practice, adding that the boosts for popular models and rebates and special financing arrangements for others indicated that these were signs of consumer sovereignty, that there was more competition in the marketplace than many realized, and that all this was to the good of everyone concerned.

True, the corporations were offering rebate programs to lure buyers to the showrooms, but they didn't ease the pain. Given a close to five-digit price tag, American automobile purchasers tended to overlook national loyalties and even comfort and performance. What they wanted was value, and it was on this battlefield that the Japanese and Americans fought it out, with both sides from the outset knowing that the Japanese had a decided edge in both products and perceptions. It would be irresponsible to predict that either national industry will ultimately triumph, for the matter is too complex to permit such a simple resolution, and as will be seen, it well might be that such distinctions will become moot by the end of the decade. Still, Detroit's performance earned only a mixed rating.

By late 1981, for example, it appeared that Chrysler would indeed be saved, and that the K-car "platforms" could be utilized as the base for other, more expensive, profitable models. Iacocca had pioneered this concept at Ford, when he developed the "pony cars" out of the Falcon, and now he was repeating the effort with no little success. Similarly, Ford had in its Escort/Lynx, the best-selling model in the world, and was preparing to bring new models from Germany to replace its fading Fairmont/Zephyr. Its 1983 mid-size Tempo/Topaz and the new Thunderbird and LTD were successes, and industry observers noted a sharp increase in productivity and better quality control. Ford hired W. Edwards Deming as a consultant and experimented with quality circles and other Japanese techniques, while moving toward greater cooperation with the UAW than at any time in the corporation's history.

Much of this had to do with the simple need to survive, and was reported on in depth in industry and general interest publications. "As long as there is a good unit coming off the line, I've got a paycheck," said one Ford worker. A midwestern plant manager noted that a few years ago "we wouldn't tell the union people what our schedules were until one week in advance." Now his plant was "pretty well committed" to a cooperative effort. "This is a fight for survival," offered Paul Guy, a Ford engineering and systems director. "I've been here 25 years, and have never seen such dedication."

As always, GM was the key company. The Citation line was a sales success, but the cars' appeals were limited. The corporation's dealers were more interested in the next group, true subcompacts, the fruits of a $5 billion investment, known as the J-cars: Cavalier (from Chevrolet), J2000 (Pontiac), and Cimarron (Cadillac), with later versions from Pontiac and Oldsmobile. It was to be a true World Car, marketed as the Ascona in Germany and South Africa, as the Monza (a familiar Chevy nameplate) in Brazil, and as the Camira in Australia. Vauxhall would retain the Cavalier designation; in what was either a burst of optimism or shrewd flattery, Isuzu asked for and obtained a license to manufacture the car in Japan.

General Motors promised surprises with this line, but there really were none, since the news was leaked to and reported in trade journals weeks prior to the official unveiling. Moreover, the mission of the cars was also well defined and hardly a secret. General Motors Vice-President Robert Lund defined them just prior to the unveiling. "We are tired of hearing how the domestic industry let the Japanese take the subcompact market away from us," he told an audience comprised of dealers and media representatives. "We need an unconventional Chevrolet—an unconventional package with an unconventional marketing strategy—if we are going to do a better job against the imports, and we spell that *Japanese.* Make no mistake about it, Cavalier is an import fighter! The whole Chevrolet organization is spoiling for a fight."

These models managed to be, at the same time, unoriginal in design and bold in presentation. Unoriginal in that they were Honda Accord look-alikes and were even packaged in much the same way as that popular Japanese model by coming almost fully equipped. Thus, GM was taking a risk in inviting comparisons between them.

The initial reception was poor. The J-cars were shorter, but no lighter than the Xs; they came with a four-cylinder 1.8 engine; the Xs came with a 2.5 liters standard. From the first, customers complained of the lack of power, and as the news filtered back to Detroit, GM hastily prepared to offer a larger engine as an option. The J-cars were considered overpriced for what they offered, and the corporation "unbundled" the equipment to bring their prices down.

Industry observers considered what GM had in mind for this car. There was ample evidence that the corporation thought what attracted Americans to the Accord was the body style and so had offered an American version, which lacked the Japanese car's engineering and finish. Ironically, to an earlier generation, the Japanese had been famous for their cheap knockoffs of American products. Now it seemed that in the J-cars, General Motors was trying to do the same thing.

To compound the problem, the Js came to market at an unfortunate time. Gasoline prices were softening in 1982, and there was a sudden loss of interest in small, fuel-efficient American models, which was what the Js, with an average fuel economy of almost 30 mpg, were advertised as being. Only 127,000 of them were sold in the 1981 model year, by the end of which it had become clear that without sudden increases in gasoline prices and changed perceptions, the cars would fail. And so they did. By 1983, the Js had become a major embarrassment at GM, which was seeking some dignified way to abandon the line. Thus, the corporation's attempt to manufacture and sell a Honda Accord look-alike did poorly. By 1984 most of the problems had been rectified and the Js were selling, but the sour taste remained.

So complex were the GM offerings that the disappointments of the Js were compensated for, in part, by the success of the new, mid-size A-body models, led by the Chevrolet Celebrity, which was one and one-half feet longer than the Citation, but only 286 pounds heavier; the price was approximately $2,000 higher. To the car buyers of 1983, the Celebrity seemed a fairly average-size, moderately priced car, but with a difference: its essential shape emanated from GM's German design team. It was as though the corporation, having failed to create an American Honda in its Cavalier, was now turning to Europe for suggestions and models. Nor was GM alone in this. Ford's 1983 Tempo/Topaz, too, was a product of German design and engineering, as were the new LTD and Thunderbird. What more than this could testify to the arrival of the World Car—or Detroit's crisis of confidence in the early 1980s?

Equally troublesome was the matter of price. The person who in 1976 purchased a Chevelle and in 1983 was trading it in for the Celebrity, a vehicle comparable in size, would have found the changes both impressive and startling. The mid-size Celebrity was smaller and offered less performance than the 1973 Nova, which was considered a compact. And of course, the Celebrity was considerably more expensive.

The full-size Monte Carlo, Impala, and Caprice also did well, as GM, whipsawed by the market, nonetheless was able to turn a profit. Similarly, fewer than 9,000 Cadillac Cimarrons were sold, as old-time owners shied from purchasing what was in effect a high-toned Cavalier, but the luxurious Eldorado posted a sales gain in a dismal year. Other A-cars—the Pontiac 6000 and Buick Century—also sold well, whereas the Oldsmobile Cutlass Ciera was the corporation's outstanding performer.

This temporary turning away from subcompacts and compacts buffeted Ford and Chrysler, too. Ford switched resources

SELECTED STATISTICS FOR THE 1973 NOVA,
1976 CHEVELLE, AND 1983 CELEBRITY

	NOVA	CHEVELLE	CELEBRITY
Weight	3,279 pounds	4,215 pounds	2,800 pounds
Overall length	195 inches	210 inches	188 inches
Engine (cc.)	250	305	151
Miles per gallon (av.)	19	17.5	23.5
Price (equipped)	$3,010	$5,116	$8,207

SOURCE: *Ward's Automotive Yearbooks, 1973, 1976, 1983.*

into Thunderbird and LTD, while Chrysler, lacking such flexibility, had little choice but to wait it out. Reflecting upon the situation in the spring of 1983, Iacocca said, "Four years ago Congress told us we built gas-guzzlers, and it was true. So Chrysler went to smaller engines. And now we're almost 100 percent front-wheel drive. The only reason we still have one rear-wheel drive, which is our worst gas-guzzler, is that it is also our hottest seller." By summer, however, Chrysler's new E-cars, which were really stretched-out Ks, were doing quite well.

That subcompacts still commanded a following was demonstrated by American Motors' Alliance, which, as the name indicates, was the first product of the partnership with Renault. Really a redesigned French model, the Alliance was roomy for its external dimensions, had a reasonably smooth ride despite its low weight, and had an EPA city mileage rating of 37 mpg, one of the best for an American sedan. With a base sticker price of under $5,600 it wasn't a moneymaker, but like other companies, AM-Renault was prepared to sacrifice immediate profits to obtain market share. The Alliance was a winner; by mid-1983, AM's sales were better than twice what they had been the previous year and the corporation was showing a profit and planning to bring over additional French cars in 1984 and later.

By early 1982, it was evident that GM's strategy involved concentrating on the broad central segment of the market. The corporation, which under Sloan and his successors had turned out models for all income groups, was now abandoning the lower levels—or, more precisely, it would no longer manufacture basic economy cars, but rather market models turned out by allied corporations for such customers. And the allies would be Japanese firms.

After prolonged, but fruitless discussions with Ford, Toyota entered into a $300 million compact with GM in 1982 to manufacture 200,000 Corollas a year in a shuttered California facility owned by GM. Among other things, this move would enable GM to study Toyota's manufacturing techniques. General Motors also invested another $200 million in Isuzu, and in 1983 announced it would import 200,000 of that company's small ST sedans the following year and also convert one of its midwestern factories to put together 300,000 more of them. But Isuzu was to be permitted to come to the United States itself, primarily to sell its small trucks. In addition, GM purchased a 5 percent equity position in motorcycle and mini-car manufacturer Suzuki, intending to bring over 90,000 of that company's small cars initially, with more to come if they caught on with Americans. All these autos would be sold through GM dealers—alongside the domestic models.

Thus, the American leader signaled, without stating outright, its withdrawal from the subcompact area. Since Chrysler clearly intended to rely upon Mitsubishi, this left Ford alone of the Big Three to compete with its Escort/Lynx. But for how long? Already in 1984 there was talk that Ford intended to bring over a new subcompact manufactured by Taunus as a backup for its much-vaunted World Car. Thus, the American and Japanese auto industries moved toward a symbiotic relationship, to the benefit of each side. Detroit would not concentrate on compacts and above and would rely increasingly on European designs, whereas the Japanese had the large market for subcompacts plus all they could get of the others. Implicit in all this was the expectation that the Americans would be accommodating when it came to lobbying in Congress for tariffs and quotas.

By and large, then, the GM strategy regarding its product line worked and would continue to do so as the industry struggled to reshape itself. In addition, GM would stress quality as well as style in its advertisements and provide extended warranties to indicate confidence in its products. Because of customer resistance and a slowing of inflation, prices rose more slowly after 1981. General Motors conducted several rebate programs and offered low finance charges, presenting a wide line of cars so as to be able to adjust to changing circumstances.

Ford and Chrysler generally followed GM in the matter of sales lures and prices, but as has been indicated, they took different paths to regain their old positions and compete with the Japanese.

The key to all of this was Lee Iacocca. There had been no shortage of job offers for him after he left Ford; Iacocca could have moved into the CEO spot at any of a dozen Fortune 500 companies had this been his ambition. Ford had presented him with a handsome settlement—$1.5 million, tied to a noncompetitive clause, meaning that the dismissed executive would have to accept a position outside the industry to collect it.

Prudence would have dictated taking the money and the attached condition, but Iacocca, well known for his pride and now eager to make Henry Ford II look like a fool for having let him go, played with the idea of reentering the automobile business on his own terms.

After more than three decades in the industry, Iacocca knew it better than all but a handful of individuals. He realized there could never be anything for him at GM, he wasn't interested in AM, and as had been known almost from the first, he understood how his talents might be used at Chrysler.

Iacocca watched the situation there unravel and was kept informed of developments relating to the potential insolvency. Watching from a distance, he mused that Chrysler might not be able to survive on its own, but that this was the condition of a majority of the world's auto manufacturers. In some respects, the situation resembled that of the pre–World War I period, when William Durant brought together dozens of corporations to form GM and Benjamin Briscoe tried to do the same when he created the short-lived United States Motors.

What Iacocca had in mind was to do the same on a world scale—to create an entity that might be known as Global Motors. Chrysler would provide the foundation, to which would be added AM. Perhaps VW or Fiat would enter as the European partner, with others joining later. Such a firm could compete head-on with GM and what Iacocca believed would eventually become a confederated Japanese industry, perhaps as one of the world's Big Three, to replace the more modest American version of an earlier period.

Nothing came of this concept; Iacocca, of course, went on to take over at Chrysler, which would remain American, and not join up with AM or VW. But although Global Motors did not come into being—at least not in this version or by the mid-1980s—the thought was sound. By then, most of the major and peripheral companies had gone global, for reasons of economy and also to prepare for what most believed would be a wave of import restrictions.

The working arrangements between the American Big Three and Japanese companies have been discussed; more are on the way. General Motors retained its ownership of Vauxhall in the United Kingdom and Opel in West Germany, as well as manufacturing, fabrication, and supply operations throughout the world. Ford remained tied to Toyo Kogyo, while Ford (United Kingdom) and Fordwerke in West Germany were dominant forces in their markets. The corporation was a leading factor in Spain and Latin America, the most internationally minded of the Big Three. During its crisis period, Chrysler relinquished control of Simca and Rootes and sold off its overseas facilities, but it did retain the Mitsubishi connection, although, as has been seen, the Japanese obtained the right to enter the American market on their own.

All the American companies expanded their overseas commitments. So did several European companies. As noted, the Ford Tempo/Topaz was created in Germany; the new Toyota Celica was a product of a team of American designers working out of California. A world industry was in the making. World Cars were being sold in the early 1980s.

The Japanese also participated in this reshuffling, which is transforming auto manufacturing. In 1982, Nissan made two significant announcements: It would phase out the Datsun nameplate and market cars as Nissans, this a symbolic move to harmonize world strategies. More concretely, it intended to assemble trucks at a $320 million facility to be erected in Smyrna, Tennessee, and it obtained a foothold in Europe through the purchase of an equity interest in Motor Iberica, a

Spanish manufacturer of trucks, vans, and buses. Toyota announced that it intended to assemble heavy trucks in the United States. Both firms made it quite clear that these plants could be the first of several, with more to come if everything worked out well.

In Europe, Nissan formed an alliance with Italian specialty car manufacturer Alfa Romeo to manufacture small cars in an Alfa plant, while opening negotiations with Volkswagen to do the same in one of that company's German facilities, in return for which VW would turn out Rabbits and Dashers in Japan. Upon concluding the arrangement, VW Chairman Carl Hahn indicated that his company's motives were not unlike those of GM. The Germans wanted to work with and learn from their partner. "For 20 years the Japanese learned from us," he said. "Now we are learning from them."

Rebuffed by Toyota, Ford negotiated several arrangements with Toyo Kogyo, the most important being one whereby the Japanese firm would manufacture diesels to be fitted into the next generation of Fords. Bypassing its German subsidiary, Ford also agreed to purchase diesels from BMW. Daimler Benz purchased American truck manufacturer Freightliner from Consolidated Freightways for $284 million. Lancia and Saab were to unite to design and manufacture a passenger car, and Alfa and Fiat would exchange component technology. Honda worked out deals with British Leyland to produce several lines of its cars in the United Kingdom, with Daimler Benz to co-manufacture a small sedan in South Africa, with Peugeot in mopeds for Western Europe, and with Yugoslavia's Mio Standard to manufacture engines. The company even entered the Chinese market through a collaborative venture in motorcycle production, with the understanding that, in time, automobiles as well might be manufactured on the mainland.

Toyota purchased a one-eighth interest in Britain's Group Lotus, the manufacturer of high-priced sports cars. Renault went international in a way that, had it been attempted thirty years earlier, might have made it a much more powerful entry and may even have aborted the German and Japanese invasions of the American market. Together with Volvo and Peugeot, it agreed to develop and manufacture a new engine. Renault was to assemble Fords in Australia. Two Renault partners, AM and Volvo, considered entering into a compact to bring some of the Swedish corporation's small cars to the United States, whereas the French company took an equity interest in Mack Trucks.

In 1983, a revived Chrysler not only agreed to purchase VW's Sterling Heights, Michigan, plant (in which a new full-size "H-car" was to be manufactured), but Iacocca also initiated discussions with Hahn for a closer relationship between their two companies and began negotiations with Mitsubishi to manufacture a new subcompact jointly. Chrysler and Peugeot planned a car to replace the Omni/Horizon. Soon after learning of the GM-Toyota partnership, Iacocca mused, "I wish Toyota had come to us first."

That summer Iacocca created a four-person Office of the Chairman, its purpose being to free him from day-to-day problems so that he could concentrate on long-term strategy, a major element of which was to be the hammering together of additional joint ventures, from which would emerge a version of Global Motors.

The old idea that there were products that might be considered American, Japanese, German, or Italian was going by the boards. In the late 1970's, one might sympathize with the American who wanted to help his country by purchasing a Ford Fiesta, rather than a VW Rabbit—not knowing that the Fiesta was manufactured in Germany and the Rabbit in the United States. A few years later, that same person might avoid a desirable Toyota in order to protect American jobs, and once again not understand that the Corolla, too, had taken on an American flavor. American legislators continued talking about restricting imports at a time when more American components were being used by the Japanese and the Big Three purchased parts and technology from several Japanese corporations.

Industry insiders understood this, as did the business

314

press. The Japanese talked knowingly of a coming American invasion of their markets, led by the next generation of compacts. The uninitiated thought this hyperbole was meant to lull the United States into a sense of security. Perhaps so; in the summer of 1983, Japan announced that the voluntary restriction of auto exports to the United States would end the following year—citing Detroit's revival as the reason. The Americans protested, but couldn't deny that the outlook was better and morale higher than in years.

Still, it was evident that the Japanese were prepared to alter their stance regarding the industry. In the late 1970s, MITI had all but proclaimed automobiles a mature industry, no longer the leading edge of Japan's world economic offensive. Just as textiles rose and then fell, so would automobiles, to be replaced as a favored industry by computers, microchips, esoteric industrial ceramics, and electronic gear and the products of molecular biology and genetic engineering. Indeed, the Japanese automobile manufacturers were now concerned with competition from countries with low labor costs and a craving to enter the markets on their own. In 1972, for example, the Republic of Korea produced 18,500 motor vehicles; seven years later, its plants turned out 203,000 almost all for domestic use, but the Koreans were already seeking markets abroad. Mexico's production rose from 225,000 to 445,000 in the same period. Brazil, hardly considered a major producer, manufactured more than 1 million cars, buses, and trucks in 1972, and was considering exports, especially of its alcohol-burning Volkswagen Beetles, to pay for purchases of industrial equipment.

All these countries had low labor costs, large internal markets, and a craving to sell abroad. They also had plants controlled by foreigners—VW and Ford were big in Brazil and Chrysler in Mexico, whereas the Japanese were all over, in manufacturing, assembly, and parts, intent on not being left out when protectionism took over.

These were bold steps for the Japanese industry, long famous for its caution and prudence. Leaders at most of the companies would have moved more slowly were it not for the fact that Honda had entered the market and showed the way. That corporation continued to be the leading innovator among the Japanese companies, insofar as breaking the cake of custom was concerned. Toyota and Nissan might have decided to come to America to manufacture cars, in any event, but the fact remains that Honda did it. Yet that company's lessons were not only for the Japanese; Detroit, too, was obliged to change some of its ways as a result of the Honda experience.

In 1981 Honda announced it would produce some of its 1983 Accords at a new plant in Marysville, Ohio, and by the following year was turning out Japanese cars there at the rate of 150,000 annually. Like other Japanese facilities in the United States, the Marysville plant had no union and the workers there were inculcated with Japanese-style concepts of teamwork. Although the wages at Honda were 20 percent below those paid at GM and Ford, all attempts at unionization were rejected by the rank and file. Interestingly enough for those who earlier had claimed Japanese methods could not work in America, Honda succeeded. "In the union shop it's every man for himself out on the floor, and everybody against management," reflected one Honda worker. "That may lead to more pay, but it also makes for lousy work conditions. I prefer what we have here, which is a lot healthier, and I see no need for a union." The company's American personnel manager told a reporter, "We have no guarantees about the future. But if history is any kind of guide, a job at Honda can be considered secure."

The smooth operations at the new Honda factory and other Japanese-owned and Japanese-operated installations in the United States led to drastic reconsiderations of the nature of the work force and the role—even the survival—of the United Auto Workers. It had long been assumed that American workers were motivated more by economic rewards than by anything else. The tacit understanding between management and labor was that the former would attempt to get all the productivity it could from the latter, whereas labor would attempt to maximize its wage and benefits package, cutting back as much as possible on actual time put in at the plant.

In such a system, the UAW was supposed to represent the workers in such a way as to obtain as much as feasible from the companies, while making as few concessions as possible. Management went through the motions of seeming to be deeply concerned about worker loyalty and well-being and a few executives—Charles Wilson and George Romney being the exemplars—truly believed that management-labor relations had to transcend simple economic considerations, but most felt otherwise. A great majority of assembly-line jobs required few skills that could not be learned in a matter of days or at most weeks, and they were dull and repetitive. The plant manager at one GM installation told a writer, "We solved problems by using our authority and imposing discipline." Another said that the workers "know what they are getting into" when they apply for such positions. "If they have such a strong desire [to seek more satisfactory work] they could just evacuate the buildings and leave." To which a bitter union official responded, "We are as important to them as a chair or ashtray." But it was different at Honda, and later, at other Japanese-owned and Japanese-managed factories. As indicated, worker satisfaction and morale were high. Production and quality control were not only satisfactory but in some cases better than those at Japanese factories.

What did this indicate? Were the Americans so accepting of Japanese ways because they were grateful to find jobs during a recession? Or might it be that several of the key assumptions regarding the work force were either exaggerated or simply wrong? Probably both contained elements of truth. Unemployed workers flocked to the Japanese installations seeking work, apparently willing to jettison old concepts and prejudices. Within a short period, however, they demonstrated a real enthusiasm for their work and an appreciation of the Japanese factory system. The conclusion was inescapable: American management had done a poor job of motivating workers.

In 1983, the Aspen Institute conducted a study of worker

morale and motivation in several European countries, the United States, and Japan, and the results were surprising. Fifty-two percent of those American workers surveyed agreed with the statement, "I have an inner need to do the best I can regardless of pay," which was 2 percent more than the Japanese sample (compared with 17 percent in Britain, 26 percent in West Germany, and 45 percent in Sweden). Three out of four thought the reason they didn't perform better was the failure of management to motivate them. This, perhaps, was why only 22 percent thought that they were working at full capacity and 44 percent thought that they didn't do much more than was required to keep their jobs. "It doesn't surprise me at all," said labor expert Sar Levitan. "The whole idea that Americans have given up on the work ethic is based on very little fact." Another scholar, John Immerwahr, reflected that "On the one hand, American workers say they want to work hard and do the best possible job. On the other hand, they say they are holding back and giving less than they could."

Other responses, however, indicated the economic motive wasn't dead. For example, only 22 percent of the American sample saw a close link between what they were paid and their performance on the job. The most important difference between the American and the Japanese work forces was revealed in answers to a question as to whether the workers thought they would benefit from increases in productivity. Only 9 percent of the Americans believed they would be rewarded, against 93 percent of the Japanese.

The Aspen study reinforced conclusions that Detroit had arrived at earlier and provided additional ammunition to those within the industry who believed drastic changes were needed in labor-management relations and the structure of the workplace. This was not because of the Japanese challenge, however, and initially, at least, it came in response to problems of a different sort.

The industry's leaders were reluctant, at first, even to discuss the matter of worker participation in any aspect of management; in 1968, for example, all GM's top executives but President Edward Cole voted to reject a proposal to study the possibility of greater worker participation in decision making, and line executives made no secret of their dislike for the project. All attempts on the part of the UAW to conduct experiments based on European experiences in worker-management cooperation were rebuffed.

This attitude changed in the mid-1970s, when quality control deteriorated and worker espionage began at several GM facilities. Distressed, the management agreed to the establishment of what such academic theorists as Deming, Juran, and Feigenbaum called "Quality of Work Life programs." These were nothing more than gatherings of workers to discuss common problems and means of improving both working conditions and productivity. Somewhat similar to the Japanese Quality Circles, they nonetheless had a particularly American nature in that they were informal, without the often rigid rules under which the Japanese operated.

But was this really so? Workers at GM's Bowling Green, Kentucky, facility might have thought otherwise. Engaged in fabricating the new Corvette, they participated in group exercises and even wore Japanese-style coveralls, complete with the Corvette insignia. The factory's floor was painted white. "This will give you an idea of how we feel about creating a clean, constructive environment," said a Chevrolet spokesman, who probably would not have felt out of place at Honda's Ohio installation. Thus proceeded the "Japanning of Detroit."

By the end of the decade, there were some 700 Quality of Work Life programs in place at American corporations. General Motors institutionalized them in several of its plants, starting in 1977, and by 1981, 74 of the corporation's 155 collective bargaining units had them in one form or another. By then, too, all the American auto companies had ongoing experiments with Quality Circles. Morale improved markedly; absenteeism dropped by 50 percent on the average, and in some plants, by as much as 90 percent. Worker complaints regarding management were down by as much as 75 percent at some plants; a survey completed in mid-1983 indicated that 82 percent of auto workers were fully satisfied with their jobs, as against 58 percent four years earlier. Doubtless recession-bred fears accounted for part of the increase, but most could be attributed to the new programs.

In the mid-1980s, it wasn't at all unusual for managers at the Big Three and AM to meet informally with workers after hours and even socialize with them. This isn't to suggest, however, that this kind of radical transformation occurred throughout the industry or that the prerogatives of management were easily relinquished or even gladly shared. Nor were the workers convinced management had become an ally or that the UAW was less necessary than earlier. Still, something drastic had to be done at a time when the industry was so seriously threatened, when every indication was that the American public considered domestically manufactured cars inferior to the imports. If Douglas Fraser could sit on the board of Chrysler, why couldn't management and labor cooperate to make the factories more pleasant places and the cars turned out from them better products?

Indications were that the UAW would cooperate fully toward the establishment of a new path in labor-management relations, one informed by but not imitative of the Japanese tradition. In February 1982, the union entered into an agreement with Ford under which it accepted a 30-month wage freeze, deferred cost-of-living increases, and agreed to reductions in paid time off. In return for this, the company guaranteed a base income for "tenured" workers until they retired and a profit-sharing plan, the former similar to the Japan lifetime employment principle, the latter not unlike bonus and profit-sharing plans often found in Japanese industry. Furthermore, Ford agreed not to close any more American plants for the next two years. "The wave of the future . . . is greater participation by our work force in the business process," said a Ford vice-president, whereas the corporation's chief negotiator Peter Pestillo said that "we aren't willing to treat our hourly people as the most variable cost we have." Soon thereafter, GM entered into a similar pact with its bargaining units. When Chrysler paid off the last of its loan guarantees in July 1983, Iacocca hinted that soon thereafter arrears might be cleared on the preferred stock, this a prelude to the reintroduction of a common stock dividend, which took place in 1984. Although the Chrysler UAW bargaining teams were then seeking parity with GM and Ford, they said nothing about the payouts, apparently realizing that they were necessary if Chrysler were to obtain a better credit rating, without which its recovery could be aborted.

In recent years, Professor William Abernathy of Harvard University, one of the leading academic experts on the auto business, has argued for what he had given the somewhat awkward name of "dematurization" of the industry, by which he meant its revival through restudy and reinvention. This is taking place in Detroit today. Alfred Sloan once remarked that the automobile of 1960 wasn't that much different from the one of thirty years earlier. In contrast, the 1985 models are a quantum jump ahead of those of a decade earlier. Low-carbon steel is being replaced by lighter, stronger materials such as aluminum and plastics; today's cars contain around 200 pounds of aluminum, twice that of four years earlier, and approximately 300 pounds of plastics to the 3 pounds in 1981. More is to come. Aluminum radiators will soon replace brass ones, and radiators may disappear completely once the radical new ceramic engine is perfected. This power plant, fabricated in whole or part of high-temperature, tough ceramics developed in the space program, will last for more than 100,000 miles and its supporters claim that it will get better than 80 mpg because of the aerodynamic chassis designs that have made their appearance.

Research in these areas is being conducted in Europe and Japan, as well as in the United States, as all major companies are participating in the dematurization process. The changes might be seen at the new factories—the Buick installation in Flint, Chrysler's new minivan complex in Canada, and Ford's revamped engine plant near Dearborn are among the most modern in the world.

With all of this there have been large-scale plant closings, as the industry streamlined and slimmed down. Since 1980, the Big Three have shuttered ten major facilities, slashing the industry's capacity by more than 2 million units. In addition, dozens of parts facilities were sold or dismantled; Chrysler now purchases 70 percent of its supplies, a third more than in 1980. Back-office personnel were dismissed on a wholesale basis. Ford cut its North American salaried work force by 21,000, or close to 30 percent, and Chrysler dismissed 11,000. General Motors eliminated 137,000 North American staff positions. All of this enabled the firms to save more than $2.5 billion. Costs all along the line have been cut drastically: the break-even point at GM declined from 5.6 million units in 1978 to 4.3 million in 1983, and those at Ford went from 4.2 million to 2.6 million. The most drastic improvement was at Chrysler. In 1978 the figure had been 2.4 million, which Iacocca—with the aid of the unions—was able to slash to 1.1 million in 1983.

Nor is this the end of it; all the American companies are more cost-conscious now than at any time since the Great Depression. "We aren't saying we can keep costs from rising at all," said Chrysler Vice-Chairman Gerald Greenwald. "But when somebody comes into my office asking for a bigger budget, he damn well better have a good reason." To which GM Chairman Smith added, "We took our industry apart and put it back together again."

And it is a different kind of domestic industry, one that is increasingly more international. By 1984 Ford was erecting a $500 million plant in Mexico to manufacture 130,000 subcompacts annually beginning in three years, AM was working with Renault to perfect a new subcompact, while Chrysler cooperated with Mitsubishi in designing a model to replace the Omni/Horizon. General Motors finally obtained approval for its joint venture with Toyota in California, but hedged its bets by designing an all-American subcompact, known as the Saturn.

Despite the much-ballyhooed Saturn, it now appears Detroit has abandoned the subcompact area to the foreigners and will be content to import them from abroad or manufacture them locally in cooperation with European and Japanese firms. More significant than the Saturn, for example, may be GM's arrangement with Korean automaker Daewoo to import its models sometime after 1986, and a subsequent purchase of half of Daewoo's stock. Not to be outdone, Ford entered into arrangements with another Korean firm, Hyundai. Talk of an American-Korean alliance disturbed the Japanese, who by 1984 were talking of a possible assault on their own domestic markets.

Because of a reversal of the negative factors of the previous four years Detroit experienced a much-welcomed boom in 1983, which carried over into 1984. The inflation rate had receded from the double digits down to slightly more than 3 percent, and a strong economic recovery brought the unemployment rate from 10.8 percent in late 1982 to under 8 percent by the end of 1983. Fuel was plentiful, and prices actually declined during the year.

REVENUES AND EARNINGS OF THE AMERICAN AUTO FIRMS, 1980–1983

	(millions of dollars)			
COMPANY	1980	1981	1982	1983
GENERAL MOTORS				
Revenues	57729	62699	60026	74582
Earnings	(762)	333	963	3730
FORD				
Revenues	37086	38247	37067	44455
Earnings	(1545)	(1060)	(658)	1867
CHRYSLER				
Revenues	9225	10822	10045	13240
Earnings	(1710)	(476)	(69)	526
AMERICAN MOTORS				
Revenues	2684	2589	2878	3272
Earnings	(156)	(137)	(154)	(259)

SOURCE: General Motors, Ford, Chrysler, and American Motors, *Annual Reports*, 1983.

More than 6.8 million cars were sold, an increase better than 17 percent over the previous year's figure. When the 2.4 million imports were included, the total came to 9.2 million, which was 15 percent more than 1982, and the best year since 1979. The Big Three earned more than $6 billion among them, and entered 1984 with more confidence than at any time since the mid-1970s. Only ailing American Motors remained in the red, but the success of that company's Alliance augured well for the future.

That there is a healthier and more optimistic spirit in Detroit cannot be doubted by anyone who has observed the business over the years. And in the factories, too, where the work force understands the challenge and knows what must be done. This was best typified by an exchange between Douglas Fraser and a worker at the Chrysler plant when the first K-car rolled off the assembly line, with Iacocca at the wheel and Fraser at his side. "Build 'em good," said the UAW President and Chrysler board member, to which the reply was, "We will. We have to."

Notes

CHAPTER 1
The Age of Detroit Baroque

DeLorean thus transformed: Then and later on, DeLorean criticized Detroit for turning out embroidered and outsized cars, claiming he had opposed the tendency. All of which would surprise anyone who remembers the cars of the period. J. Patrick Wright, *On a Clear Day You Can See General Motors* (Grosse Pointe, Mich.: Wright Enterprises, 1979), 87–89ff.

The outlook was bleak: Michael Moritz and Barrett Seaman, *Going for Broke: The Chrysler Story* (Garden City, N.Y.: Doubleday, 1981), 7.

wasn't really a sports car: Allan Nevins and Frank Hill, *Ford: Decline and Rebirth, 1933–1962* (New York: Scribner's, 1962), 380.

"distinctive" car: John Brooks, *Business Adventures* (New York: Weybright & Talley, 1969), 25–75 *passim.*

CHAPTER 2
Miracle at Wolfsburg

By then, the British: Peter Dunnett, *The Decline of the British Motor Industry* (London: Croom Helm, 1980), 20; Eric Toder, *Trade Policy and the U.S. Automobile Industry* (New York: Praeger, 1978), 9.

"Perhaps it would be best": Walter Nelson, *Small Wonder* (2d ed., Boston: Little, Brown, 1967), 3–4.

At the time the British: K. B. Hopfinger, *The Volkswagen Story* (2d ed., Cambridge, Mass.: Robert Bentley, 1971), 151–170 *passim.*

"I brushed away all temptation": Nelson, *Small Wonder,* 145.

CHAPTER 3
The German Onslaught

VW's chief executive: Nelson, *Small Wonder,* 172–176.

Nordhoff finally found: Hopfinger, *Beyond Expectation: The Volkswagen Story* (London: Fowles, 1954), 165.

To place the matter: Jerry Heasley, *The Production Figure Book for U.S. Cars* (Osceola, Wis.: Motorbooks International, 1977).

CHAPTER 4
The Coming of the Compact

popular legend holds: For example, see John Rae, *The American Automobile: A Brief History* (Chicago: University of Chicago Press, 1965), 202.

The Metropolitan's statistics: Tom Mahoney, *The Story of George Romney* (New York: Harper & Brothers, 1960), 200–203.

Nash's old distributorships: When, in 1951, Mason presented the Nash-Healy, a sports car with an English body, many Nash dealers refused to accept delivery, and more of them were sold in foreign car supermarkets than by these dealers. Ironically, sales of the Nash-Healey were quite profitable.

"American Motors could": *Ibid.*, 170.

CHAPTER 5
The Big Three Think Small

Simca proved: Undaunted, Colbert, and then Townsend, pressed ahead in Europe, and invariably wound up the loser. Six years after taking a position in Simca, Chrysler purchased 30 percent of Rootes, a British company whose Hillmans, Humbers, Singers, and Sunbeams all were in decline, between them accounting for less than 10 percent of their domestic market. Rootes was in worse shape than Chrysler, adding more buckets of red ink to the Chrysler balance sheets and pushing the corporation further down the road to collapse. More overseas forays would follow, with all but one ending in failure. The sole exception was a tie-in with Mitsubishi, and this was mishandled by the Americans, who it would appear didn't really know what they were doing or what a prize they might have had.

"always be 5 percent": Robert Sheehan, "A Big Year for the Small Cars," *Fortune* (August 1957), 197.

"Thus far it has not been": Lawrence White, *The Automobile Industry Since 1945* (Cambridge: Harvard University Press, 1971), 184–185.

If these new cars proved successful: William Harris, "Detroit Shoots the Works," *Fortune* (June 1959), 99–102.

CHAPTER 6
Sunrise in Nippon

"I recommend urgently": Theodore McNelly, *Contemporary Government in Japan* (Boston: Little, Brown, 1963), 130–132; C. S. Chang, *The Japanese Auto Industry and the U.S. Market* (New York: Praeger, 1981), 48–49.

"It is meaningless": *Ibid.*, 49.

In 1924, for example: *Historical Statistics of the United States*, 716; William Lockwood, *The Economic Development of Japan* (Princeton: Princeton University Press, 1968), 107; Shotaro Kamiya, *My Life with Toyota* (Tokyo: Toyota Corporation, 1976), 103.

Depending on how *zaibatsu*: William Irvine, *Japan as an Automotive Market U.S. Dept. of Commerce: Special Agent Series No. 217* (Washington, D.C.: Government Printing Office, 1918), 30ff.

The new, independent companies: Chang, *Japanese Auto Industry*, 187.

Yoshida eventually produced: William Duncan, *U.S.-Japan Automobile Diplomacy* (Cambridge, Mass.: Ballinger, 1973), 55–56.

In all, Tokyo Motors: Chang, *Japanese Auto Industry*, 188.

Masujiro Hashimoto: Duncan, *Automobile Diplomacy*, 56, 183.

Meanwhile, several established: Chang, *Japanese Auto Industry*, 192–193; U.S., Strategic Bombing Survey, Military Supplies Division, October–November, 1945; *Japanese Motor Vehicle Industry* (Washington, D.C.: Government Printing Office, 1946), 4.

"Your father served": Duncan, *Automobile Diplomacy*, 185.

Although there have been some: Bradley Richardson and Taizo Ueda, eds., *Business and Society in Japan* (New York: Praeger, 1981), 10–11ff.

The large *zaibatsu*: Chang, *Japanese Auto Industry*, 200.

Why this change in spelling?: Kamiya, *My Life with Toyota*, 109.

Japanese truck production: *Ibid.*, 110.

Unlike Toyoda, Aikawa: Chang, *Japanese Auto Industry*, 26–32; Duncan, *Automobile Diplomacy*, 63–65; John Rae, *Nissan/-Datsun: A History of Nissan Motor Corporation in U.S.A., 1960–1980* (New York: McGraw-Hill, 1981), 8; Chalmers Johnson, *MITI and the Japanese Miracle The Growth of Industrial Policy, 1925–1975* (Stanford, Calif.: Stanford University Press, 1982), 131.

In the peak year: Chang, *Japanese Auto Industry*, 200–201.

CHAPTER 7
The United States as Number One

Ford-Japan was organized: Mira Wilkins and Frank Hill, *American Business Abroad: Ford on Six Continents* (Detroit: Wayne State University Press, 1964), 150–151; Kamiya, *My Life with Toyota*, 102–104.

"When that day comes": Chang, *Japanese Auto Industry*, 16.

By 1934, for example: *Ibid.*, 200.

"He had convinced the government": Wilkins and Hill, *American Business Abroad*, 255.

Between them, the two companies: Chang, *Japanese Auto Industry*, 200.

"Never in history": Douglas MacArthur, *Reminiscences* (New York: McGraw-Hill, 1964), 280–281.

Fortunately for both Japan: See William Manchester, *American Caesar: Douglas MacArthur, 1880–1964* (Boston: Little, Brown, 1978), chap. 8, for a summary of the early MacArthur viceregency.

powerful Ministry of Commerce: Murray Sayle, "Explaining Japan to America—and Vice Versa," *Harper's* (November 1982), 32; Johnson, *MITI and the Japanese Miracle*, 18.

restrictions on automobile manufacture: Chang, *Japanese Auto Industry*, 202; Kamiya, *My Life with Toyota*, 112–113.

At Toyota, for example, the newly named president: Kamiya, *My Life with Toyota*, 50–63 *passim*.

"The United States created": "How the Japanese Blitzed the California Auto Market," *Forbes* (September 15, 1971), 28.

CHAPTER 8
The Japanese Difference

Professor Warren Hunsberger: Institute of International Development in testimony before Joint Economic Committee of Congress, November 20, 1961.

To those with long memories: An extensive literature informed Americans what they were doing wrong and the Japanese were doing right, and how they could learn from the Japanese experience. The most typical and accessible of these are Ezra Vogel, *Japan as Number One: Lessons for America* (New York: Harper & Row, 1979); William Ouchi, *Theory Z: How American Business Can Meet the Japanese Challenge* (Reading, Mass.: Addison-Wesley, 1981); and Richard Pascale and Anthony Athos, *The Art of Japanese Management: Applications for American Executives* (New York: Simon & Schuster, 1981).

"For 20 years the Japanese": John Holusha, "Japan's Car Makers Facing Tests Abroad as Industry's Leader," *The New York Times*, April 1, 1983.

"They invent few things": Kurt Singer, *Mirror, Sword, and Jewel: The Geometry of Japanese Life* (Tokyo: Kodansha, 1973), 98.

During the 1950s: Nomura Research Institute, *Investing in Japan* (London: Woodhead-Faulkner, 1976), 9.

"The guiding principles": *Ibid.*, 99–100.

At Toyota, all the workers: Satoshi Kamata, *Japan in the Passing Lane: An Insider's Account of Life in a Japanese Auto Factory* (New York: Pantheon, 1982), 10–11.

"I get the impression": Robert Hayes, "Why Japanese Factories Work," Harvard Business Review, ed., *Survival Strategies for American Industry* (New York: John Wiley, 1983), 241.

conflicts with MITI: There were major revisions in the Antimonopoly Law in 1977, when the government decided that the reduction of competition was inflationary, and under the circumstances may have been overdone. Nomura Research Institute, *Investing in Japan*, 48–49.

"In 1950, when I was a young shop steward": John Holusha, "Japan's Productive Car Unions," *The New York Times*, March 30, 1983.

level of cooperation: Robert Cole, *Japanese Blue Collar: The Changing Tradition* (Berkeley: University of California Press, 1971), 101–270 *passim*.

student of the situation: Kamata, *Japan in the Passing Lane*, xxvii.

One of the goals: In particular, see A. V. Feigenbaum, *Total Quality Control: Engineering and Management* (New York: McGraw-Hill, 1961).

The Japanese adapted: Robert Cole, *Work, Mobility and Participation* (Berkeley: University of California Press, 1979), 136.

What later had been thought: James Lincoln, *A New Approach to Industrial Economics* (New York: Devin-Adair, 1961).

W. Edwards Deming brought the doctrine: W. Edwards Deming, "What Happened in Japan," *Industrial Quality Control* (August 1967); W. Edwards Deming, "The Statistical Control of Quality," *Quality* (February 1980).

"You had so many good things": John Simmons and William Mares, *Working Together* (New York: Knopf, 1983), 97.

Toyota, for example, owns: *The Oriental Economist, Japan Company Handbook, 1st half 1983* (Tokyo: The Oriental Economist, 1983).

"Normally, you don't want": John Holusha, "Just-in-Time System Cuts Japan's Auto Costs," *The New York Times*, March 25, 1983.

Several American analysts have: Compare the Japanese situation to a recent description of Chrysler operations in 1970. "The new parts clogged up the aisles in the plants, overflowed out the doors and frequently had to be stored in boxcars, for which the company had to pay demurrage. Chrysler was almost in two businesses. One assembled automobiles, the other stored parts." Moritz and Seaman, *Going for Broke*, 102.

"We had been half-prepared": William Abernathy, Kim Clark, and Alan Kantrow, *Industrial Renaissance: Producing a Competitive Future in America* (New York: Basic Books, 1983), 76.

"The keynote of Toyota rationalization": Kamiya, *Japan in the Passing Lane*, 199–200.

In 1960, firms with: Johannes Hirschmeier and Tsunehiko Yui, *The Development of Japanese Business, 1600–1973* (Cambridge, Mass.: Harvard University Press, 1975), 234.

Could Japanese techniques: In 1980, the Japan Productivity Center formed the Association to Rescue the United States (later more tactfully renamed the Association to Encourage the United States), the purpose of which was to instruct Americans in techniques they had imbibed from American sources since World War II. Simmons and Mares, *Working Together*, 101.

CHAPTER 9
The Japanese Stumble

For 1956–1958, Japan sold: U.S. Congress. Senate. Joint Economic Committee. Subcommittee on Foreign Economic Policy, *Japan in United States Foreign Economic Policy* by Warren Hunsberger, 87th Cong., 1st sess. (Washington, D.C.: Government Printing Office, 1961), 7.

performance of the Japanese economy: Isaiah Frank and Ryokichi Hirono, eds., *How the United States and Japan See Each Other's Economy* (New York: Committee for Economic Development, 1974), 13, 23.

the United States was closer: Motor Manufacturing Economic Development Councils, *Japan: Its Motor Industry and Market* (London: Her Majesty's Stationery Office, 1971), 53.

MITI could hardly permit: Duncan, *Automobile Diplomacy*, 75.

cooperation was short-lived: Jack Baranson, *The Japanese Challenge to U.S. Industry* (Lexington, Mass.: Lexington Books, 1981), 152–153.

None of these contracts: Ira Magaziner and Thomas Hout, *Japanese Industrial Policy* (Berkeley: Institute of International Studies, University of California Press, 1979), 68–69.

"Whenever I see": Seisi Kato, *My Years with Toyota* (Toyota City: Toyota Motor Sales, 1981), 65–66.

"Toyota impressed me": "He Who Lasts Longest," *Toyota Today* (November 1982), 2–3.

"We were counting": *Ibid.*, 69.

"This car is really": *Road and Track* (December 1958), 22.

CHAPTER 10
The Beachhead

three out of every four: Motor Manufacturing EDC, *Japan: Its Motor Industry and Market*, 14.

In 1960, only 1.2 percent: Japan Automobile Manufacturers Association, *Motor Vehicle Statistics of Japan, 1971* as quoted in Duncan, *Automobile Diplomacy*, 76, 151.

In 1950, fewer than: There is no little irony in the fact that the Japanese now prefer bigger, more luxurious cars. Americans visiting Japan expecting to see roads filled with compacts are surprised to see the Nissan President and Toyota Century, two relatively large and more expensive cars the Japanese do not export to the United States. Why don't they buy standard-size American cars? Not because of quotas and tariffs, but rather because they believe that their quality is unacceptable.

"The Datsun is a product": *Road and Track* (May 1960), 42.

"Whereas the car": *Road and Track* (March 1961), 36.

"Especially difficult for the engineers": *Toyota: The First Twenty Years in the U.S.A.* (Torrance, Calif.: Toyota Motor Sales, 1977), 31.

The company approached Ford: That Toyota would have quality control and design problems and seek American assistance in such matters must astonish those who are convinced the Japanese automakers are close to infallible. Kato, *My Years with Toyota*, 75–82.

"It was, if I": *Ibid.*, 76.

"The Corona's engine": *Consumer Reports* (October 1966), 505–511.

CHAPTER 11
Reshaping the Industry

There were three: Miyake Sadeo, "The Japanese Motor Industry," *Japan Quarterly* (January–March 1968), 100–103.

The Big Two: David Friedman, "Beyond the Age of Ford: The Strategic Basis of the Japanese Success in Automobiles," in John Zysman and Laura Tyson, *American Industry in International Competition: Government Policies and Corporate Strategies* (Ithaca, N.Y.: Cornell University Press, 1983), 364–365.

Such was the case: Toyo Kogyo, Ltd., *Guide to Toyo Kogyo* (Tokyo: Toyo Kogyo, 1983), 2.

both financial institutions: Mitsubishi continued on as Honda's banker when the company became a factor in the automobile industry, while serving in the identical capacity for Mitsubishi Motors. To appreciate what this means, one must imagine the Bank of America owning substantial shares in both Ford and GM, being privy to both companies' secrets, and provoking no reaction from the Justice Department.

he stressed individualism: Sol Sanders, *Honda: The Man and His Machines* (Boston: Little, Brown, 1975), 67.

its first product: The best study of Honda is Tetsuo Sakiya, *Honda Motor: The Men, the Management, and the Machines* (Tokyo: Kodansha, 1982).

the companies themselves: One of the auto firm CEOs remarked, "In the council I am a member, but when I return to my company I am president. The adjustment between conception and reality is difficult." Duncan, *Automobile Diplomacy*, 87.

Kono Fumihiko: *Ibid.*, 83–89; Magaziner and Hout, *Japanese Industrial Policy*, 75–77.

Japanese automakers: As MITI's vice-minister for international affairs would put it in 1980, when Detroit had virtually conceded the small-car market to Japan, "The American auto industry seems to perceive the Japanese competition as stronger than it actually is." *Japan Times* (November 9, 1980), as quoted in Mary Saso and Stuart Kirby, *Japanese Industrial Competition to 1990* (Cambridge, Mass.: Abt Books, 1982), 83.

"For over a century": Ralph Nader, *Unsafe at Any Speed* (New York: Grossman, 1965).

The Ford suspension arm: *Ibid.*, 1–41, 56.

detectives were directed: Thomas Whiteside, *The Investigation of Ralph Nader* (New York: Pocket Books, 1972), 43.

"It is our regular": *Los Angeles Times*, May 13, 1969, as quoted in Cray, *Chrome Colossus*, 427.

"there would be no": Moritz and Seaman, *Going for Broke*, 155.

"What the workers want": Simmons and Mares, *Working Together*, 45. The most striking exposition of this phenomenon, from one who sympathized with the antitechnology bent of the period, is Emma Rothschild, *Paradise Lost: The Decline of the Auto-Industrial Age* (New York: Random House, 1973).

"It is impossible": Duncan, *Automobile Diplomacy*, 93.

a Mitsubishi sedan: Chrysler dealers had been trying vainly to sell small cars manufactured by the corporation's Simca and Rootes companies and welcomed the Colts, which, although never a threat to Toyota and Datsun, immediately outsold the trouble-prone, Rootes-manufactured Crickets.

corporation lacked the funds: Moritz and Seaman, *Going for Broke*, 115–116; Stephen Young and Neil Hood, *Chrysler U.K.: A Corporation in Transition* (New York: Praeger, 1977), 51, 54.

Wankel rotary engine: Duncan, *Automobile Diplomacy*, 48.

CHAPTER 12
Success in America

Japan exported: Motor Manufacturing Economic Development Council (EDC), *Japan: Its Motor Industry and Market*, 19.

Fiat, with 12 percent: "Renault: Heading for the Pits," *The Economist* (June 18, 1983), 77–78.

The engine: Robert Ayres and Richard McKenna, *Alternatives to the Internal Combustion Engine: Impact on Environmental Quality* (Baltimore: Johns Hopkins University Press, 1972), 113–117.

Detroit clasped: Charles Burck, "A Car that May Reshape the Industry's Future," *Fortune* (July 1972), 74–79; "Wangle Yourself a Wankel," *Forbes* (December 15, 1972), 24–27.

"The experiences": *Consumer Reports* (April 1973), 285.

"Driving a car": Sanders, *Honda*, 119–121.

"Honda CVCC have": *Ward's Automotive Yearbook, 1973*, 33.

CHAPTER 13
The Challenge Recognized

fuel costs: It would later be alleged that the refiners orchestrated the subsequent energy crisis to obtain higher prices. The debate on the matter still rages, and the only possible verdict at this time is "not proven." Independent Petroleum Association of America, *United States Petroleum Statistics, 1982* (New York: Petroleum Association of America, 1982), 4.

several government agencies: Tad Szulc, *The Energy Crisis* (New York: Franklin Watt, 1974); Fred Allvine and James Patterson, *Highway Robbery: An Analysis of the Gasoline Crisis* (Bloomington: Indiana University Press, 1974).

cars that gulped gasoline: The fleet average for 1973 American cars was 13 mpg, an all-time low. Moritz and Seaman, *Going for Broke*, 164.

at $0.60 a gallon: *Time* (December 31, 1973), 18.

"as long as most": Cray, *Chrome Colossus*, 485.

sales of that small: "Detroit Thinks Small," *Newsweek* (April 1, 1974), 55.

company executives wondered: On the other hand, GM and Ford earned money in 1973–1974, whereas Chrysler's losses were modest. The decline in sales was compensated for, in part, by higher prices. In 1974, GM earned $950 million, Ford $261 million, and Chrysler lost $52.1 million.

Toyota and Nissan sales: Sanders, *Honda,* 180–181.

"Although there has": William Tucker, "The Wreck of the Auto Industry," *Harper's* (November 1980), 52.

they sponsored: Arabinda Ghosh, *OPEC, The Petroleum Industry, and United States Energy Policy* (Westport, Conn.: Greenwood Press, 1983), chap. 10.

antitrust probe: The probe would end in 1981. At that time the FTC's acting chairman, David Clanton, said, "Given the industry's continuing slump it made no sense to pursue the inquiry." Yet for four and a half years, Detroit had to combat the Japanese at a time when it appeared Washington had allied itself with the adversary.

mandate to downsize: *Consumer Reports* (April 1973), 271.

"This has all the elements": *Business Week* (October 23, 1976), 43.

"Imported cars": *Ward's Automotive Yearbook, 1976,* 23–24.

CHAPTER 14
The American Malaise

approximately $666: Murray Weidenbaum, *Government Mandated Price Increases: A Neglected Aspect of Inflation* (Washington: American Enterprise Institute, 1975), 24; *The Future of Business Regulation* (New York: AMACOM, 1979), 12–14.

The market shifted: An alternative explanation was that only the wealthy could afford to buy new cars during the stagflation, which accounted for the shift in the market. A similar situation had existed during the Great Depression, when big luxury cars retained their followings, and those who prior to that time had wanted medium-price cars downgraded to the economies of that era. In 1974, however, sales of economy models also declined.

The New York Times: Motor Trend (August 1973); *Consumer*

Reports (February 1974); *The New York Times,* March 12, 1974.

This failure was: Moritz and Seaman, *Going for Broke,* 15–16.

"not acceptable,": *Consumer Reports* (June 1978), 377.

The Chevette delivered: Jim Dunne and Ray Hill, "Mini-Compacts: Chevette Meets the Competition," *Popular Science* (January 1976), 26, 32–36; *Consumer Reports* (May 1975), 298–305, (April 1976), 208–211.

"We are on": Simmons and Mares, *Working Together,* 43.

CHAPTER 15
The Victory Secured

General Motors rushed: This need not have been. General Motors' Japanese partner, Isuzu, had been one of the pioneers in the diesel field, turning them out since 1935. Yet GM elected to manufacture its own engines rather than purchase them from Isuzu.

engine of the future: General Motors which earlier had gone overboard on the Wankel, did so on the diesel too, predicting that by 1985, 15 percent of its cars would be so equipped, and indeed the 1981 Chevette had the engine as an option. It was too late to cash in on the craze, however. Stable gasoline prices of the early 1980s and the increase in the price of diesel fuel made the engines less popular. Brown, Flavin, and Norman, *Running on Empty,* 58–59.

midst of a turnabout: *Ward's Automotive Yearbook, 1978,* 31.

Rabbit had problems: Robert Ball, "Volkswagen Hops a Rabbit Back to Prosperity," *Fortune* (August 13, 1979), 120–128.

Fuji's reluctance: Because Security & Exchange Commission regulations oblige financial disclosure, we know that Subaru's 1978 revenues came to $440 million on sales of 76,210 vehicles. Similar figures aren't available for the other Japanese automobile companies. Subaru of America, *1978 Annual Report.*

"a bicycle economy": *The New York Times,* May 24, 1973.

Mazda would not fulfill: Yoshi Tsurumi, "How to Handle the Next Chrysler," *Fortune* (June 16, 1980), 87.

"one of the best": *Consumer Reports* (January 1977), 32.

Honda had created: Arthur Louis, "Honda's Happy Predicament," *Fortune* (July 30, 1979), 92–93.

CHAPTER 16
The American Response

"the most ambitious": John Holusha, "General Motors: A Giant in Transition," *The New York Times Magazine* (November 14, 1982), 79.

Cimarron was correctly viewed: It will be recalled that in the early postwar period, when the Packard came out in a lower-priced model (complete with a six-cylinder engine), it lost that special cachet as a luxury car. The same could have happened when the Cimarron made its debut, and indications today are that Cadillac has lost much of its luster.

American Motors became: Renault excluded Quebec from the arrangement, this in recognition of the special relationship that province had with France.

then named Renault's: It should be noted, however, that even before World War II, American components manufacturers had entered into similar relationships with European and Japanese corporations.

"for 12,000 miles": Moritz and Seaman, *Going for Broke*, 125.

"salvaging of Chrysler": The Chrysler saga and the Iacocca story have been well covered in the popular press and in several books, and will not be recounted in detail here. For the details, see *ibid.* and David Abodaher, *Iacocca: A Biography* (New York: The Macmillan Company, 1982).

receiving warrants: The rights, which represented 9 percent of the capitalization, were sold by the government in 1983, after Chrysler was salvaged.

All this took place: Paul Lawrence and Davis Dyer, *Renewing American Industry* (New York: Free Press, 1983), 18–19.

"Today, we are caught": *The Wall Street Journal*, June 19, 1980.

"This is the beginning": Moritz and Seaman, *Going for Broke*, 323.

"These days": Joseph Kraft, "Annals of Industry: The Downsizing Decision," *The New Yorker* (May 5, 1980), 135.

average 1983 American car: "The Beat Is Back in the Motown Sound," *The Economist* (July 30, 1983), 59–60.

benefited from the importation: Toyota U.S.A., *Toyota and the American Society* (Torrance, Calif.: Toyota Motor Sales U.S.A., 1982).

"Imports have been drawn": "U.S.-Japan Trade Relations: Reaching an Accommodation," in Robert Cole, ed., *The Japanese Automobile Industry: Model and Challenge for the Future? The Changing Tradition* (Ann Arbor: University of Michigan Press, 1981), 19.

"The agreement that came": *The New York Times*, March 25, 1981.

"We automakers understood": *The Wall Street Journal*, May 2, 1981; "Japan and the United States: A Time of Testing," *Fortune* (August 22, 1983), 42.

CHAPTER 17
The Shape of Things to Come

"They are GM's": John Teakin, Jr., "GM Increases Prices by an Average of $186; 2.2. Pct. Hike Had Been Expected," *Automotive News* (April 7, 1982), 3.

"As long as": John Holusha, "Detroit's New Labor Strategy," *The New York Times*, May 13, 1983; John Dorfman, "Make or Break," *Forbes* (April 25, 1983), 104; Noel Grove, "Swing Low, Sweet Chariot," *National Geographic* (July 1983), 27.

"We are tired": Brock Yates, *The Decline and Fall of the American Automobile Industry* (New York: Empire, 1983), 14–15.

J-cars were considered: Within a year a fully equipped Accord sold for around $8,000, whereas a "loaded" Cavalier could go as high as $11,000. There were long waiting lists for Accords, and discounts on the Cavaliers. *Ibid.*, 66.

"Four years ago": Grove, "Swing Low, Sweet Chariot," 28.

compact with GM: "Toyota Takes a Foreign Trip with General Motors," *The Economist* (February 5, 1983), 65–66.

"For 20 years": John Holusha, "Japanese Car Makers Facing Tests Abroad as Industry's Leader," *The New York Times*, April 1, 1983.

Ford negotiated: Malcolm Salter and Mark Fuller, "Profile of the World Automotive Industry" (unpublished, 1980), quoted in National Research Council, *The Competitive Status of the U.S. Auto Industry* (Washington, D.C.: National Academy Press, 1982), 65.

All these countries: Jean-Pierre Bardou, Jean-Jacques Chanaron, and Patrick Fridenson; James Laux, ed., *The Automobile Revolution: The Impact of an Industry* (Chapel Hill: University of North Carolina Press, 1982), 192.

"In the union shop": "Japanese Cars Find Ohio Roots," *Newsday*, December 5, 1982.

"We solved problems": Simmons and Mares, *Working Together*, 62; Rothschild, *Paradise Lost*, 132–133.

Fifty-two percent: Robert Reno, "U.S. Workers More Willing than Able," *Newsday*, July 10, 1983.

This attitude changed: American managers still reject the notion they have much to learn from the Japanese. The superintendent at the Japanese Kawasaki factory in Lincoln, Nebraska, told a scholar, "We don't do it the Japanese way; we do it the American way here." Simmons and Mares, *Working Together*, 103.

Workers at GM's: Yates, *Decline and Fall of the American Automobile Industry*, 242.

700 Quality of Work Life programs: Simmons and Mares, *Working Together*, 51.

"The wave of the future": Frank Gibney, *Miracle by Design* (New York: Times Books, 1982), 218.

"dematurization" of the industry: Abernathy, Clark, and Kantrow, *Industrial Renaissance*, 107–110.

"We aren't saying": Robert Simison and John Koten,

"Auto Makers' Earnings Are Increasing Sharply Despite Mediocre Sales," *The Wall Street Journal*, December 19, 1983.

Detroit has abandoned: "The All-American Small Car Is Fading," *Business Week* (March 12, 1984), 88–90.

More than 6.8 million: *The New York Times*, January 6, 1984.

"Build 'em good": Moritz and Seaman, *Going for Broke*, 323.

Selected
Bibliography

Invaluable for a work of this nature have been the better-known industry publications and magazines devoted to cars, such as *Ward's Automotive Reports, Ward's Auto World, Car and Driver, Motor Trend, The Wheel Extended,* and *Automotive News. Consumer Reports,* whose well-followed analyses of new cars often has proved to reflect informed public tastes, was utilized for that purpose. Unless otherwise indicated, all statistical material referred to has been taken from these sources.

I have also consulted the popular press and business magazines, the most important being *The Wall Street Journal, The New York Times, Business Week, Fortune, Barron's, Forbes, The Economist* and, to a lesser extent, *Newsweek, Time,* and *U.S. News and World Report.* The specialized journals included *Business Asia* [Hong Kong], *Financial Times* [London], *Asia and the Pacific, Japan Quarterly, Oriental Economist, Banker* [London], *Survey of Current Business, Journal of Commerce, Far Eastern Economic Review* [Hong

Kong], *Japan Economic Journal,* and *Industrial Review of Japan.* In addition I have studied the relevant government documents.

These and the works listed below are meant as a guide to future research. Published materials dealing with the Japanese economy are growing exponentially, as are works dealing with the crisis in the American automobile industry. This list is by no means exhaustive.

Finally, I have been assisted by the American affiliates of Toyota, Nissan, Toyo Kogyo, Fuji Heavy Industries, and Honda, who have provided relevant information and advice on how to better understand their operations.

BOOKS

ABBEGGLEN, JAMES, ed. *Business Strategies for Japan.* Tokyo: Sophia University Press, 1970.

ABERNATHY, WILLIAM. *The Productivity Dilemma: Roadblocks to Innovation.* Baltimore: Johns Hopkins University Press, 1978.

———, CLARK, KIM, and KANTROW, ALAN, *Industrial Renaissance: Producing a Competitive Future for America.* New York: Basic Books, 1983.

———, and Ginsberg, Douglass, eds. *Government, Technology, and the Future of the Automobile.* New York: McGraw-Hill, 1979.

ABODAHER, DAVID. *Iacocca: A Biography.* New York: The Macmillan Company, 1982.

ADAMS, T. F. M., and KOBAYASHI, N. *The World of Japanese Business.* Tokyo: Kodansha International, 1969.

ALLEN, GEORGE. *Japan as a Market and Source of Supply.* Oxford: Pergamon, 1967.

———. *The Japanese Economy.* New York: St. Martin's, 1981.

———. *Japan's Economic Expansion.* London: Oxford University Press, 1965.

———. *Japan's Place in Trade Strategy.* London: Moor House, 1968.

344

———. *A Short Economic History of Modern Japan.* Cambridge: Harvard University Press, 1967.

ALLVINE, FRED, and PATTERSON, JAMES. *Highway Robbery: An Analysis of the Gasoline Crisis.* Bloomington: Indiana University Press, 1974.

American Enterprise Institute. *The Japan-U.S. Assembly: Proceedings of a Conference on Japan-U.S. Economic Policy.* Washington, D.C.: American Enterprise Institute, 1975.

ANGEL, D. DUANE. *Romney: A Political Biography.* New York: Exposition, 1967.

AYRES, ROBERT, and MCKENNA, RICHARD. *Alternatives to the Internal Combustion Engine: Impacts on Environmental Quality.* Baltimore: Johns Hopkins University Press, 1972.

BALASSA, BELA, ed. *Studies in Trade Liberalization, Problems and Prospects for the Industrial Countries.* Baltimore: Johns Hopkins University Press, 1967.

———. *Trade Liberalization Among Industrial Countries: Objective and Alternatives.* New York: McGraw-Hill, 1967.

BALLON, ROBERT. *The Japanese Employee.* Tokyo: Charles Tuttle, 1969.

———, ed. *Joint Ventures and Japan.* Tokyo: Sophia University Press, 1967.

BALZER, RICHARD. *Clockwork: Life in and Outside an American Factory.* New York: Doubleday, 1976.

BARANSON, JACK. *The Japanese Challenge to U.S. Industry.* Lexington, Mass.: Lexington Books, 1981.

BEARDSLEY, R. K. *Studies on Economic Life of Japan.* Ann Arbor: University of Michigan Press, 1964.

BEASLEY, NORMAN. *Knudsen: A Biography.* New York: McGraw-Hill, 1947.

BENEDICT, RUTH. *The Chrysanthemum and the Sword.* Boston: Houghton Mifflin, 1946.

BENJAMIN, ROGER, and ORI, KAN. *Tradition and Change in Postindustrial Japan.* New York: Praeger, 1981.

BHASKAR, KRISH. *The Future of the World Motor Industry.* London: Kogan Page, 1980.

BIEDA, KEN. *The Structure and Operation of the Japanese Economy.* Sydney: John Wiley, 1970.

BLOOMFIELD, GERALD. *The World Automotive Industry.* North Pomfret, Vt.: David & Charles, 1978.

BOLTHO, ANDREA. *Japan: An Economic Survey, 1953–1973.* London: Oxford University Press, 1975.

British Central Policy Review Staff. *The Future of the British Car Industry.* London: Her Majesty's Stationery Office, 1974.

BROADBRIDGE, SEYMOUR. *Industrial Dualism in Japan.* London: Frank Case, 1966.

BROOKS, JOHN. *Business Adventures.* New York: Weybright & Talley, 1969.

BROWN, LESTER, FLAVIN, CHRISTOPHER, and NORMAN, COLIN. *Running on Empty: The Future of the Automobile in an Oil-Short World.* New York: Norton, 1979.

BRZEZINSKI, ZBIGNIEW. *The Fragile Blossom: Crisis and Change in Japan.* New York: Harper & Row, 1972.

BUNGE, FREDERICA, ed. *Japan: A Country Study.* Washington, D.C.: Government Printing Office, 1983.

BURBY, JOHN. *The Great American Motion Sickness.* New York: Doubleday, 1958.

CHANDLER, ALFRED, JR. *Giant Enterprise: Ford, General Motors, and the Automobile Industry.* New York: Harcourt, Brace, 1964.

CHANG, C. S. *The Japanese Auto Industry and the U.S. Market.* New York: Praeger, 1981.

CHINOY, ELY. *Automobile Workers and the American Dream.* New York: Doubleday, 1955.

CHRISTOPHER, ROBERT. *The Japanese Mind: The Goliath Explained.* New York: Simon & Schuster, 1983.

CLARK, RODNEY. *The Japanese Company.* New Haven: Yale University Press, 1979.

COHEN, J. B. *Japan's Postwar Economy.* Bloomington: Indiana University Press, 1958.

COLE, ROBERT, ed. *The Japanese Automobile Industry: Model and Challenge for the Future?* Ann Arbor: University of Michigan Press, 1981.

————. *Japanese Blue Collar: The Changing Tradition.* Los Angeles: University of California Press, 1971.

————. *Work, Mobility and Participation.* Berkeley: University of California Press, 1979.

CRAY, ED. *Chrome Colossus.* New York: McGraw-Hill, 1980.

CROSBY, PHILIP. *Quality Is Free: The Art of Making Quality Certain.* New York: McGraw-Hill, 1979.

CUNNINGHAM, WILLIAM. *Segmentation in the United States Compact-Car Market.* Austin: University of Texas Press, 1972.

DARK, HARRIS. *The Wankel Rotary Engine.* Bloomington: Indiana University Press, 1975.

DEMING, W. EDWARDS. *Elementary Principles of Statistical Control of Quality.* Tokyo: Nippon Kagaku Gijutsu Renmei, 1950.

DENISON, EDWARD, AND CHUNG, WILLIAM. *How Japan's Economy Grew So Fast: The Sources of Postwar Expansion.* Washington, D.C.: Brookings Institution, 1976.

DESTLER, I. M., FUKUI, HARUHIRO, and SATO, HIDEO. *The Textile Wrangle: Conflict in Japanese-American Relations, 1969–1971.* Ithaca: Cornell University Press, 1979.

DIMOCK, MARSHALL. *The Japanese Technocracy.* New York: Walker/Weatherhill, 1968.

DONNER, FREDERIC. *The World-Wide Industrial Enterprise: Its Challenge and Promise.* New York: McGraw-Hill, 1976.

DORE, RONALD. *British Factory–Japanese Factory: The Origins of National Diversity in Industrial Relations.* Berkeley: University of California Press, 1973.

DRUCKER, PETER. *Adventures of a Bystander.* New York: Harper & Row, 1978.

————. *The Changing World of the Executive.* New York: Times Books, 1982.

————. *Concept of the Corporation.* New York: John Day, 1946.

————. *The Practice of Management.* New York: Harper & Row, 1954.

————. *The Unseen Revolution: How Pension Plan Socialism Came to America.* New York: Harper & Row, 1979.

DUNCAN, WILLIAM. *U.S.-Japan Automobile Diplomacy: A Study in Economic Confrontation.* Cambridge, Mass.: Ballinger, 1973.

DUNNETT, PETER. *The Decline of the British Motor Industry.* London: Croom Helm, 1980.

EDWARDS, CHARLES. *The Dynamics of the American Automobile In-

dustry. Columbia, S.C.: University of South Carolina Press, 1965.

EDWARDS, RICHARD. _Contested Terrain: The Transformation of the Workplace._ New York: Basic Books, 1979.

FEARY, ROBERT. _The Occupation of Japan, Second Phase: 1948–1950._ Westport, Conn.: Greenwood, 1970.

FEIGENBAUM, A. V. _Total Quality Control: Engineering and Management._ New York: McGraw-Hill, 1961.

FINE, SIDNEY. _Sit Down! The General Motors' Strike of 1936–1937._ Ann Arbor: University of Michigan Press, 1969.

FLINK, JAMES. _The Car Culture._ Cambridge: MIT Press, 1975.

FLINT, JERRY. _The Dream Machine: The Golden Age of American Automobiles, 1946–1965._ New York: Quadrangle, 1976.

FORM, WILLIAM. _Blue Collar Stratification: Autoworkers in Four Countries._ Princeton: Princeton University Press, 1976.

FOUNTAIN, CLAYTON. _Union Guy._ New York: The Viking Press, 1949.

FRANK, ISAIAH, ed. _The Japanese Economy in International Perspective._ Baltimore: Johns Hopkins University Press, 1975.

————, and HIRONO, RYOKICHI, eds. _How the United States and Japan See Each Other's Economy._ New York: Committee for Economic Development, 1974.

FRIEDMAN, HARRY, and MEREDEEN, SANDER. _The Dynamics of Industrial Conflict: Lessons from Ford._ London: Croom Helm, 1980.

FUKEDA, HARAKA. _Japan and World Trade: The Years Ahead._ Farnborough, U.K.: Saxon House, 1973.

FUKUTAKE, TADASHI. _Japanese Society Today._ Tokyo: University of Tokyo, 1981.

FULLER, RICHARD. _George Romney and Michigan._ New York: Vantage, 1966.

GASEYGER, CURT. _Japan and the Atlantic World._ Paris: Saxon House, 1972.

GIBNEY, FRANK. _Miracle by Design: The Real Reasons Behind Japan's Economic Success._ New York: Times Books, 1982.

GINSBURG, DOUGLAS, and ABERNATHY, WILLIAM. _Government, Technology, and the Future of the Automobile._ New York: McGraw-Hill, 1978.

GRAD, FRANK, et al. *The Automobile and the Regulation of Its Impact on the Environment.* Norman: University of Oklahoma Press, 1975.

GYLLENHAMMAR, PEHR. *People at Work.* Reading, Mass.: Addison-Wesley, 1977.

HADLEY, ELEANOR. *Antitrust in Japan.* Princeton: Princeton University Press, 1970.

HAITANI, KANJI. *The Japanese Economic System: An Institutional Approach.* Lexington, Mass.: Lexington Books, 1976.

HALL, ROBERT. *Driving the Productivity Machine: Production and Control in Japan.* Falls Church, Va.: American Production and Inventory Control Society, 1981.

HALL, R. B. *Japan, Industrial Power of Asia.* New York: Van Nostrand, 1963.

HARRIS, T. GEORGE. *Romney's Way: A Man and an Idea.* New York: Prentice-Hall, 1967.

Harvard Business Review. *Survival Strategies for American Industry.* New York: John Wiley, 1983.

HEASLEY, JERRY. *The Production Figure Book for U.S. Cars.* Osceola, Wis.: Motorbooks International, 1977.

HICKERSON, J. MEL. *Ernie Breech.* New York: Meredith, 1968.

HIRSCHMEIER, JOHANNES, and YUI, TSUNEHIKO. *The Development of Japanese Business.* Cambridge Mass.: Harvard University Press, 1975.

HO, ALFRED. *Japan's Trade Liberalization in the 1960s.* White Plains, N.Y.: International Arts & Sciences, 1974.

HOLLERMAN, LEON. *Japan's Dependence on the World Economy: An Approach Toward Economic Liberalization.* Princeton: Princeton University Press, 1967.

HOPFINGER, K. B. *Beyond Expectation: The Volkswagen Story.* London: Foulis, 1954.

———. *The Volkswagen Story.* Cambridge: Robert Bentley, 1971.

HUNSBERGER, WARREN. *Japan and the United States in World Trade.* New York: Harper & Row, 1964.

———. *Japan: Lessons in Enterprise.* New York: Curriculum Research, 1963.

———. *Japan: New Industrial Giant.* New York: American-Asian Educational Exchange, 1972.

———. *Recent Difficulties in Japan's Economic Development.* Rome: Banca Nazionale del Lavoro, 1969.

Institute of Pacific Relations. *Industrial Japan.* New York: Institute of Pacific Relations, 1941.

IRVINE, WILLIAM. *Japan as an Automotive Market: U.S. Dept. of Commerce Special Agent Series No. 207.* Washington, D.C.: Government Printing Office, 1918.

JANSEN, MARIUS, ed. *Changing Japanese Attitudes Toward Modernization.* Princeton: Princeton University Press, 1965.

JOHNSON, CHALMERS. *MITI and the Japanese Miracle: The Growth of Industrial Policy, 1925–1975.* Stanford, Calif.: Stanford University Press, 1982.

JURAN, JOSEPH. *Quality Control Handbook.* 3rd ed. New York: McGraw-Hill, 1974.

———. *Quality Planning and Analysis from Product Development Through Use.* New York: McGraw-Hill, 1974.

KAHN, HERMAN. *The Emerging Japanese Superstate: Challenge and Response.* Englewood Cliffs, N.J.: Prentice-Hall, 1970.

KAMATA, SATOSHI. *Japan in the Passing Lane: An Insider's Account of Life in a Japanese Auto Factory.* New York: Pantheon, 1982.

KAPLAN, EUGENE. *Japan, the Government-Business Relationship.* Washington, D.C.: Dept. of Commerce, 1972.

KATO, SEISI. *My Years with Toyota.* Toyota City: Toyota Motor Sales, 1981.

KAWAI, KAZUO. *Japan's American Interlude.* Chicago: University of Chicago Press, 1960.

KEATS, JOHN. *The Insolent Chariots.* Philadelphia: Lippincott, 1958.

KIPPING, N. V. *The Japanese Economy.* London: Economic Intelligence Unit, *The Economist,* 1962.

KLEIN, LAWRENCE, and OHKAWA, KAZUSHI, eds. *Economic Growth: The Japanese Experience Since the Meiji Era.* Homewood, Ill.: Irwin, 1968.

KOMIYA, RYUTARO, ed. *Postwar Economic Growth in Japan.* Berkeley: University of California Press, 1966.

KRAUS, HENRY. *The Many and the Few.* Los Angeles: Plantin, 1947.

KUJAWA, DUANE. *International Labor Relations Management in the Automotive Industry: A Comparative Study of Chrysler, Ford and General Motors.* New York: Praeger, 1971.

LANGWORTH, RICHARD. *Kaiser-Frazer: The Last Onslaught on Detroit.* New York: Automobile Quarterly, 1975.

LASKY, VICTOR. *Never Complain, Never Explain: The Story of Henry Ford II.* New York: Marek, 1981.

LAWRENCE, PAUL, and DYER, DAVIS. *Renewing American Industry.* New York: Free Press, 1983.

LEE, CHAE-JIN, and SATO, HIDEO. *U.S. Policy Toward Japan and Korea: A Changing Influence Relationship.* New York: Praeger, 1982.

LEE, S. M., and SCHWENDIMAN, GARY. *Management by Japanese Systems.* New York: Praeger, 1982.

LEVINE, GARY. *The Car Solution: The Steam Engine Comes of Age.* New York: Horizon, 1974.

LINCOLN, JAMES. *A New Approach to Industrial Economics.* New York: Devin-Adair, 1961.

LOCKWOOD, WILLIAM. *The Economic Development of Japan: Growth and Structural Change.* Princeton: Princeton University Press, 1968.

———, ed. *The State and Economic Enterprise in Japan.* Princeton: Princeton University Press, 1965.

LONGSTREET, STEPHEN. *A Century on Wheels: The Story of Studebaker.* New York: Holt, 1952.

LYNCH, JOHN. *Toward an Orderly Market.* Tokyo: Sophia University Press, 1968.

MCNELLY, THEODORE. *Contemporary Government in Japan.* Boston: Little, Brown, 1963.

MACARTHUR, DOUGLAS. *Reminiscences.* New York: McGraw-Hill, 1964.

MAGAZINER, IRA, and HOUT, THOMAS. *Japanese Industrial Policy.* Berkeley: University of California Press, 1979.

MAHONEY, TOM. *The Story of George Romney.* New York: Harper & Brothers, 1960.

MALMGREN, HAROLD, ed. *Pacific Basin Development: The American Interests.* Lexington, Mass.: Lexington Books, 1972.

MANNARI, HIROSHI. *The Japanese Business Leaders.* Tokyo: University of Tokyo Press, 1974.

MANCHESTER, WILLIAM. *American Caesar: Douglas MacArthur, 1880–1964.* Boston: Little, Brown, 1978.

MANDELL, LEON. *Driven: The American Four-Wheeled Love Affair.* New York: Stein & Day, 1977.

MAXCY, GEORGE. *The Multinational Automobile Industry.* New York: St. Martin's, 1981.

——. *The Multinational Motor Industry.* London: Croom Helm, 1981.

MAY, GEORGE. *A Most Unique Machine.* Grand Rapids: Eerdmans, 1975.

MOLLENHOFF, CLARK. *George Romney: Mormon in Politics.* New York: Meredith, 1968.

MONROE, WILBUR, and SAKAKIBARA, EISUKE. *The Japanese Industrial Society: Organizational Cultural and Economic Underpinnings.* Austin: University of Texas Press, 1977.

MORISHIMA, MICHIO. *Why Has Japan "Succeeded"?* Cambridge: Cambridge University Press, 1982.

MORITZ, MICHAEL, and SEAMAN, BARRETT. *Going for Broke: The Chrysler Story.* New York: Doubleday, 1981.

Motor Manufacturing Economic Development Council. *Japan: Its Motor Industry and Market.* London: Her Majesty's Stationery Office, 1971.

Motor Vehicles Manufacturers of the United States. *Automobiles of America.* Detroit: Wayne University Press, 1974.

NADER, RALPH. *Unsafe at Any Speed.* New York: Grossman, 1965.

NAKAMURA, TAKAFUSA. *The Postwar Japanese Economy: Its Development and Structure.* Translated by JACQUELINE KAMINSKI. Tokyo: University of Tokyo Press, 1981.

National Academy of Engineering. *The Competitive Status of the U.S. Auto Industry: A Study of the Influences of Technology in Determining International Industrial Competitive Advantage.* Washington, D.C.: National Academy, 1982.

National Economic Development Council. *Japan: Its Motor Industry and Market.* London: Her Majesty's Stationery Office, 1971.

NELSON, RICHARD, ed. *Government and Technological Change: A Cross Industry Analysis.* New York: New York University Press, 1982.

NEVINS, ALLAN, and HILL, FRANK. *Ford: Decline and Rebirth, 1933–1962.* New York: Scribner's, 1963.

Nissan Motor Co. *History of Nissan Motor Co. Ltd., 1933–1963.* Tokyo: Nissan Motor Co., 1965.

Nomura Research Institute. *Investing In Japan.* London: Woodhead-Faulkner, 1976.

OHKAWA, KAZUSHI, and ROSOVSKY, HENRY. *Japanese Economic Growth: Trend Acceleration in the Twentieth Century.* Stanford, Calif.: Stanford University Press, 1973.

Organization for Economic Cooperation and Development. *The Industrial Policy of Japan.* New York: OECD, 1971.

OUCHI, WILLIAM. *Theory Z: How American Business Can Meet the Japanese Challenge.* Reading, Mass.: Addison-Wesley, 1981.

OZAWA, TERUTOMO. *Japan's Technological Challenge to the West, 1950–1974: Motivation and Accomplishment.* Cambridge: MIT Press, 1974.

PASCALE, RICHARD, and ATHOS, ANTHONY. *The Art of Japanese Management: Applications for American Executives.* New York: Simon & Schuster, 1981.

PASSIN, HERBERT. *Encounter with Japan.* New York: Kodansha/-Harper & Row, 1983.

————. *Society and Education in Japan.* New York: Teacher's College Press, 1965.

PATRICK, HUGH. *Monetary Policy and Central Banking in Contemporary Japan.* Bombay: University of Bombay, 1962.

————. *Japanese Industrialization and Its Social Consequences.* Berkeley: University of California Press, 1976.

————, and ROSOVSKY, HENRY, eds. *Asia's New Giant: How the Japanese Economy Works.* Washington, D.C.: Brookings Institution, 1976.

PHILLIPS, RICHARD, and WAY, ARTHUR. *Auto Industries of Europe, United States, and Japan.* Cambridge, Mass.: Abt Books, 1982.

PORSCHE, FERRY (with JOHN BENTLEY). *We at Porsche: The Autobiography of Dr. Ing. h.c. Ferry Porsche.* New York: Doubleday, 1976.

RADER, JAMES. *Penetrating the U.S. Auto Market: German and Japanese Strategies, 1965–1976.* Ann Arbor: UMI Research, 1980.

RAE, JOHN. *The American Automobile: A Brief History.* Chicago: University of Chicago Press, 1965.

————. *Nissan/Datsun: A History of Nissan Motor Corporation in U.S.A., 1960–1980.* New York: McGraw-Hill, 1981.

REUTHER, VICTOR. *The Brothers Reuther and the Story of the UAW: A Memoir.* Boston: Houghton Mifflin, 1976.

RICHARDSON, BRADLEY, and UEDA, TAIZO, eds. *Business and Society in Japan.* New York: Praeger, 1981.

ROSE, MARK. *Interstate: Express Highway Politics.* Lawrence: Regents Press of Kansas, 1979.

ROSENBERG, NATHAN. *Perspectives on Technology.* Cambridge: Cambridge University Press, 1976.

ROSOVSKY, HENRY. *Capital Formation in Japan, 1868–1940.* New York: Free Press, 1961.

ROTHSCHILD, EMMA. *Paradise Lost: The Decline of the Auto-Industrial Age.* New York: Random House, 1973.

SAKIYA, TETSUO. *Honda Motor: The Men, The Management, The Machines.* Tokyo: Kodansha, 1982.

SANDERS, SOL. *Honda: The Man and His Machines.* Boston: Little, Brown, 1975.

SASO, MARY, and KIRBY, STUART. *Japanese Industrial Competition to 1990.* Cambridge, Mass.: Abt Books, 1982.

SATO, KAZUO, ed. *Industry and Business in Japan.* White Plains, N.Y.: M.E. Sharpe, 1980.

SAXONHOUSE, GARY. *Economic Statistics and Information Concerning the Japanese Auto Industry.* Cambridge, Mass.: Department of Transportation, 1979.

SCHNAPP, JOHN. *Corporate Strategies of the Automotive Manufacturers.* Lexington, Mass.: Lexington Books, 1979.

SCHONBERGER, RICHARD. *Japanese Manufacturing Techniques: Nine Hidden Lessons in Simplicity*. New York: Free Press, 1982.

SCHRANK, ROBERT. *Ten Thousand Working Days*. Cambridge: MIT Press, 1978.

SEABURY, PAUL. *America's Stake in the Pacific*. Washington, D.C.: Ethics and Public Policy Center, 1981.

SELTZER, LAWRENCE. *A Financial History of the American Automobile Industry*. Boston: Houghton Mifflin, 1928.

SERRIN, WILLIAM. *The Company and the Union*. New York: Knopf, 1973.

SHINGO, SHIGEO. *Study of Toyota Production System*. Tokyo: Japan Management Association, 1981.

SHIVELY, DONALD. *Tradition and Modernization in Japanese Culture*. Princeton: Princeton University Press, 1971.

SIMMONS, JOHN, and MARES, WILLIAM. *Working Together*. New York: Knopf, 1983.

SINGER, KURT. *Mirror, Sword and Jewel*. Tokyo: Kodansha, 1973.

SLOAN, ALFRED, JR. *Adventures of a White Collar Man*. New York: Doubleday, Doran, 1941.

————. *My Years with General Motors*. New York: Doubleday, 1964.

SLOAN, ALLAN. *Three Plus One Equals Billions: The Bendix-Martin Marietta War*. New York: Arbor House, 1983.

SMITH, PHILIP. *Wheels Within Wheels: A Short History of American Motor Car Manufacturing*. New York: Funk & Wagnalls, 1968.

SMITH, R. P. *Consumer Demand for Cars in the USA*. Cambridge: Cambridge University Press, 1975.

SOBEL, ROBERT. *The Fallen Colossus*. New York: Weybright & Talley, 1977.

————. *The Worldly Economists*. New York: Free Press, 1980.

STOCKWIN, J. A. A. *Japan: Divided Politics in a Growth Economy*. New York: Norton, 1975.

STOKES, HENRY. *The Japanese Competitor*. London: Financial Times, 1976.

STUART, REGINALD. *Bailout: The Story Behind America's Billion Dol-*

lar Gamble on the "New" Chrysler Corporation. New York: And Books, 1980.

SUTTON, ANTHONY. *Energy: The Created Crisis.* New York: Books in Focus, 1979.

SWADOS, HARVEY. *On the Line.* Boston: Little, Brown, 1957.

SZULC, TAD. *The Energy Crisis.* New York: Franklin Watts, 1974.

TARRANT, JOHN. *Drucker: The Man Who Invented the Corporate Society.* Boston: Tarrant, 1976.

TASCA, DIANE, ed. *U.S.-Japanese Economic Relations: Cooperation, Competition, and Confrontation.* New York: Pergamon, 1980.

TERKEL, STUDS. *Working: People Talk About What They Do All Day and How They Feel About What They Do.* New York: Pantheon, 1973.

THOMAS, ROY. *Japan: The Growth of an Industrial Power.* Toronto: McGraw-Hill, 1971.

TODER, ERIC (with NICHOLAS CARDELL and ELLEN BURTON). *Trade Policy and the U.S. Automobile Industry.* New York: Praeger, 1978.

TOYO KOGYO. *Guide to Toyo Kogyo.* Tokyo: Toyo Kogyo, 1983.

Toyota Motors Sales, U.S.A. *Toyota: The First Twenty Years in the U.S.A.* Torrance, Calif.: Toyota Motor Sales U.S.A., 1977.

TSOUKALIS, LOUKAS, and WHITE, MAUREEN. *Japan and Western Europe: Conflict and Cooperation.* New York: St. Martin's, 1982.

TSURUMI, YOSHI (with TSURUMI, REBECCA). *Sogoshosha: Engines of Export-Based Growth.* Montreal: The Institute for Research on Public Policy, 1980.

VERNON, RAYMOND. *Storm over the Multinationals: The Real Issues.* Cambridge: Harvard University Press, 1977.

VOGEL, EZRA. *Japan as Number One: Lessons for America.* New York: Harper & Row, 1979.

—————, ed. *Modern Japanese Organization and Decision-Making.* Berkeley: University of California Press, 1975.

WALKER, CHARLES, and GUEST, ROBERT. *The Man on the Assembly Line.* New York: Arno, 1979.

WARD, ROBERT, ed. *Political Development in Modern Japan.* Princeton: Princeton University Press, 1968.

WHITE, JAMES. *The Sokagakkai and Mass Society.* Stanford, Calif.: Stanford University Press, 1970.

WHITE, LAWRENCE. *The Automobile Industry Since 1945.* Cambridge: Harvard University Press, 1971.

WHITESIDE, THOMAS. *The Investigation of Ralph Nader.* New York: Pocket Books, 1972.

WIDICK, B. J., ed. *Auto Work and its Discontents.* Baltimore: Johns Hopkins University Press, 1976.

———. *Labor Today.* Boston: Houghton Mifflin, 1964.

WILKINS, MIRA, and HILL, FRANK. *American Business Abroad: Ford on Six Continents.* Detroit: Wayne State University Press, 1964.

WILLOUGHBY, CHARLES, and CHAMBERLAIN, JOHN. *MacArthur, 1941–1951.* New York: McGraw-Hill, 1954.

WRIGHT, J. PATRICK. *On a Clear Day You Can See General Motors: John Z. DeLorean's Look Inside the Automotive Giant.* Grosse Pointe, Mich.: Wright Enterprises, 1979.

YAMAMURA, K. *Economic Policy in Postwar Japan.* Berkeley: University of California Press, 1967.

YANAGA, CHITOSHI. *Big Business in Japanese Politics.* New Haven: Yale University Press, 1968.

YATES, BROCK. *The Decline and Fall of the American Automobile Industry.* New York: Empire, 1983.

YERGIN, DANIEL, ed. *The Dependence Dilemma: Gasoline Consumption and America's Security.* Cambridge: Harvard University Press, 1980.

YOSHINO, MICHAEL. *Japan's Managerial System: Tradition and Innovation.* Cambridge: MIT Press, 1968.

YOUNG, ALEXANDER. *The Sogo Shosha: Japan's Multinational Trading Companies.* Boulder, Colo.: Westview, 1979.

YOUNG, STEPHEN, and HOOD, NEIL. *Chrysler U.K.: A Corporation in Transition.* New York: Praeger, 1977.

ZYSMAN, JOHN, and TYSON, LAURA, eds. *American Industry in International Competition: Government Policies and Corporate Strategies.* Ithaca, N.Y.: Cornell University Press, 1983.

STATISTICAL SOURCES

Automobile Manufacturers Association. *Automobile Facts and Figures.* 1967–1981 eds. Detroit: Automobile Manufacturers Association, 1968–1982.

Bank of Japan. *Economic Statistics Annual.* 1965–1982 eds. Tokyo: Bank of Japan, 1966–1983.

Japan Automobile Manufacturers Association. *Motor Vehicle Statistics of Japan.* 1971–1981 eds. Tokyo: Japan Automobile Manufacturers Association, 1971–1981.

Japan Motor Industrial Federation, Inc. *Guide to the Motor Industry of Japan.* 1971–1981 eds. Tokyo: Japan Motor Industrial Federation, 1971–1981.

The Oriental Economist. *Japan Company Yearbook.* 1963–1982 eds. Tokyo: The Oriental Economist, 1963–1982.

————. *Japan Economic Yearbook.* 1965–1982 eds. Tokyo: The Oriental Economist, 1964–1981.

Ward's Communications Inc. *Ward's Automotive Yearbook.* 1955–1982 eds. Detroit: Ward's Communications, 1955–1982.

Yamaichi Securities Co. *Company Financial Data.* 2 vols. Tokyo: Yamaichi Securities, 1970.

DOCUMENTS

Organization for Economic Cooperation and Development. *OECD Economic Surveys. Japan.* Paris: OECD, 1973–1983.

U.S. Strategic Bombing Survey, Military Supplies Division, October–November, 1945. *Japanese Motor Vehicle Industry.* Washington, D.C.: Government Printing Office, 1946.

U.S. Congress. Senate. *Hearings on the Confirmation of Charles E. Wilson as Secretary of Defense.* 83rd Cong., 1st sess. Washington, D.C.: GPO, 1953.

U.S. Congress. Senate. Subcommittee of the Committee on Interstate and Foreign Commerce. *Automobile Marketing*

Practices. 84th Cong., 2nd sess. Washington, D.C.: GPO, 1956.

U.S. Congress. Senate. Subcommittee of the Committee on Interstate and Foreign Commerce. *Automobile Marketing Practices—Finance and Insurance.* 85th Cong., 2nd sess. Washington, D.C.: GPO, 1958.

U.S. Congress. Senate. Joint Economic Committee. Subcommittee on Foreign Economic Policy. *Japan in United States Foreign Economic Policy, by Warren Hunsberger.* 87th Cong., 1st sess. Washington, D.C.: GPO, 1961.

U.S. Congress. Senate. Committee on Finance. Subcommittee on International Trade. *Issues Relating to the Domestic Auto Industry.* 97th Cong., 1st sess. Washington, D.C.: GPO, 1981.

U.S. Department of Transportation, *The U.S. Automobile Industry, 1980.* Washington, D.C.: GPO, 1981.

U.S. *Historical Statistics of the United States, Colonial Times to 1970.* Washington, D.C.: GPO, 1975.

Index

NOTE: Page numbers in *italics* refer to tables.

364